RICK
RUBIN

RICK RUBIN

IN THE STUDIO

JAKE BROWN

Published by ECW Press
2120 Queen Street East, Suite 200, Toronto, Ontario, Canada M4E 1E2
416-694-3348 / info@ecwpress.com

LIBRARY AND ARCHIVES CANADA CATALOGUING IN PUBLICATION

Brown, Jake
Rick Rubin : in the studio / Jake Brown.

ISBN-10: 1-55022-875-7 / ISBN-13: 978-1-55022-875-5
ALSO ISSUED AS: 978-1-55490-875-2 (PDF); 978-1-55490-440-2 (EPUB)

1. Rubin, Rick — Biography. 2. Sound recording executives and producers —
United States — Biography. I. Title.

ML429.R896B87 2009   781.66'092   C2008-907563-3

Editor for the press: Crissy Boylan
Cover and text design: Tania Craan
Typesetting: Gail Nina
Front cover photo: Kevin Estrada
Printing: Rapido   9

PRINTED AND BOUND IN CANADA

ECW PRESS
ecwpress.com

This book is dedicated to my childhood friends — like Alex Schuchard (Danzig, *Less Than Zero*), Tim Woolsey (Beasties, Run-DMC), and Britton Clapp — who grew up with me on Rick Rubin records!

Table of Contents

Introduction

There is no greater an enigma than Rick Rubin working in record production today, but one thing is crystal clear: the records he produces are sonically and stylistically beyond reproach. Rubin has rejected the comfort and complacency of working in a niche, instead taking on artistic collaborations that are truly original and which often lead the artists to their first commercial or critical breakthrough. His career began in hip hop; Rubin co-founded Def Jam Records with Russell Simmons in 1984, producing LL Cool J's *Radio* and the seminal 1986 Beastie Boys album *Licensed to Ill*, not only rap's first number one album, but also widely credited for launching hip hop as a viable commercial medium. Not only a producer who could launch new groups, Rubin proved early on in his career that he had an ability to breathe new life into old acts, giving Aerosmith a new chapter in their history with "Walk This Way," their Run-DMC collaboration.

Refusing to play it safe, Rubin jumped ship from rap to metal, leaving Def Jam to found his own label, Def American, where he signed and produced groundbreaking acts like Danzig and Slayer. His eclectic taste was nowhere better reflected than in 1987's *Less Than Zero* soundtrack. Rubin also proved his mettle as a top A&R man, executive-producing controversial but commercially successful acts like Public Enemy, the Geto Boys, and comedian Andrew Dice Clay. After his work on the hugely successful and critically acclaimed *Blood Sugar Sex Magik*, Rubin was only seven years into his career and already a living legend for his ability to break a band like the Red Hot Chili Peppers into the mainstream while respecting their musical roots and simultaneously pushing them to new heights. Though he worked with legends like Mick Jagger, AC/DC, and Tom Petty in the early 1990s, it was his recordings with Johnny Cash that still stand out as his most astonishing and studied collaboration. A partnership that began in 1993, it gave Cash renewed credibility and its commercial success allowed Rubin to be selective about who he worked with, choosing diverse artists like Donovan, Rancid, Sheryl Crow, and System of a Down and returning to those he'd produced before, most notably on the Red Hot Chili Peppers' *Californication*.

By the turn of the century, Rubin had invented, reinvented, or re-defined so many musical genres that there was no way to categorize his style — every producer's dream. Despite Rubin's stoic persona, the critics had caught on to the producer's legacy in the making, with *USA Today* commenting, "Rick Rubin may be as impossible to pigeonhole as the starry and swollen catalog of music he has produced," *Rolling Stone* singling him out as "the most successful producer of any genre," and *Esquire* concluding that there were "four words we trust: *Produced by Rick Rubin*." But the praise and album sales didn't shake Rubin's focus as he dedicated himself to artist after artist. In 2002, the Rubin-produced Audioslave debut was released and once again he had helped to launch a new statement in rock 'n' roll: the supergroup. By 2005, MTV would hail him as "the most important producer of the last 20 years," and Rick Rubin continued to live up to that title, by resurrecting the career of pop-crooning legend Neil Diamond, helping to shape the solo career of Justin Timberlake, and working with the Dixie Chicks on their comeback album, *Taking the Long Way*. Grammy nominations and awards poured in as 2007 began, including a Producer of the Year win, but Rick Rubin, workaholic and recluse, found himself too busy to attend, hard at work on Linkin Park's *Minutes to Midnight*. Not surpris-ingly, that album was a massive critical and commercial success upon its release. Rubin had already turned his sights to what some argued would be his greatest challenges yet: producing heavy metal monsters Metallica and taking a new position as head of Columbia Records.

As this generation's most legendary record man remains focused on the future of a business he has been instrumental in revolution-izing, *Rick Rubin: In the Studio* looks back at more than two decades of sonic supremacy, offering the stories behind volume one of Rubin's greatest hits.

"My production style involves being in tune with everything. You can't do it by listening to music. Pro-wrestling is really important. Movies. You know, everything. You have to make records the way you live your life."

— RICK RUBIN

PART I

In the Beginning

CHAPTER 1

Production by Reduction

Rubin's Approach in the Studio

WHEN RICK RUBIN ENTERS THE STUDIO, his goal is to record music in "its most basic and purest form" — no extra bells and whistles; all wheat, no chaff. "When I started producing [minimalism] was my thing," he explained to *Music Wizard*. "My first record actually says, instead of produced by Rick Rubin, it says, 'reduced by Rick Rubin.' . . . It's still a natural part of me not to have a lot of extra stuff involved that doesn't add to the production, and [to get] to the essence of what the music is. . . . You want to feel like you have a relationship with the artist when you're done listening to their record."

That relationship between listener and artist begins with Rubin's own relationship with the artist. As he told MTV.com in 2007, "I have to really like them as people first and foremost. Then I talk to them and hear their vision for the project, see what's going on in their life and see if it feels like a potential there for great work to come." Finding that potential and seeing how to realize it, he told *Mix* in 2000, "can be the best part. And then the actual work of having to get it there is just going through the process. Once you hear it in your head, it's like being a carpenter — trying to build the thing when you already know what it is."

Rubin's job as producer is to "find what's good about [a band] and help bring it out. And I'm clearly involved in what it sounds like, but it's almost more like I join a band when I produce a record. But, I'm unlike all the other members of the band, who each have their own personal agenda. The bass player is concerned about the bass part; everyone is concerned about their own part. I'm the only member of the band that doesn't care about any of those particulars. I just care that the whole thing is as good as it can be." Claiming to the *Washington Post* that he doesn't "even know what a traditional producer is or does," Rubin is clear on what *he* brings to his work. "I feel like the job is like being a coach, building good work habits and building trust. You want to get to a point where you can say anything and talk about anything. There needs to be a real connection. My goal is to just get out of the way and let the people I'm working with be their best."

Because he is in such high demand, Rubin has to assess projects to see "whether the potential is there to warrant the investment. It's so different, case by case, and I like so little in the first place. Very few records come out that interest me at all, very few bands do I ever see that interest me at all. I have to be honest, I don't really think about it that much. I just kind of do it. A lot of times I'm overworked. I'm a workaholic." It's not easy to peak Rubin's interest, as he explained to *Shark* magazine. "I guess I'm bored by regular stuff. Things really excite me or else they mean nothing to me. I don't like anything that's mediocre. I'd never talk about anything, 'Oh, that was okay.' I hate it or I love it." He described himself as "attracted to bizarre things. I'd like to call them progressive things . . . I like extreme things — good, bad. I like it when people take things to their limits, regardless of whether or not I agree. Because I think that's the only way we find out about new things."

Famous for his ability to move between musical genres, Rubin draws creative energy from this experimentation. "I love having a variety, as far as styles go. I feel like it keeps me fresh. I get to work a lot, but I never really get bogged down, because every time I go to the studio with a different style of artist, it forces me to start from square one and really tune in to what the artist is about. If all I did was make hip hop records or metal records, I feel like it would run its course," he told MTV.com.

Expanding on that same point to *Music Wizard*, Rubin revealed he sometimes gets flak from artists for moving on. "Almost anytime I've had success doing a particular kind of music, I end up doing something else next, as opposed to staying with what I've had success in. I've had complaints from people I've worked with who say, 'Why change? You had so much success doing rap records. Why aren't you making rap records?' I'm not feeling rap records where at the time I was doing them it was really a different time. It was an exciting movement for me at that time. It was a new exciting community that I was a part of. I don't feel rap now. I still like it, but I don't have the same relationship to it that I did before. And the same is true as time goes on, with always trying to do new things, and really trying not to get stuck with, 'Well, you do this.' I've never had that tag. I've broken through enough times of what I'm supposed to do that people now luckily let me do what I want to do, and leave me alone."

Ultimately, the bottom line for Rubin to take on any project is, as he told *Mix*, "falling in love. I'm not looking for any type of anything or to fit any mold. I'm not looking for the next Prince or something. It's really an emotional connection that transcends any genre." More than a decade before that, he told *MTV News* in 1989 that he was "not trying to find great new stars, I'm just being true to what I like." That strategy has worked for him, with Rubin maintaining, "Usually when I'm in the studio, it feels special. In fact, I try to work on projects that feel special before we get in the studio whenever possible."

The fundamental element Rubin values in a project seems obvious but is far too often overlooked in commercial music recording. As he said to MTV.com as the 2007 Grammys approached, "I tend to believe overall in the quality of content over everything else. . . . So we spend a great deal of time working on material long before we ever think about going into a recording studio. It's about finding songs and writings songs and really exhausting that before thinking about things like performance and what the album's going to sound like." The importance of the material is something he emphasized in a *New York Times* profile: "Whether it's producing, or signing an artist, [it] always starts with the songs. When I'm listening, I'm looking for a balance that you could see in anything. Whether it's a great painting, or a building, or a sunset. There's just a natural human element to a great song that feels immediately satisfying. I like the song to create a mood." One of his primary functions as producer "is to hear through production and look at a song."

An avid and career-long advocate of pre-production, Rubin first focuses on working out the songs before heading into principal production. Speaking to *Billboard* about a project with Metallica, Rubin explained his approach: "We really have to feel secure about the music and know it's good. Then in the studio, we're free to only worry about performance and not worry about writing a song. Hopefully, we've done our homework." That homework, in what could be compared to a masters course in songwriting, is tackled from a particular perspective. "I try to get [a band] in the mindset that they're not writing music for an album," he detailed to *Time*. "They're writing music because they're writers and that's what they do." By encouraging his artists to experiment and take some joy in the process of songwriting, Rubin hopes to end up with better material for the eventual album. "I try to get the artist to feel like they are writing songs for the ages rather than songs for an album. As they write, they come over and play the songs for me. For some reason, most people will write 10 songs and think, 'That's enough for a record. I'm done.' When they play the songs for me, invariably the last two songs they've written are the best. I'll then say, 'You have two songs, go back and write eight more.'" Rubin feels the real work of making an album is in the songwriting, but that work can be drudgery. "Writing is dull and unglamorous stuff. For most people, it's really pretty miserable. But if you write 30 songs, there's a better chance that the 10 on your album will be better than if you just write 10."

"What we do is really a big experiment, and there's no reason not to try different things," Rubin said to *Mix*. "If it doesn't work, we all know it doesn't work. Usually. And we get in the habit of trying a lot of different things. You get everyone thinking in terms of 'nothing's in stone, there's the potential for more.' Usually." And one trick of the trade of songwriting, particularly when approaching it in this organic way, is to get "artists those little cassette recorders that you can carry around with you — the little tiny ones. I tell them to keep the recorder in the car and in case something comes to mind because ideas do go away quickly."

In the case of most bands, a brainstorming approach is ideal creatively: "It's really a completely collaborative effort. Anyone who's got a good idea, if it makes the record better, we use it." Rubin told the *LA Times*, "It's one of the things we talk about at the beginning of a project. 'Let's try every idea and see where it takes us, not prejudge it.' Sometimes it still comes up where someone in the band makes a suggestion and part of me says, 'That's a bad idea. Let's not waste time on that.' I stop myself and think, 'Let's try it and see what it sounds like,' and very often it sounds good." If Rubin feels a song is headed in the wrong direction, "I may start by pointing to one line and suggesting it's not as good as the rest, and the artist may say something like, 'I think it's the best line in the song.' So, I'll just keep gently pressing the point until I get to where I can see the artist isn't going to change. In this case, I might say, 'It doesn't resonate with me. What is it you like about it, how does it fit the song?' and so forth. You're not always successful. Ultimately, it's their album, not mine." Since he can't fight over every point, Rubin chooses his battles and is known and respected for being forthcoming with his highly valued opinion. Rubin outlined his trademark no-nonsense style to *Mix*: "If I think something can make or break the song, I'm more emphatic. But ultimately, it is the artist's record. . . . There's nothing better than telling the truth. When I start working with a band, I explain, 'Look, I'm just going to tell you everything I think. I'm telling you that, not in any way to criticize what you do, but to do my job.' . . . And they can listen to what I say, accept it, and try it, or they can say, 'You know what? What you don't like about this is what I like about it. Fuck you, it's fine.'"

Rubin concedes that some artists are more pleasant to work with than others, and his theory is that it boils down to confidence: "The more confident a band or an artist is, the easier they are to work with. . . . The more insecure they are, the more they tend to hold onto things that don't really matter. Before Roy Orbison died, I did a track with him, and he was willing to try anything. Because he knew, no matter what I had him do, it wasn't going to take away from him being Roy Orbison. Sometimes young artists, or insecure artists, hold onto things that don't matter because they feel, 'This is what makes me "me."' They have this image that some little thing they do makes them what they are. But it doesn't." Self-taught in the art of production and a self-described amateur in technical production, one of Rubin's most valuable qualities is his own confidence — in his perspective on music and his ability to convince an artist of the validity of that opinion.

During pre-production, Rubin tries to steer his artists away from the distraction and pressure of the Hollywood spotlight and striving for commercial success. A principal part of his job is "taking away any fears [artists] had about what they were doing and not let anything get to them to where they would soft-pedal anything in any way." Rubin challenges artists to do their best for the sake of the work rather than succumbing to industry pressure. "So much is about the process and pleasing ourselves, not thinking, 'Can it get on the radio, will it be done in time?'" he told *USA Today*. "I try to erase all the restrictions that I've seen impede great art over and over. If the album is great, everything else will follow."

What can be challenging for both artist and producer is the pressure from record companies to have commercially viable songs. Rubin feels that no one "is good at trying to figure out what will be a hit. The best thing you can do is reach for something that excites you and the artist." Creating these records is "not an accident. You already know what the sculpture is, but you have to do all that work of chipping the stone away, and that's not the fun part. The fun part is knowing what it is. But no one else gets to know what it is unless you do the work." A good test of a song's mettle is stripping it down to its basics; as he explained to *Time*, "If a song is great on an acoustic guitar, you can make a hundred different versions of that song and it'll still be great."

As detailed and lengthy as the pre-production process can be, Rubin's productions tend to be quite short on actual in-studio time, as he told *Mix*. "I often make records faster than a lot of other people. It usually has to do with how prepared we are in advance. . . . But it's the pre-production time that really makes the difference. Sometimes that's a couple of weeks, sometimes it's a few months, sometimes it's a year of getting ready to go into the studio and cut the whole album in a week. The preference is always to get as much done before you go in the studio as possible."

A former night owl, after more than 20 years of record producing, Rubin's personal preparatory process now begins in the morning and outdoors. "When I wake up in the morning now . . . [I spend] 20 minutes in the sun. When it was suggested to me, it sounded like jumping off a cliff. I always slept late, wore dark glasses, spent more time up and out at night. But I changed my hours [in 2004], so I wake up in the shock of the sun before nine, and there's more natural light, and I really love it," he told the *Washington Post*.

Another staple of Rubin's routine is meditation, which he got into when he was just 14 years old at the recommendation of his pediatrician. Finding it beneficial to all aspects of his life, meditation helps Rubin with his focus and with the creative process, as he explained to the *LA Times*. "I think the act of creation is a spiritual act. The more involved we are with nature and the spiritual side of life, the more it seems to have a good effect on creativity. I think about how seeing the sunset can take your breath away. That's the same feeling I get when I hear a beautiful line in a song or a great guitar solo. I don't think great songs stem from us. They are just kind of in the universe. The best artists are the ones with the best antennae that draw it in, and meditation helps get rid of tension and tune into the ideas that are out there." Meditation allows Rubin "to stay open and really listen. I know in the production process often, I feel like I don't really know what I'm saying, but when I hear [the resulting recording], it sounds right."

"The more artists I work with," said Rubin, "the more I see whether they understand it, like Donovan who really understands his spirituality, or Johnny Cash, who [was] a very religious person.

There are some artists who don't know where it comes from, but it comes." That ability is oftentimes part of a larger "star quality," which draws audiences in and renders tolerable whatever shortcomings the artist may have. "We're talking about those people with that special magic, the people who light up a dark room; you have to be prepared to take whatever comes along with it," Rubin explained to *Shark*.

Once in the studio, Rubin continues to rally his collaborators, asking that they set their expectations of themselves high. "We put everything we have into it all the time, whatever it takes," he told the *Washington Post* in 2006. "If we're going to do it, let's aim for greatness. Because, honestly, the physical act of documenting the ideas that you have is not fun. So if it's not going to be great, I'd much rather go swimming. Really. I might rather go swimming anyway. But at least aiming for greatness is a good foil for not being in the water." On the eve of the 2007 Grammys, Rubin explained to the *LA Times* how strength of conviction has helped him and the artists he works with consistently achieve greatness: "You and the band have to believe what you are doing together is the most important thing in the world. . . . [but] you never want them to think that what they are doing *today* is most important. You don't want them to ever think, 'Oh my God, I have to get it right today or else.'" To create that sense, Rubin doesn't adhere to strict schedules for projects, instead opting to experiment and see how the process evolves.

Having established a work ethic that combines freedom as well as determination, performance becomes the focus, with Rubin encouraging experimentation in the studio. "There's a humanity to a great performance," he told the Associated Press. "It's more like jazz. It could be a pop song, or a rock song, or a country song, but we approach it more from the standpoint of jazz, and try to get this special interactive moment. We know the tunes, we know the songs, now we're trying to get that special magic moment."

As Rubin described to *Music Wizard*, "In terms of getting a performance from an artist, if they play a song 50 times, it is waiting until that *one* to happen. You can have the same person sing the same song over and over again, but one time it's magic, and everything is in it. All the emotion is behind it, and you don't know why that happens, but you just know it. And it happens with pretty much every artist I work with. You play along and wait, while fishing for those moments of when that magic happens. And we look at each other like, there it is. . . . We just try to work together, and go through the experimentation of trying a lot of different songs, and helping the artist find their voice."

The recording primarily takes place in Rubin's state-of-the-art studio and creative mecca in his Laurel Canyon home, behind a sign that reads, "Quiet please, meditation in progress." Before his work was based there, he preferred traditional recording venues. Rubin described those studios to *Music Angle*: "Most of the studios I [work] in were built in the '50s or '60s and they sound amazing. Modern recording studios sound horrible. It's not just the equipment; it's the room itself. Now, like the CD, they are spec'd out properly. Before they were kind of magically, with smoke and mirrors, made to sound good by people with good ears. Now everything is computer generated. Now it's perfect, but there's no vibe at all . . . I work at Cello, which used to be Ocean Way, which used to be Western Electric. All of the Beach Boys albums, a lot of Frank Sinatra, all the Wrecking Crew stuff was recorded there. A classic studio." Part of creating the right sound is creating the right vibe in the studio. Red Hot Chili Peppers' Anthony Kiedis described Rubin's setup to *Time*: "He basically goes into the engineer's booth, removes everything in the room and has his people bring in the most comfortable couch-bed-type object that you'll ever see. Then he'll cover it with pillows and blankets, and that becomes his station."

From Rubin's experience working with both veteran recording artists and those starting out, he's developed an understanding of the particular challenges each faces — an overzealousness on one hand, and recording-by-rote on the other. "When you're making your first or second album, it's a really big deal," said Rubin. "It's the most important thing in your life. It was the dream for most of your life and you're finally getting to do it. When you've made 20 albums you have a different relationship to it. It can be just another album. An artist's life gets on a certain rhythm where you tour for this long, you're off for this long, you record an album, you go back out on the road and there's this kind of cycle. Once that cycle is firmly in place, it kind of takes over and if you need to take a year to write the songs to make your album to be all that it is, well that's not in the cycle — or two years — whatever it is. . . . I think it's a human nature thing, just when you get into a certain pattern, you just stay on the pattern."

Breaking that pattern is difficult as "most [artists], especially the ones that are established and have had success, tend to be in a little bit of a vacuum, because most people tell them what they do is great. But there's a lack of reality in that world and it's not beneficial to the artist to be in that world." Rubin is anything but a yes-man, which makes him "good with artists . . . whom a lot of people consider difficult," he told *Shark*, "because I understand the way they think. I hate all the same shit they hate." To clear any impediment to being creative, Rubin tries "to be a support system for the artists that I work with. If an artist doesn't have a manager, if the stress of that is getting in the way of their art, I'll set up meetings with a manager and arrange everything . . . so the artists can do their best work." While the producer is "not a babysitter" and doesn't "do hand-holding," he is a facilitator of the creative process and thus tries "to run interference and refocus everything on the art and the artist's truth." Once Rubin has the artist's trust, a key part of his job is simply listening, as he explained to AP, "A lot of artists really like having someone to bounce things off of, because it's hard to know."

As much as Rubin has his opinions, his focus is on adhering to the artist's vision for the album, rather than his own. Justin Timberlake recalled to MTV.com the first time he met Rubin: "The cool thing about Rick is when we first met, he said to me, 'Look, I don't influence you one way or the other. You do whatever it is that you do and I'll just come in and tell you what I think and move stuff in a direction that seems conducive to what you do.' And that's such a comforting thing because you know you're in good hands." When working with artists with a long career behind them, Rubin doesn't try to reinvent the wheel, knowing that, from a fan's perspective, you don't want to hear your favorite artists without their signature sounds. "You don't really want to hear Elvis without the 'slap' [echo]. It's part of the Elvis sound. You really wouldn't want to hear Robert Plant without the delay he uses. There are just certain artists that use effects and have kind of created a sound for themselves."

Once principal tracking is complete, Rubin hits the part of the process he finds especially trying: mixing and mastering. "The fact of the matter is if you're sitting in front of speakers for eight or 10 hours a day, often listening to the same song for days at a time, it really messes with your head. So it's hard. After that you don't want to come home and put on even your favorite record. You need a palette cleanser of some kind," he explained to *Music Angle*. Rubin revealed, "One of the problems I have is that I'm in the studio so much that I don't have so much time to listen to music for pleasure, and when I do, I'm listening to so much loud music during the day, I'll often listen to classical music or . . . the '60s channel on XM." One unusual practice he employs in this stage of production is doing "shoot-outs all the time," with "as many as five different mastering engineers mastering the same album and then we 'A/B' them." Rubin outlined the rationale behind that strategy to the *LA Times*: "If you know the greatest mixer in the world mixed one track and the guy who is making coffee on the project mixed [another], you're liable, psychologically, to think the famous engineer's mix is bound to be the best. But if you don't know who did what, the playing field is clear and even, and you are really picking based on what sounds good. And very often we're surprised. Very often."

Rubin's method — and its success — is underscored by his constant struggle to remain open-minded throughout the process. But there is one arena he is rather closed off to: live performance. As he told *Music Angle*, "I feel like — I don't want to say 'perfection' but there's an ideal that's reached in recorded music that I very rarely see live. It happens on occasion, but I think if there's an artist that you see live who's great and the record isn't so good . . . I would blame the people in the record-making process for not doing their job. . . . There's nothing like sitting in the room with a piano and hearing the piano and the overtones and the nature of that instrument . . . it's never going to be the same coming out of the speaker as it is just from a sonic perspective, [that's] the nature of the beast. But from a performance perspective and the things that you can do in the record-making process and the clarity of what you can hear, it's very hard to get that same experience [live]. I don't go out to see a lot of music live because I'm always so disappointed. I'd rather stay home and listen to my CDs."

At the core of record production, Rubin feels so much boils down to common sense, but he doesn't take for granted the lessons experience and open-mindedness have taught him over his many years (and multi-platinum albums) in the business. And though he's a very private person, Rubin doesn't shy away from making his professional life very personal, telling the *Washington Post* that his work develops from "learning about myself and being a better person." Rubin's career choices haven't been deliberately plotted but follow "an intuitive process." As he described to *Music Wizard*, "I'm doing things that touch me personally, and that I feel and am moved by. I've been lucky in my career that things that have moved me have luckily moved other people too. But it hasn't been any planning or trying to imagine what someone else is going to like, or what's going to be successful. It's really natural and pure. I try to be as pure as I can and just feel what I feel, and like what I like, and be true to that."

Admittedly, his journey of self-development isn't over; he's called himself a "spiritual quester," a "work in progress" who has "revelations every day." But since his early days as a producer, he has changed, and for the better: "In the beginning — I don't remember, but I've been told — I was much more of a tyrant." Rubin's progression has been part and parcel of his work crossing musical boundaries. "I allow my tastes to change and not say, 'Oh, I sold millions of records making rap records, I have to keep making them.' I'm happy to say, 'Oh well, I like speed metal this week, so I'm going to make speed metal records. And fuck it, I don't care if my speed metal records sell or don't, this is what I want to do.' . . . Like treading new ground, like doing something that's not what's already on the radio. Rather than doing something that's already on the radio, so that's what we should do because then we'll get on the radio too. That's not valid." And this refusal to simply recreate "hit sounds" has kept his work from getting stale. "If you listen to my records, they don't really sound the same," he told *Shark*. "Unlike a Stock-Aitken-Waterman record where the artists are interchangeable, or Desmond Child — I think all of his records sound the same, whether it's Alice Cooper or Bon Jovi singin' them, it's a Desmond Child song. I try not to fall into that trap because I think it's limiting. I think it's short-term."

How he regards his own role in creating an album helps him move from one sound to the next, an ability at the heart of his career's longevity. Rubin doesn't think of a record he produces as a "Rick Rubin album. I think of it as a really great Neil Diamond album, or a really great Johnny Cash album. . . . These are people that I love and [I'm] trying to get them to be what I imagine they could be." After so many years, Rubin is very clear on what his strengths and limitations are. "I do not know how to work a board. I don't turn knobs. I have no technical ability whatsoever," he unabashedly admitted to the *New York Times*. "But I'm there when [artists] need me to be there. My primary asset is I know when I like something or not. It always comes down to taste. . . . I'm there for any key creative decisions." He summed up the drive behind his life's work very simply: "I'm just trying to make my favorite music. That's how I work; I just do things based on the way they feel to me."

Rubin's work in the studio has moved millions of music fans around the world, but the producer has bittersweet feelings about his accomplishments. "It feels nice that all the work we've done over the years has built up to this point," he said to the *Washington Post*. "It's a testament to hard work; we're really not fooling around. . . . I've really lived the last 20 years of my life in a recording studio. It's yielded great artistic results, but I don't know how good it's been for my life. I can't say it's always the happiest existence."

Rubin continues to approach "every record as a fan and I don't give up. Each step of the way, I ask myself, 'Am I satisfied with what I'm hearing?' If not, I'm still a fan. I'm just not satisfied." His distinctive style continues to produce success after success, and undoubtedly there are countless artists hoping that one day Rubin will work with them as a "professional fan."

CHAPTER 2

Growing Up in Long Island

BORN ON MARCH 10, 1963, in the Lido Beach area of Long Island, New York, to parents Mickey and Linda, Frederick Jay Rubin spent his formative years in the hard rock glory days of the 1970s listening to bands like Led Zeppelin, Black Sabbath, Aerosmith, and AC/DC. Those bands had grown up on rock 'n' roll's first generation — the Rolling Stones, the Beatles, Cream, The Who, and Jimi Hendrix — and were its new pioneers, refining and re-defining hard rock and heavy metal. Rubin witnessed this evolution exploding out of amplifiers and over the radio airwaves. One band in particular spoke to the seventh grader: AC/DC. The producer wrote in the April 2004 issue of *Rolling Stone*: "When I was in junior high in 1979, my classmates all liked Led Zeppelin. But I loved AC/DC. I got turned on to them when I heard them play 'Problem Child' on *The Midnight Special*. Like Zeppelin, they were rooted in American R&B, but AC/DC took it to a minimal extreme that had never been heard before. Of course, I didn't know that back then. I only knew that they sounded better than any other band. . . . I'll go on record as saying they're the greatest rock 'n' roll band of all time. They didn't write emotional lyrics. They didn't play emotional songs. The emotion is all in that groove. And that groove is timeless."

Listening to the band as a teenager, Rubin was unwittingly developing his ear and his production style. The group's minimalist approach would show up years later in his sonic approach to recording rock records, and even earlier in the way he constructed hip hop albums, which sampled bands like AC/DC. "*Highway to Hell* is probably the most natural-sounding rock record I've ever heard," Rubin wrote. "There's so little adornment. Nothing gets in the way of the push-and-pull between the guitarists Angus and Malcolm Young, bassist Cliff Williams, and drummer Phil Rudd. . . . When I'm producing a rock band, I try to create albums that sound as powerful as *Highway to Hell*." Acknowledging the man who captured the sound of *Highway to Hell* and other classic AC/DC albums, Rubin counts Mutt Lange among the producers whose work he respects the most, "I really like the way he [got] a very pure sound . . . and I think he really captured the spirit of what that group was about."

As a teenager, Rubin immersed himself in the world of rock 'n' roll; he had the requisite long hair, leather jacket, and position as lead guitarist in a punk band called The Pricks. But one part of that lifestyle he avoided entirely was alcohol and drugs. Rubin had a discipline and focus rare for someone his age. "Kids I knew did drugs or got drunk out of boredom. I didn't want to give up my time," he told *USA Today*. Being "deeply into something" kept Rubin — as a youth and through adulthood — from the need to distract or entertain himself that way. Before music, his deep focus was on magic.

"From the time I was nine years old, I loved magic. I was an only child, and I think that had a big impact on me. I always had grown-up friends even though I was a little kid. I would take the train from Lido Beach into Manhattan, and I'd hang out in magic shops. When I was 14, I had magician friends who were 60. I learned a lot from them — I still think about magic all the time," Rubin told the *New York Times*. "I always think about how things work, the mechanics of a situation — that's the nature of being a magician." Training as a magician helped turn Rubin into a studio wizard in a more spiritual sense as well: "When you're that age [nine years old], you don't know the difference between magic, spirituality, and the occult. It's all kind of the same — they're all other realms. I feel like those realms play a role in everything. The spiritual connection that I have plays a big role in my ability to do my job."

Rubin's fascination with and love for magic and music was something that delighted his endlessly supportive parents, who showed the same devotion to their son as he did to his passions. Rubin's mother would drive him to concerts in New York City, wait outside the venue until the show was over, no matter how late the hour, and then drive her son home for a few precious hours of sleep before waking him for school the next day. His suburban upbringing affected his musical tastes, which by his senior year had begun to shift from rock to the burgeoning hip hop scene in New York. Rubin recalled that as a teenager, "I wished that I was in Manhattan. But in retrospect, I think it very much played a role in who I am and gave me a different perspective . . . [it] probably led me to [have] more commercial taste."

Another formative moment in Rubin's musical development was seeing the Godfather of Soul perform. "I first saw James Brown around 1980, between my junior and senior years in high school. It was in Boston. The show was in a catering hall, with folding chairs. And it was one of the greatest musical experiences of my life. His dancing and singing were incredible, and he played a Hammond B3 organ tufted with red leather, with godfather in studs written across the front," Rubin wrote in *Rolling Stone*. That performance and the recordings of James Brown had a profound impact on Rubin as he tried to understand "the feeling you get when you listen to those grooves" and capture that in the records he was soon to produce.

In 1981, Rubin graduated from Long Beach High School and enrolled in New York University as a philosophy major with law school in mind for his future career. But his intentions were clear for anyone who read his senior yearbook. His graduation quote prophetically read: "I wanna play loud, I wanna be heard, I want all to know, I'm not one of the herd." Rubin's ability to make people listen would soon radically change the sound of rap and rock.

"Really, the key to it is doing what
you believe in, as opposed to
what you think is going to work.
There were never any plans to make
anything happen. I just did what I
liked and believed in it, and
luckily it all worked out."

— RICK RUBIN

PART II

The 1980s

CHAPTER 3

DJ Double R and the Birth of Def Jam

AT NEW YORK UNIVERSITY (the only college he applied to) in 1981, Rubin studied by day and hit the burgeoning hip hop scene by night. Rubin was still a regular at punk clubs but had gotten into hip hop before it was even a blip on white America's radar. As the producer recalled, "I'd go to clubs and hear this music and love it." Rubin told the *Washington Post* in 2006, "For a long time I was the only white person in that world. But it wasn't like I was let into a secret society. I was just the only one who cared. It was such a little underground scene at that point."

Like many of his legendary contemporaries from Dr. Dre to Timbaland, Rubin began his career as a DJ, throwing parties in his legendary NYU dorm and soon thereafter at the hottest underground hip hop clubs in New York. The enterprise gave him first-hand feedback, seeing which records got a response from the crowd when he played them. The move from DJ to producer resulted from the dearth of good material for him to play: "There weren't a lot of rap records coming out, and the rap records that were coming out weren't representative of what the rap scene really was." Rubin explained the failing of those records to the *AV Club*: "My favorite group at the time was Treacherous Three, and I met with one of the guys in the band. I didn't know anything about the record business, but I recognized that the hip hop records that were coming out that I would buy as a fan, and the music I would hear when I'd go to the club, were two different things. The music in the club was much more breakbeat, scratching, raw, kind of rock-based. The hip hop records that were coming out at the time were really like disco or R&B, but with a person rapping on it instead of a girl singing on it. I guess what I set out to do as a fan was to make records that sounded like what I liked about going to a hip hop club, and trying to document that scene." Buying all the new hip hop records each week (around three to five singles), Rubin thought the problem with them was in the attempt to try and sound like a record, rather than *record* what the actual music was like in the club atmosphere.

Straddling the worlds of rock/punk (touring with his band Hose) and hip hop/rap, Rubin quickly found that hip hop wasn't so far off from his other musical interest. "I used to go to the rap clubs in New York . . . and they'd be playing rock 'n' roll records with guys rapping over them. Like 'Walk This Way' was an original record that every rap DJ would have and use. Billy Squier's 'Big Beat' was another one. . . . I saw this void and starting making those records, just because I was a fan and wanted them to exist," he told *Shark* magazine.

By October 1983, Rubin was DJing for the Beastie Boys under the name DJ Double R and met his first producer-mentor, DJ Jazzy Jay — a DJ in Afrika Bambaataa's Soulsonic Force group — who "just had the best taste." A few months later, in December, the pair set about to produce a single together. The song was "It's Yours," written by T La Rock and his brother Special K of the Treacherous Three. As T La Rock recalled, "Originally Special K was supposed to do that record and Louie Lou was supposed to do the scratching. My brother kept telling me, 'Man you need to do this record.' I didn't even want to make records, I had a job at a pharmacy making good money. K hooked me up with Rick Rubin and that was it." Rubin, the Beastie Boys' Ad-Rock, T La Rock, and Jazzy Jay gathered to record the track at Jazzy's house in

Rick Rubin (second from left) with his college band Hose in the early '80s.
(© Monica Dee/Retna Ltd.)

Queens, using Rubin's Roland 808 drum machine. Rubin approached the production of "It's Yours" "just from a fan's point of view."

Rubin borrowed $5,000 from his parents to press the single, imprinting "Def Jam Records" on it; it's the first hip hop record to bear the logo of the future company. "The way it started was, the first record I made, I was planning on putting it out myself strictly for the purpose of breaking even — making back my costs, that was always the plan — and I sold it to Streetwise Records, who offered me more than I thought I was going to make if I'd sold as many as I wanted to," Rubin explained. "Then, as it turned out, it was a hit; it sold, I don't know, 100,000 12-inches in the New York area, which was a big deal." Released in 1984 on independent label Streetwise/Party Time Records, the single's sleeve listed Rubin's NYU address and launched an onslaught of demos being mailed to him, which helped to fuel the fires of Def Jam. "It's Yours" was featured in the Harry Belafonte–produced film *Beat Street*, but despite the song's success, Rubin never made a dime on the record.

Enter Russell Simmons. On the recommendation of Tuff City Records owner Aaron Fuchs who said of Simmons, "No one promotes rap records better," Rubin first met him in the hopes of moving "It's Yours." Familiar with Simmons' work with groups like , Davy DMX, Jimmy Spicer, and Orange Crush, as well as his stable of the coast's hottest rappers at the time, Rubin felt that while most of the rap records of the time weren't very good, those that were always had Russell Simmons' name on them.

The partnership that would revolutionize hip hop began with a simple meeting. "We met at a party . . . a few months after ['It's Yours'] came out, and he said it was his favorite record, and he was so excited to meet me, and couldn't believe that I was white. There was nobody white doing anything in hip hop, and here was his favorite hip hop record made by a white guy. I was really excited to meet him, because his name was on all these great records, like Kurtis Blow. He was already a mogul of rap music, even though there was no business. It was just a small, underground scene. He was already kind of the focal point," Rubin explained to *AV Club*. The two crossed paths again on a local New York hip hop television show, *Graffiti Rock*, promoting singles. After hearing a series of unfinished beats Rubin had produced, which awaited a new crop of rappers to flow overtop, Simmons called the beats "hit records in the making." The two became fast friends, with Simmons saying of the early days, "We did everything together. We'd be at the studio every night; if it wasn't the studio, we were in Danceteria. I used to take him to Disco Fever in the South Bronx. I took him everywhere."

Rubin and Simmons shared a love for hip hop, a vision of where they felt it should head both musically and commercially, and one other thing — both had hit records under their belts but no profit to show for it. As Rubin recalled, Simmons "had made about 20 hit records that sold a lot, and he was broke. He never got paid either. So

I said, 'This is dumb. [The independent record labels are] not really doing much for us, and they're not paying us, so let's do it ourselves. At least we can make sure we get paid and our artists get paid.'" The formation of Def Jam as a record company proper grew out of the knowledge that Rubin and Simmons could take care of their artists and get the job done. Rubin explained to *Shark* that Def Jam was a better setup to overcome business obstacles: "Instead of going to somebody and asking them to do the things that needed to get done, and not getting them done, it was easier to just take on the responsibility. It was just not going to get done unless [we] did it." A senior at NYU by this time, Rubin asked Simmons to be his partner in Def Jam in 1984. "Russell was five years older, and he was established," the producer explained to the *New York Times*. "By myself, I was just a kid making records. He gave me credibility."

And Rubin had just the right artist to launch the new formalized partnership, a young rapper whose demo was one of hundreds that had been sent to his dorm room. A&R houseguest Adam "Ad-Rock" Horovitz sorted through Rubin's bins and boxes of demo tapes and discovered the first artist Def Jam would sign. While the tapes were mostly "horrible," Ad-Rock came across LL Cool J's demo, which Rubin admitted he wouldn't describe as "great, but it was different, and I liked it. There was something about it that just struck us as funny, and we wanted to hear it over and over again." Rubin brought the demo to the attention of partner Russell Simmons, and LL was the first person Rubin ever called based on a demo tape and became "the foundation of the company." Taking a chance on signing an unknown as Def Jam's first act seems like more of a risk from today's perspective than it was at the time. As Rubin explained, "There were no stars in rap music. It was really just a work of passion. Everyone who was doing it was doing it because they loved it, not because anyone thought it was a career. We didn't even think about having a hit single. We just tried to do something we liked. There were no expectations whatsoever. The only hope was that we'd sell enough records to make enough money to make another record. If it didn't cost us money to have Def Jam, we'd be happy. If it supported itself, and we could keep doing it, we'd be doing it."

With LL Cool J on board, Rubin set out to record his first single, "I Need a Beat." The approach Rubin took on producing this single was perhaps the secret to Def Jam's commercial success and became the blueprint for hip hop's first commercial explosion. "Before Def Jam, hip hop records were typically really long, and they rarely had a hook. Those songs didn't deliver in the way the Beatles did. By making our rap records sound more like pop songs, we changed the form," explained Rubin to the *New York Times*. Using a classic song structure and applying his philosophy — "the less going on in a record, and the clearer and more in-your-face it is, the better" — Rubin and LL Cool J cooked up a demo version of "I Need a Beat," the strength of which convinced Simmons they had made the right choice. Even today it's held dear by Rubin who described the song as "a really sparse record, pretty much all one drum machine, vocals, and a couple of little musical nuances here and there, a little bit of scratching." Rubin put together the track for LL striving to "make music that suited the artist and reflected the signature of that artist, and was very representative of who they were." Recorded on a nominal budget of $7,000 at Chung King Studios and pressed at Soundworks in New Jersey, LL Cool J's first single, "I Need a Beat," was released in November 1984. For Rubin, that single was "the real birth of Def Jam."

Rubin then passed the baton to Simmons, whose promotional expertise pushed the fresh new sound of the single onto the airwaves of local New York hip hop stations and into the city's hip hop clubs. With Simmons' talent in old-school hustling and based on his reputation and past successes, "I Need a Beat" moved enough units to catch the attention of execs at CBS Records, who were looking to jump on the hip hop bandwagon, which had been steadily gaining mainstream attention. CBS offered what amounted to a development deal with a $600,000 advance, and Simmons and Rubin seized the opportunity to expose their new brand of hip hop to a national audience. Time would prove this deal to be merely a foot in the door they would kick open a year later, but for 20-year-old Rick Rubin, it was a major milestone: "I sent a Xerox of the check to my parents. That's when this stopped being a hobby." Just as Def Jam started to take off on the success of LL's single, Rick Rubin was slated to graduate from New York University, but according to production partner and college buddy George Drakoulias, "We were still in the dorms and Rick didn't want to leave. He got college credits for running the record company. He stayed until he graduated." Rubin continued working with LL Cool J on his full-length studio LP and had a new project on the go: the soundtrack to the movie *Krush Groove*.

Krush Groove was a marketing vehicle Russell Simmons dreamed up — before securing a deal for financing or release — to introduce their label and its artist roster (which included the Fat Boys, LL Cool J, the Beastie Boys, and Simmons' brother's group, Run-DMC) to mainstream America. The soundtrack featured these newcomers bolstered by a who's who of New York hip hop and R&B — Kurtis Blow, Sheila E., and New Edition. The buzz on Def Jam was already so hot that these relative upstart producers were able to pull big names already. Directed by Michael Schultz, the film drew inspiration from Harry Belafonte's *Beat Street* and was essentially a semi-autobiographical story about the struggles of an NYC hip hop producer and his burgeoning label. *L.A. Law*'s Blair Underwood played the Russell Simmons character, and Rubin played the fictionalized version of himself. "Russell really cared about finding new ways to expose the music to a bigger audience," explained Rubin. *Krush Groove* was certainly innovative if not 100 percent factual. "It's maybe 50 percent accurate. . . . That was definitely a Hollywood version. But the basic story is similar," said Rubin.

The success of LL Cool J's "I Need a Beat" was pivotal to convincing movie executives, including Warner Bros. Pictures President Marc Canton, to finance the $3 million film budget. The picture's green light coupled with the buzz created by LL's single led CBS to change the terms of their original development deal with Def Jam, signing the label to a $2 million distribution deal in September 1985, in what Simmons described as "the greatest opportunity in the whole world."

The spring and summer of 1985 Rubin spent juggling the filming of *Krush Groove* at Silvercup Studios in Long Island City, production duties on the soundtrack, and LL's debut LP. George Drakoulias recalled what it was like working with Rubin in those early days: "I didn't know what I was doing and Rick didn't know much more, I don't think. He was just paying for the studio time and kind of had a vision. He would write these beats, and the studio was totally manual, so you had four or five people on the board holding things down, waiting for something to come up. 'Is that coming? Okay, next one.' You might accidentally put the kick drum on half a beat early, but it would be okay. You always broke it down to the high-hat at one point. There were certain things you just automatically followed. There would be a guy yelling in one room and a drum machine and a lot of reverb. You never knew what was gonna happen."

When fall arrived, Rubin hadn't had time to find an apartment but was finally forced to move out of his dorm room at Weinstein Hall. The producer wound up moving into a loft between Houston Street and Brice, at 594 Broadway, and Def Jam's offices officially relocated to 40 East 19th Street, sharing space with Russell Simmons' Rush Management offices.

With his office and home settled, Rubin just needed to find the right studio to record in. LL Cool J's album had been recorded at Chung King Studios. The studio was originally called Secret Society Records, but as it was housed in a former Chinese restaurant, Rubin took to calling it the Chung King House of Metal and the name stuck. Rubin remembers the studio as "such a dump, it was like an embarrassing place to record. . . . So we made up this fictional name." *Blender* described Chung King as "the home away from home for many of the artists signed to Def Jam. . . . Owned by John King, a musician and friend of Rubin's since the two first met at the New York club Danceteria, Chung King was a single-room sixth-floor studio measuring about 13 feet by 18 feet, with fresh graffiti on the walls." It may have been a dump but it came to be known as the Abbey Road of Rap. Rubin felt the studio was "rock 'n' roll. . . . It was like stepping back in time, something in a film noir. . . . The studio had a really free vibe." All of LL Cool J's *Radio* LP and much of the material for the Beastie Boys' and Run-DMC's LPS were recorded at Chung King, but when Def Jam spent part of their $600,000 CBS advance on a four-story building at 298 Elizabeth Street in June 1986, the producer was excited to turn the building's basement into a state-of-the-art recording studio. Aside from producing platinum albums, Rubin's goal was to never go "to Chung King again." But with that studio still just a dream, Rubin was forced to complete these seminal projects there.

Krush Groove hit theaters in October 1985, grossing $11 million, three times its production budget, and making overnight stars of Def Jam's artist roster and its management. Riding high on the success of the film, Def Jam released LL Cool J's *Radio* on November 18. The album sold 900,000 copies upon its release (and was eventually certified platinum), earning back the $7,000 recording costs and bumping up the label's reputation with CBS, the hip hop community, and bolstering Rubin's and Simmons' confidence.

On a promotional trip to London, Rubin and Simmons caught a show by British rapper Slick Rick, and the producer declared afterward that he should be the next Def Jam artist, no matter what efforts were required to sign him. Simmons focused on the business of signing Slick Rick and promoting Def Jam's artists and the brand itself, while Rubin returned to his domain of mastery — the studio. Thanks to the trust he and Simmons had placed in one another, Rubin retained complete autonomy as in-house producer for Def Jam.

Rubin's goal was for the music Def Jam released "to be as cutting-edge and radical as it could be, but we weren't elitist about it. We didn't want people not to be able to have it. We would focus on making music, and [CBS would] focus on selling it and getting [it] into stores, exposing and advertising it." Rubin and Simmons were the eyes and ears on the street for what everyone else in the industry heard on record and saw on MTV. "There was a synergy, where anything that was going on in hip hop was coming out of our office, one way or another," Rubin said of the time. In addition to LL Cool J's album, Def Jam's first year of releases was scheduled to include the debut LP from the newly signed Beastie Boys. As Rubin began work on demos for the Beastie Boys, he also started work on Run-DMC's third LP.

Run-DMC was signed to Profile Records with Russell Simmons managing the group, but with Rubin's stock as the hottest hip hop producer on the East Coast fast on the rise, it was a foregone conclusion he would produce the rap group's next album. Rubin's desire to work with Run-DMC dated back to the early '80s, when Rubin, upon hearing the group's first single, "It's Like That"/"Sucker MCs," had boldly commented, "This is the real shit. [But] *I* could do this better." With *Raising Hell*, he would have his opportunity.

CHAPTER 4

Run-DMC

Raising Hell and Making History

BEFORE EVER WORKING TOGETHER, Rick Rubin and Run-DMC were tight on a personal level. "Through my friendship with Russell, I started hanging out with Run and D and Jay," explained Rubin to *AV Club*. "We just became friends, and when it was time to make their next album, they really loved what I was doing with LL and with the Beastie Boys, so they asked me to help." Run felt Rubin was "a multi-talent deserving of acclaim."

Talking to VH1 in 2002, Rubin described the group's process for developing songs: "They always had live routines that would start as a freestyle routine, and they would evolve into the kernel of an idea that would become a song. It was always good when they were out on the road, because Run would say one thing one night, then he and DMC would look at each other and think, 'Put that in the catalog!' The next night, he might expand upon it. It was stuff written through improvisation in front of an audience. . . . Sometimes there would be a lyrical hook or a particular sample or break that we liked. We'd try to create a new song using that element. *Raising Hell* was one of the first albums to create a montage of existing bits of music together to make something new."

Rubin's vision for the album sonically and conceptually was to capture something "raw, musical, and ferocious. It's very stripped down but there's more music going on than on anyone else's records at the time. It's 'less is more' — but it's the right less! It's easy for a hip hop album to start sounding very same-y, because you don't have the advantage of melody. We were drawing from all different styles of music — from James Brown's funky drumming to new wave — but there was a concerted effort for each track to stand on its own. The music that we liked in the clubs didn't sound glossy and shiny. It sounded rough and raw. So part of what made this album special was we recorded it at a really crummy studio. The drum machine was supposed to sound like a crummy drum machine. We wanted sounds that sounded like crummy toys with soul. That was more important than making it sound pretty or perfect. It was raw, like a documentary."

Once production on the LP was nearly wrapped, Rubin had one more idea up his sleeve that he felt would be "a nice little kicker to the album." He suggested to the rap group that they pair with rock legends Aerosmith for a re-imagining of the band's 1975 song "Walk This Way," which a decade earlier had hit #10 on the Billboard Hot 100. Initially Run-DMC just wanted to sample the song. "They all each had two copies of the record but had never heard past the first seven seconds of the song. That intro beat was the part that always got played. Their idea was 'Okay, well, let's use the beat but write a new Run-DMC song using the beat.' I felt like the whole purpose of exposing this music to a greater audience had to do with the familiarity of the song," Rubin told VH1. Russell Simmons recalled the genesis of the idea, "We were gonna cut the beat back and forth, that's how we gonna make this record. It's not gonna be any singing or any of that crap. Rick Rubin was like, 'No, let's call up Aerosmith.' I said, 'Who?' 'Aerosmith.' 'Who are they?' 'That's the people from *Toys in the Attic*; that's the band.' Run and DMC were not for the idea. I was a little more in the middle about it, 'Are you gonna rap those lyrics?' But we had a lot of fun making it." Convincing Aerosmith to do the collaboration was relatively easy. The

Run-DMC with Rick Rubin and Russell Simmons at The Ritz in New York City on January 28, 1988. (© Ebet Roberts/Getty Images)

former supergroup was at a low point in their career, having recently released an unsuccessful album. More accessible to the upstart producer, Aerosmith were also keen to participate as they had always been fans and supporters of R&B and black music.

Rubin sold both groups on the idea, and once they were together, "it was interesting because it was two very different cultures. We were all kids but Aerosmith was already Aerosmith. They carried themselves in a different way than we did 'cause they were real rock stars and we were like college students. It was an awe-inspiring experience for me because I grew up on Aerosmith and loved them. I also knew how great they were, so I became fairly demanding with what I asked them to play and contribute. . . . Both sides didn't really know what to make of it."

While many people at the time were staunch believers that "rap wasn't music," Rubin saw a natural musical compatibility between the two genres of rock and rap, and his production of "Walk This Way" helped the general public "open their eyes to hip hop." Rubin elaborated, "The idea of covering 'Walk This Way' was to give hip hop a context. It would show people outside of the really small hip hop community that if you saw it in a different light maybe you could discover the music's secret. . . . It was a shortcut to get people to see it." It was a move that would complete Run-DMC's launch into the pop-culture stratosphere and revitalize Aerosmith's career in the process.

Rubin described the album's overall stylistic vibe to *AV Club*: "It wasn't slick, and it wasn't mainstream, but it was alternative, edgy, raw music. There's a homemade and handmade quality to it." The groundbreaking album had a great impact on hip hop as a genre commercially, pushing further the traditional pop song structure that Run-DMC had begun experimenting with in *King of Rock*. Far from the "old school" six- to nine-minute 12-inch singles, the songs on *Raising Hell* took hip hop into unchartered territory.

The album reached #3 on the Billboard Top 200 Album Chart on September 20, 1986. It was the first hip hop album to reach Billboard's Top 10 and the first to garner a five-star review from *Rolling Stone*; the magazine called the LP "the first truly consistent rap album," declaring that Run-DMC "transcend the limitations of their genre," and that "for every outrageous boast and randy pun, these MCs have an angry insight and a wicked rhyme, while DJ Jam Master Jay works the turntables like a brain surgeon turned mad scientist."

Looking back close to 20 years later, Rick Rubin shared his perspective on the seminal nature of the album: "*Raising Hell* was like a Coasters album. People don't like to say that, but *Raising Hell* fused what was great about hip hop with a deeper understanding of song structure. That's why it crossed those boundaries. The timing was also critical. Run-DMC was the most credible hip hop group in the world. Before the record came out, they were already the Beatles of hip hop. Hip hop had already been around for a couple of years, so it was less alien to people. And they're great songs: they transcend genre. It's bigger than hip hop."

Raising Hell secured Rubin's position as the hottest producer in hip hop. Given that he had already produced a hit LP for LL Cool J, the Village Voice, in a November 1986 feature on Def Jam, hailed Rubin as the King of Rap. That title would be further validated with Def Jam's next release, arguably Rubin's most successful and groundbreaking production of the 1980s: the Beastie Boys' Licensed to Ill.

CHAPTER 5

Beastie Boys

Licensed to Ill

A CREATIVE PLAYGROUND FOR RICK RUBIN, *Licensed to Ill* marked his opportunity to further blend rock and rap, picking up where he left off with Run-DMC's *Raising Hell*. Recorded at Chung King Studios over the summer and fall of 1986, Rubin and the Beastie Boys put together a seminal album, one that would establish hip hop as a commercially viable force. The incorporation of rock riff samples over hip hop beats, a fusion that Rick Rubin had first popularized, became Def Jam's blueprint throughout the second half of the 1980s, and it made the Beastie Boys true pioneers of the rap-rock format. The breakthrough hip hop album by a white act, *Licensed to Ill* is the foundation of all the rap-rock derivatives that followed: Anthrax's *I'm the Man*, Faith No More's *Epic*, Limp Bizkit, and Kid Rock. It all began with the collaboration between the Beastie Boys and Rick Rubin, which also marked the final step in rap's growth from an underground, urban genre into the mainstream and America's suburbs. With the success of *Licensed to Ill*, hip hop began its evolution into the huge industry and pop-culture-driving phenomenon it is today.

The Beastie Boys began as a hardcore punk-rock act with elements of rap in their performance. Ad-Rock explained to *Guitar World*, "When we'd play a show, the first 15 minutes would be hardcore, then Rick Rubin would come up and we'd start to rap. Eventually, we switched over to doing only rap. But it was a mellow transition for us. Half our act was rap anyway." The jump from one genre to the next was a no-brainer for the boys. "When you think about it, hardcore and hip hop aren't really that different. In hardcore, you've got your verse and your chorus. In a rap song, it's kind of the same thing. And the attitude is the same — it's a city attitude." Mike D expressed a similar opinion to *Newsday*: "Attitude wise, hardcore and rap are remarkably similar. The energy is the same. And you can express yourself without having had to study music for 15 years. I used to say that the only difference was that with punk rock you had to have funny haircuts, whereas with rap, you have funny hats."

And Rubin was on the same page as the Beasties. With his own punk band past and long-time love of rock 'n' roll, Rubin "liked punk-rock music and for me, hip hop was black punk, and I like white punk and black punk equally. I like fringe music. It just seemed like, at the moment in time while I was at NYU, the punk scene was kind of waning and the hip hop scene was thriving. If it had been five years before, I probably would have produced punk rock first." Rubin had first met the Beastie Boys — when they were still a punk outfit made up of Adam Yauch (MCA), Michael Diamond (Mike D), Kate Schellenbach, and John Berry — at a benefit held at CBGBs. The bill also featured Adam Horovitz's band The Young and the Useless. Shortly after that show, Adam "Ad-Rock" Horovitz left his punk band to join the Beastie Boys, and they recorded the *Cooky Puss* 12-inch in 1983. As MCA recalled, "After we did *Cooky Puss*, we were still a rock band, and we decided we wanted to work some rap into our set, and this DJ said we ought to meet this guy Rick. It was Christmas, and we wanted to have a bubble machine and a smoke machine and Rick had both. So there was a part of our show when Mike was playing the drums, and Kate, who was our drummer, played the bass and Rick [DJ Double R] was scratching and me and Ad-Rock were trying to rap."

Rubin recalled those early days: "I was chairman of the social committee [at NYU] and a DJ and the Beastie Boys started coming to these parties at my dorm. They asked me to DJ for them since I was a friend of theirs and I had a bubble machine." Mike D elaborated on the relationship, "Rick came into the picture after we did the record *Cooky Puss*. That was sort of weird, it was right after Malcolm McLaren was making his records and we were just having a good time. We'd been listening to hip hop in rock clubs since day one, asking rock DJs to play the records, then we decided to do our own jam." The Beasties and Rubin joining forces moved the group's sound toward what would eventually end up on *Licensed to Ill*. "We hooked up with Rick Rubin because we wanted to MC in our live shows and needed a DJ to do so, and he had turntables," explained Mike D. "He definitely swayed us in that he told us to forget the other stuff we were doing and just concentrate on the rap stuff. He had this PA in the room and we'd listen to all the new 12-inch singles in there and Horovitz would make beats on his drum machine."

With Rubin giving the group a shove from punk to rap, there were also changes to the line-up of the group. Drummer Kate Schellenbach, who went on to Luscious Jackson, explained, "We actually had gone into the studio and started recording a rap tune. But Rick didn't like me and I didn't really like him and he didn't like women rapping, the sound of women's voices rapping or something ridiculous. So Yauch was like, 'All right, this is what's happening. Rick's kind of like, it's either me or you.' Either Rick or Kate, basically, was what it was." Friend of the Beastie Boys, actress Nadia Dajani recalled, "Rick was the one who influenced them to say it should be boys, and it should just be rap. He didn't want Kate in the band and that was tough. They felt completely remorseful, but I think they sort of understood that it made sense at that time for them. Rick had to convince them, but they absolutely felt shitty about it."

Rubin and Ad-Rock seemed to have the most instant connection, with Ad-Rock hanging out every day at Rubin's NYU dorm room (a.k.a. the headquarters of Def Jam) flipping through boxes of demo tapes and sometimes finding gold — like LL Cool J's demo. Of those

They be illin': the Beastie Boys in August 1984 in New York City. (Rick Rubin, aka DJ Double R, is standing center.) (© Josh Cheuse/Retna Ltd.)

early days, Rubin recalled, "We all hung out, but me and Adam Horovitz were together a lot, more than the other guys. The summer right before the *Licensed to Ill* album, it seemed like we were living together at the dorm, and we would just write rhymes all the time. Anywhere we'd go, we'd think of good ideas for rhymes, and have all these scraps of paper loaded with rhymes." Then-publicist for Def Jam Records Bill Adler explained, "I think pretty early on Rick decided that Ad-Rock was the dominant, creative force in the group, and so he was just gonna get very tight with Ad-Rock. . . . They just hung out a lot together, in Rick's dorm room, in the studio." Out of those hours spent together came many of the ideas for *Licensed to Ill*; Rubin and Ad-Rock wrote "Girls" on an Amtrak ride between DC and New York, inspired by the Isley Brothers hit "Shout," in what Rubin described as "kind of a reductionist take on that breed of music."

One of the first songs the producer and group recorded together was "Rock Hard," which featured a sample from AC/DC's "Back in Black." "B-Boys liked it 'cause it was, like, really loud," said Mike D to the *Record Mirror* in 1986. "The fact that there was guitar in it didn't matter as long as it was loud. I kept saying, 'Speed up the tempo, speed up the tempo.'" MCA piped in, "We were up to 185 beats per minute and Mike's ass just started dancing." Mike D is still proud of those tracks: "There are some things that I think are really fly and still stand up."

While the Beastie Boys and Rubin were still in pre-production for *Licensed to Ill*, Russell Simmons landed the group a dream slot on Madonna's Like a Virgin tour in 1985 — it would provide massive exposure for the group, though not necessarily to the right audience demographic. MCA recalled, "Before we started *Licensed to Ill*, at that time, we had 'Slow and Low.' We went into the studio and recorded 'She's on It' when we got the Madonna tour so that we would have another song to perform live. We went and added that because all we had was 'Beastie Groove' and 'Rock Hard.' We were doing a cover of T La Rock's 'It's Yours' because we didn't have enough songs of our own." Andre "Doctor Dre" Brown, then a Beastie Boys DJ and future co-host of *Yo! MTV Raps*, recalled that "*Licensed to Ill* was written, like, in a year, all over the place. We wrote on the bus, we wrote in the studio, and then with CBS and the deal coming tighter and 'Hold It, Now Hit It' becoming such a big hit, they were forced to try to finish the album correctly."

The protracted recording schedule affected the style of the album in a beneficial way. "One of the reasons that [*Licensed to Ill*] was as diverse as it was, is that we really did it over a long period of time," Rubin explained to *liveDaily*. "We probably recorded it over two years, really slowly, writing the song and then writing another song six weeks or two months later. By taking so long, it really gave it a breadth and depth that's difficult from a typical album where an artist has six weeks to write their songs for a record."

The recording sessions at Chung King were "all fun, it wasn't serious work," said Rubin. And his former roommate, Adam Dubin, agreed, recalling the sessions having "a loose atmosphere." Nadia Dajani remembered, "The recording of *Licensed to Ill* was one big hangout. After a night of partying at Danceteria or Area or wherever we'd make our way down to Chung King studio. We would bring in sloppy White Castle burgers, someone would make a run for beer, a run for Cokes. It was a constant trickle in and out. Ad-Rock's mom would come by." Even the "corporate suits" like Bill Stephney, the GM for Def Jam Records, would "[bounce] in and out of the sessions, just seeing what was going on, and it all sounded great, a great energy." But Rubin's partner Russell Simmons was rarely around the studio. "I don't think Russell spent any time in the studio with them," said Bill Adler. "I mean, he would hear what they made. He was a great enthusiast of what was being made as it happened. But I don't think he had very much to say over what happened in the studio. Rick did that."

Rubin's autonomy over the recording sessions as producer was absolute, with the producer admitting to the *LA Times*, "In the early days of Def Jam, I was pretty dictatorial, and I think that's one of the reasons the Beastie Boys left the label. They wanted to have more of a voice in their records, and they were right." Despite that, former Beastie Boys manager Lyor Cohen felt "Rick just had this amazing vision for the group." And longtime Beastie Boys friend and *Hello Nasty* graphic designer Cey Adams — a regular during album recording sessions — positioned Rick as influential conceptually: "I really think it was Rick Rubin who came up with a lot of the hip hop ideas. For the record, anything silly was usually Rick's idea." That creative autonomy was felt by engineer Steve Ett. "Rick knows right away when something doesn't sound right. If I play him a tape, within the first 30 seconds, he'll love it or hate it. Maybe he'll help write the beat. Or if someone has a rap written and a particular lyric doesn't work, Rick will come up with a different way of saying what they wanted to say. But mostly he lets the artist have his own way." Some songs were mostly crafted — both lyrically and musically — by the Beastie Boys with Rubin citing "Hold It, Now Hit It" and "Paul Revere" as ones the boys "had a lot to do with."

The stylistic blend in the group's debut full-length album, Rubin explained, was a result of the Beastie Boys' urban style and Rubin's commercial ear. "Their musical taste was radically different from mine. I liked bands like AC/DC, Led Zeppelin — they hated those things. Because being cool kids in the city, those things were too commercial, too mainstream. So the Beastie Boys liked really underground stuff, which served them well. It was cool, and it made them who they were. But I think it was the collaboration between my more suburban, mainstream taste and their more eclectic, underground taste that made our working together so successful."

Rubin, for his part, felt his greatest contribution to rap — and by extension to constructing the Beastie Boys record — "was the structured-song element. Prior to that, a lot of rap songs were seven minutes long; the guy would keep rapping until he ran out of words." As he explained to *Shark*, Rubin also found more commercial success with the Beastie Boys because of the color of their skin: "The fact that the Beastie Boys were a white group was kind of a big deal. If a 14-year-old white girl in, oh, Alabama had brought home a Run-DMC album in those days — you know, looking at these black guys as rock 'n' roll guys or sex symbols — it would not really have been okay. Whereas, as stupid and disgusting as the Beastie Boys might have been, that was okay because they were white. Reality is, this is a very racist country, very racist. I think when they played the Beastie Boys on MTV, then it made it easier for MTV to play Run-DMC."

Digital programming technology was primitive at the time so Rubin recorded the album's groundbreaking rhythm tracks entirely on what engineer George Drakoulias described as "DMXs and 808s back then, with big AMS reverbs, a little bit of compression, and the console was a small 24 x 4 x 2, old Neve 68, and just big speakers. I don't think we ever used little monitors. And the goal was to get the record to be as loud as we could, and this was before digital, so we'd print to half-inch tape, and make a lot of edits. If someone messed up, we'd just keep going, and make the part again, and did a lot of tape editing. That was fun. And [we] played with a lot reverbs. One time we turned the tape over for a track called 'Paul Revere.' The whole thing was whoever was there back then, you *had* to be involved because everything was handmade."

Drakoulias recalled of the days spent at Chung King Studios: "It was a 16-track, 2-inch, analog studio, and the songs were handmade with no automation and the records were really simple: a drum machine, a rapper yelling, and a DJ scratching. It was very simple and basic, but what was fun was it was all mixed by hand. So what we'd do was have three or four people on a console, and I was responsible for however many hands I had, so like four buttons. And if you wanted to make a breakdown, we couldn't program the drum machine — the beat was pretty much constant — so if you wanted a breakdown you'd manually mute the kick drum or snare, whatever it was." In one instance, with the drum beat for "Fight for Your Right," Rubin and engineer Steve Ett physically hit the rubber pads of their Oberheim DMX drum with bare hands to emphasize the song's kick and snare parts.

MCA recalled, "On *Licensed to Ill*, we didn't even have any samplers. So the stuff that's looped, we actually made tape loops. We'd record [Led Zeppelin's] 'When the Levee Breaks' beat onto a quarter-inch tape, and then we'd make the loop and that tape would be spinning around the room, dangling on mic stands, going around in a big loop. And then, in order to layer that with something else, we'd have to actually synch it up, physically."

A November 1986 *Village Voice* article documented a day in the studio and the creative process of constructing a classic like "The New Style": "one of the few without a chanted chorus, but the song has peaks and breaks of tension created by the way Rubin and Ett work the mixing board. Each of the board's 24 tracks contains a separately recorded percussion element, which repeats a phrase dozens of times. Rubin and Ett press buttons to make each cowbell, high hat, snare, and bass drum track pop in and out at the precise moment. The mixing board itself acts as a polymorphic drum set, which allows an enormous amount of freedom to alter a song."

"Slow and Low" came to the Beastie Boys by way of Run-DMC. Rubin recalled they gave "the Beasties the lyrics for 'Slow and Low,' not the track. We did the musical track the same way as the rest of the album. There was a close familial relationship between the Beasties and Run-DMC — they were the premiere hip hop group in the world at that time and took the Beasties under their wing. There was a general feeling of sharing and all for one at Def Jam. There were other collaborations at this time between the different Def Jam artists — LL Cool J wrote the lyrics for a Run-DMC song during this same period." DMC remembered more pressure from Rubin: "We recorded 'Slow and Low'; we was gonna put it on our album. But they liked it so much that they wanted to do it. Rick was pressuring us, 'Yo, you gotta let my guys have it.' They put their names in there, their favorite stuff — like where we would say, 'We like McDonalds,' they would put in 'We like White Castle.'" In another case, DMC recalled, "It was Run's idea to turn the beat backwards on 'Paul Revere.' They wanted to have a slow beat, and Run was like, 'To make it outrageous you need to turn the beat backwards and rhyme over that.'"

Run-DMC's influence over the Beastie Boys' sound and style showed up in the blend of rap and rock; *Licensed to Ill* sampled rock legends including Led Zeppelin, Black Sabbath, and others. Rubin described it as his "rock 'n' roll roots coming out. . . . Much like 'Walk This Way' was really kind of different than the rest of the Run-DMC album, I really wanted to do a straight-up rock song that incorporated rap, but something that really blurred the line and that's what it did." That blurred line lead to two of the album's hit singles: "No Sleep till Brooklyn" and "Fight for Your Right." To ensure maximum authenticity, Rubin enlisted guitarist Kerry King of the just-signed thrash metal band Slayer to play lead on "No Sleep." King recalled the experience: "We just got signed to Def Jam, and we were in the same studio, and Rick Rubin was working with both of us. And he just came down and said, 'Hey, what do you think about doing the lead down the hallway?' That was about all there was to it. It took five minutes . . . and was such a whim thing to do. We were in the studio at the same time and I didn't even know any of them. They were on Def Jam and they needed a lead and I went, 'Okay!' and went down there and did it and that was it. I did get to be in their video, which was cool because

[Slayer] didn't have any videos at the time. . . . I think that I got like 200 bucks or something. I had no idea who they were or if they would be popular. . . . It might have taken two takes, because it wasn't supposed to be anything intricate. They were spoofing metal, so to speak, on 'No Sleep till Brooklyn,' so I just went in and did something, out of tune in parts, and with feedback — as just one of those totally spur-of-the-moment things. I didn't think about it at all."

On what would become the Beastie Boys' break-out song, "Fight for Your Right," Rubin placed a heavy emphasis on rock drums and guitars with its potential as a cross-over single perhaps more in mind than the group's members. MCA recalled, "Rick Rubin took the task of mixing the stuff in our absence. . . . I remember someone showing up on our tour bus with a tape of what Rick had made from our demo and playing it. Rick had replaced the drums with these big rock drums and replayed the guitar with a real Top 40, cheesy rock sound." Rubin maintained total autonomy over mixing and was in no rush, explaining to Mike D that "I would love it to be done. . . . But the reality of the creative process is it takes however long it takes to be great." Rubin later commented on the amount of time he and the Beastie Boys invested in producing *Licensed to Ill*: "If we'd have written the songs in two months, it wouldn't sound like it does. . . . It really is an episodic journey. That was the life of the project. I've always really followed the art." As for the content of the lyrics, which are undeniably juvenile and misogynist in places, looking back Rubin felt "no regrets at all. . . . Listening back to it, you can be horrified by some of the things that were said, but in the spirit it was done in at the time, it was just fun. Nothing was done with any malice or negative intent. There was a certain amount of locker-room humor, guys trying to make each other laugh. Whatever got a rise, made it to the record."

Once the album was finished and handed over to Def Jam and Columbia Records for release, Russell Simmons, who had given Rubin as much creative freedom and time as he'd required, felt the investment had paid off. The Beastie Boys and Rubin had "made an album that was great and it represented the ideas and attitudes of a lot of kids who didn't have their own rap artists yet. . . . It really took all the alternative

music and rap music and put it into a little box and made it nicely packaged."

Already riding high off the success of Run-DMC's *Raising Hell*, Def Jam rounded out the year by releasing *Licensed to Ill* in November 1986. The album reached the top of the Billboard Top 200 Album Chart on March 7, 1987, besting even Run-DMC's debut, and becoming Def Jam's — and hip hop's — first #1 album. Critics and record buyers, especially suburban and white fans, ate the Beastie Boys up with fervor, causing the *Village Voice* to observe that "the wise cracking arrogance of this record is the only rock and roll attitude that means diddley right now." *Licensed to Ill* has since been recognized not only for its great sales but as a top album of all time, appearing on *The Source*'s 100 Best Rap Albums list and on *Rolling Stone*'s 500 Greatest Albums of All Time list. In its praise for the album, *Rolling Stone* called it "one hard-rockin' cartoon, a rappin' caricature so huge only a grown-up sourpuss could take it seriously. . . . *Licensed to Ill* cuts an even wider swath musically than *Raising Hell*, and it's the brash assurance of Rubin's 'stealin' that ultimately makes these white boys more than a sophomoric joke. . . . it's time to get ill."

CHAPTER 6

Public Enemy Brings the Noise

RUBIN'S SUCCESS WITH THE BEASTIE BOYS showcased the duality of his talents — an ear of a producer and an A&R man's eye for talent. It was in the latter capacity that he pursued Chuck D, eventually signing his cutting-edge rap group Public Enemy to Def Jam in June 1986. Public Enemy founded political rap, period. It was an arena they would undisputedly dominate until Tupac Shakur entered the rap game in 1991. Group leader Chuck D's goal for Public Enemy was to "make a rap group that was as big as Run-DMC. I wanted to change how people looked at rap music. I wanted to change how black people thought of ourselves. . . . Our attitude to music is a cross between a sports team and military corps: win, crush, destroy."

It was DMC who initially turned Rick Rubin's ear onto Public Enemy. "When me and J first heard [Chuck D] and Flavor at WBAU, we ran with the tape to Rick Rubin and said, 'Rick, G-d has come down to rock the mic!' Rick was like, 'I gotta sign this dude' . . . just from that. Russell was so scared of what Chuck was talking about, believe it or not. 'People will never go for that . . . it's too radical.' Rick was like, 'This is the new thing man!'" Rubin knew he had to sign Public Enemy to Def Jam, as he told *AV Club*. "I'd heard a tape of Chuck D's college radio show, and the theme song was called 'Public Enemy No. 1,' which ended up being on the first album. I heard that and said, 'We need this guy. This needs to be Def Jam.'" Feeling on the strength of "Public Enemy No. 1" that Chuck D was "the greatest" next artist, Rubin had to convince Chuck D of that. "He considered himself a grown man, with a family and a regular job. . . . I put his phone number on a Post-it note on my phone and I would call it every day and just keep bugging him . . . saying 'We really have to make a record, it's time to make a record.' I finally tried again in about six months' time and he said, 'Maybe.'"

Chuck D's initial skepticism was that he was too old for the hip hop game; artists like LL Cool J were just 16 and he was in his early 20s. "He felt like his artist days were past," explained Rubin. "We wanted to put out music, and we were having great success, and there was nothing good. And here was something good. Finally, one day, after months, he came in with Flava Flav — I don't think Griff was there yet — and said, 'Okay, I'm ready to do it. It's called Public Enemy. Here's the whole vision.' He had it all worked out. They weren't going to be like any other hip hop group. They were going to be more like The Clash. They were going to have lyrics that meant something, and uniforms, and a militaristic feel, the whole thing." Chuck D had his reasons for his initial hesitation: "I felt I would be a better director than artist, but Rick Rubin was adamant about me being the vocalist in the group. I was in a situation where I received an offer I couldn't refuse, and I had to do it. . . . No other label would have given us the latitude. We brought so many ideas to the Def Jam table. They brought the marketing and promotional concepts that made for a perfect marriage."

Stepping back from the mixing board into an executive producer role, Rubin gave Public Enemy carte blanche in the studio, allowing them creative freedom, which suited Chuck D, who said, "I don't think it would have worked if it was a hovering situation." Def Jam's in-house engineer Steve Ett was the only member of the label's production staff involved with the recording sessions for *Yo! Bum Rush the*

Show. Shock Lee, the group's producer, explained, "Rick felt like we can retain the Def Jam sound by retaining Steve Ett. Steve had helped develop that sound with Rick. It's hard to say what it is, but you know it when you hear it. It almost feels like a heavy-metal hip hop record."

Released in January 1987, *Yo! Bum Rush the Show* became one of the year's best-selling rap albums and one that critics took notice of. Jon Pareles of the *New York Times* singled Public Enemy out for "a spirit of defiance that shades toward rage," declaring, "At a time when most rappers typecast themselves as comedy acts or party bands, Public Enemy's best moments promise something far more dangerous and subversive: reality." *Yo! Bum Rush the Show* was the first in a pair of groundbreaking LPs that served as a blueprint for future political rap albums. It was followed by 1988's *It Takes a Nation of Millions to Hold Us Back*, also a Def Jam album executive produced by Rick Rubin. In its four-and-a-half star review, *Rolling Stone* underscored the importance of the album: "Rap didn't come any heavier, harder or angrier in '88 than Public Enemy's second Molotov cocktail of nuclear scratching, gnarly minimalist electronics, and revolution rhyme . . . Public Enemy can step into your face so fiercely, challenging your courage with its conviction."

Speaking to the *Progressive* in 2005, Chuck D reflected on the album's landmark status: "*It Takes a Nation* was an album that happened to cross the roads at the right place at the right time. Rap music, as recorded work, was just eight years in. The music was ready to break nationally in album form as opposed to what it had been, which was a singles medium. The album was released by a small radical label called Def Jam. Def Jam was distributed by staunch old school institutions such as CBS and Columbia. We happened to find that loophole and use their distribution system to be able to get to the people in a brand new state of mind. We wanted to be a social critic, a community voice. We wanted everyone to know, truly understand, that our music was from the people, not above the people."

After such a dogged pursuit of the group, Rubin was overwhelmed when he first listened to *It Takes a Nation of Millions*, hearing the kernel of excellence he first witnessed in "Public Enemy No. 1" realized on that

album. "I was on the airplane listening to it and I remembered I cried. I was so proud. Because to me it just took it to a whole new level, and I just remember crying, thinking this is just such a beautiful thing that's evolving and growing. But for me it felt like that was the last one like that. That's what I always wanted from music, and I wasn't getting it from rap at that time." Rubin felt the legacy of Public Enemy was far reaching. "[Chuck D] changed the whole world of rap. When everyone was just bragging or dissing, he had serious social commentary and talked about serious things when nobody else was. I can remember when [*Yo! Bum Rush the Show*] came out. Radio stations would only play the instrumental versions, because they liked the tracks but hated Chuck's voice. And then on [*It Takes a Nation of Millions to Hold Us Back*] he said, 'Last time you played the music, this time you'll play the lyrics.' That's what he was talking about." Though Rubin didn't work with Public Enemy on their next Def Jam album (1990's *Fear of a Black Planet*) there was one other project the two forces collaborated on — "Bring the Noise" on 1987's *Less Than Zero* soundtrack.

CHAPTER 7

Rick Rubin
Goes to Hollywood

THE *LESS THAN ZERO* SOUNDTRACK *was* "Rick Rubin, all of those different kinds of records," according to his partner Russell Simmons. Showcasing his true potential as a producer of any style of music, Rubin took the opportunity to expand his production portfolio, creating a soundscape that mixed music styles to create what legendary rock publication *Circus* hailed as a "great rock soundtrack." As a Def Jam project, Rubin had complete creative freedom. "They came to us and said 'Pick the songs,'" recalled assistant producer George Drakoulias. Rubin took his expertise at reinventing classic rock hits for a new generation of fans to its next logical step. He had already mastered the art of drawing catchy samples from classic hits and using them to great effect to create hit rap singles. On the *Less Than Zero* soundtrack, Rubin took artists like The Bangles and Poison and paired them with songs to create hit cover versions. At the same time, Rubin used the soundtrack to showcase his roster of Def Jam artists: Public Enemy, Glenn Danzig, Slayer (who covered Iron Butterfly's "In-A-Gadda-Da-Vida"), and rap star LL Cool J, who scored his biggest hit to date with "Going Back to Cali."

Though the movie's subject matter and its soundtrack were edgy, Rubin and Drakoulias tried to keep the recording sessions light-hearted and encouraging for the wide array of artists. Recording a cover of Simon & Garfunkel's "A Hazy Shade of Winter," The Bangles became the first female group to work with Rick Rubin. Drakoulias recalled, "We went to see The Bangles rehearse 'Hazy Shade of Winter,' and I remember there was a lot of tension in the room. They were girls, and we hadn't worked with girls yet, and didn't know if the dynamic was there. I remember looking at Susanna Hoffs' guitar, and she had a custom-made Rickenbacker model, and I remember looking at her, and she asked, 'Oh, you play guitar?' And I said, 'Oh, not great.' And she said, 'Do you know this song?' So I said, 'Well, I know it, but . . .' And she says, 'Do you want to play it? Because I don't really wanna learn it? I just wanna sing.' And I said, 'I think you should learn it,' and so they rehearsed and got it down." Rubin recalled to *Time* of the session, "Just before recording, one of the girls completely broke down. She said, 'I don't think I can do this. I've never played on one of our records before.' Someone made her believe she wasn't good enough to play on her own records. It just made me realize that the music business is lousy at nourishing creative people but that my personality is pretty well suited for it."

As Rubin and company led the group through tracking, George Drakoulias recalled that their biggest hurdle centered around the guitar riff, which had become an issue in rehearsals. "When we were tracking 'Hazy Shade of Winter,' the main riff was a hard riff to play straight through, so we cut it into two pieces, and panned them left and right as each part came in. It's an odd riff, and Vicki [Peterson], I and another guy played the guitars on the song. We decided to split the main riff up between Vicki and I, and made it like two separate parts, like a call-response thing." That solution became the catchiest part of the song. For Drakoulias, his personal highlight was "watching them do vocals, which was fantastic, and when we recorded their harmonies, it was just a matter of figuring out how we were going to split the vocal up. And we spent a little bit of time figuring out the outro: how one person came in, and stacked, and how we'd keep that build going. We recorded the girls' vocals on an 87 and a 67, because we had them singing in two sets of twos at each other. They had glass between them, but we also had them sing two at a time in the same room on certain things, and they would look at each other when they sang."

Expanding into the technical side of tracking the album's center-piece single, Drakoulias recalled, "We recorded at an old Motown studio in Hollywood, and it had a really nice room, and we had the Wendel, which was this old late '70s, early '80s sampler. It had an 8-track cartridge that went into it, because the samples went on tape; they were taped samples. So we triggered that to the kick-drum, and I remember that was a big deal, when we discovered the Wendel, we were all in awe like, '*Wow*, the Wendel.' We also used this thing called the Russian Dragon, which was this piece of equipment that let you know if you were in time so you could set your sample. It was a brave, new world; it was a lot of fun. For that song, I remember Rick and I were like, 'We have to get the tom-toms as big as possible!'" Recording with The Bangles was a milestone moment for the production team as they navigated live rock for the first time, and the result was a #2 hit on the Billboard Hot 100.

Known to be more style than substance, hair metal mavens Poison were next into the studio to record the Kiss classic "Rock and Roll All Nite." As Drakoulias explained, "After rehearsing with The Bangles, the next day we did a rehearsal with Poison, and it was the same room, but you would have never known it, because Poison had risers and amps with their pictures on it, they were wireless, they had roadies every-where and a lighting guy — all just to rehearse the song. They were playing the song and they half-knew it, and couldn't care less because they were having a great time. They were definitely putting on a show, and musically it was awful, but we didn't care because it was a good time. That was a hard track to cut. It was a weird session and they recorded with make-up on. They had this really strange click-track, and when guitarist C.C. Deville was playing guitar, his guitar was painted and had paint over the pick-ups. I asked, 'Does that affect the sound?' And he said, 'Yeah, probably, but I owe it to my fans to play this guitar,' which I thought was the funniest thing I'd ever heard. It took us three days to get through C.C.'s solo, three nights. We were at A&M, and we'd start at six then end at seven or eight in the morning. It took about a day and a night to get the first part, and we'd just punch in constantly. I would fall asleep and wake up while he and Rick were working on it. He was just a perfectionist, and it was a simple thing, but he was very methodical and particular about going over and over it again."

From relative newbies to legends, next up was Aerosmith. The band had tried to work with Rubin a few years before, but because of their struggles with addiction, it didn't lead anywhere. As Joe Perry, lead guitarist, recalled, "I remember that Rick Rubin contacted us. Rick has always been a supporter and a fan — this was like 1985, I think. Steven and I hadn't written anything but we went ahead and booked a session with Rick. We figured we would just go in and wing it and write something on the spot. We stopped at the liquor store on the way in. I had a pocketful of drugs in one pocket and I had a couple of joints in the other. We walked in with a bottle of Jack Daniels under one arm and a couple of six packs and the next thing I know I am waking up the next day and it was all a haze. We listened back to the tape and it sucked; it was terrible. Steven and I talked to each other and said that it was not working anymore. We knew we had to do something because it just wasn't right. That was the moment — we heard a really crappy piece of music and I said, 'This has got to change.' Aside from how screwed up spiritually I was at that point, the artistic side of me just wasn't working anymore. There was really no choice."

The group had committed to sobriety and worked with Rubin and Run-DMC on the massively successful remake of "Walk This Way." After almost a decade on the sidelines of relevance, Aerosmith was back in the game. For the *Less Than Zero* soundtrack, Drakoulias recalled, "In general, [Rubin and I] tried to use humor to relax everyone, but we also used the psychology of suggestion when it got difficult. One example in particular was recording Aerosmith's 'Boogie Woogie Flu.' I remember they rehearsed it, and they were like, 'That's good.' Rick and I were like, 'Well, it's okay. Maybe it could use another part.' And they said, 'Well, what do you mean?' And I went, 'I don't know — key change solo, oldest trick in the book.' So they tried it, liked the idea, and said to Rick, 'Good thing you brought him along.' So then we go in to cut it, and it went well; we got a track pretty fast. Then Joe Perry played a few solos, and everyone at some point went, 'Okay, yeah, that's great, that's the one.' So then Joe Perry comes in the control room and says, 'What'd you think?' And I said, 'It's great man, if you want everybody to think that [Brad Whitford, rhythm guitarist] played it.' So he looked at me, said, 'Give me that guitar,' made a face, got really mad, played a solo, and then went, 'You like that one?' And that's the one we used. And I knew, okay, here's Joe Perry, an idol of mine, and that if I used sarcasm he would do a better take."

Rick Rubin recruited Glenn Danzig to write two songs for the soundtrack, one of which was for Roy Orbison. Danzig was happy to work on such a mainstream project if it meant writing for one of his idols. "Roy Orbison is real dramatic stuff. I remember saying how he's got one more serious gold, maybe platinum, album left in him: he's just waiting for the right producer. And this guy called me up one day and said, 'I've got this soundtrack and I'm going to use Roy Orbison. Do you want to write a song for him?' . . . So I said, 'Yeah! I'll do it!' I wrote the song ['Life Fades Away'] especially for him. Me and Rick did a demo in the studio, sent it out to him, he loved it, I went over there and taught it to him, and we worked on it in the studio. It turned out really good even though it was really rushed; we could've added more tracks to it. When I listened to the *Less Than Zero* stuff, I only listened to, like, four songs: Public Enemy, Roy Orbison, my song, somebody else's."

Glenn Danzig wasn't supposed to sing "You and Me (Less Than Zero)," the second song he wrote for the soundtrack. "Rick wanted me to write this song, it was a favor for Rick Rubin, the producer. He wanted me to write a song that some girl was going to sing, that kinda related to what was going on in the movie, between the main three characters. He wanted a girl to sing it, so what I did was I lay down a rough vocal track for her, so she'd be able to . . . hear how the melody went and sing it. And eventually he couldn't find a girl to sing it, whatever it was, and he played the demo for the people at CBS and they said, 'Well just have this guy sing it,' so he asked me to do it." But Danzig was reluctant. "I was very apprehensive about doing the song that I did because it was originally written for a girl to sing . . . And I was like, 'Well, I don't know, I don't usually sing this kind of stuff, although I love this kind of music.' Like the Righteous Brothers and stuff; I wanted them to get Bill Medley and they were like, 'Oh, that guy's over, he's probably a loser somewhere,' but in actuality, he's a behind-the-scenes guy who produces records and stuff. Three weeks after *Less Than Zero* came out, Bill Medley had the number one song in the country."

Drakoulias recalled the experience recording with Glenn Danzig, Roy Orbison, and Rick Rubin. "When we got out here to [L.A. to] work on the record, Glenn came out, and Rick made me share a room with him. He's intimidating, and puts on this Halloween persona, but is a sweet kid deep down. I remember he was drawing little cartoons around the room, then I said to him, 'Okay, we have to go see Roy Orbison now.' So we drove out to Malibu in the middle of the day, and it was fall, and when we got there, his wife let us in. I'd met Roy a few days earlier, and Glenn had written Roy's song for the soundtrack, so we all went out to listen to it together. So when Roy had first heard Glenn's demo on a cassette player, he said, 'Oh, that's very nice. Let's bring Glenn out to talk about it.' So when Glenn got there, he was nervous — everybody was — because it was Roy Orbison. So we're standing in his upstairs den, looking out over the ocean, and Roy walks in and says [to Glenn], 'You remind me of myself when I was your age.' So we all picked up guitars and ran through the song once. Then when we were done, Roy put his guitar down and was staring out at the ocean and looking at Glenn, and Glenn was looking at me, going, 'Does that mean he liked it?' So Glenn's nudging me like 'Do something,' so I said, 'Okay, Roy, that was great. Should we try to run it through one more time?' Then Roy looks at us both and says, 'George, you and Glenn, y'all cool dudes. But I'm gonna have to get used to you for a little while.'

"When we tracked the song, Glenn came down and played the piano, and I played guitar and bass. And when Roy did his vocal, and in the song, he kept having to push to sing higher and higher to that last note, and he really went for it. Whenever we'd say, 'You need to sing a little higher,' he'd say, 'Okay, I'll try,' and he was really great. It was really strange watching him because he doesn't move his mouth when he sings, so you hear him, but you can't tell when you look at him. He'd say, 'Shoot'; he wouldn't curse. At one point, he just couldn't hit the high note, and I said, 'You okay? What do you need?' And he said, 'I've never made a record before without a Coca-Cola,' so I ran out and got one for him, and he knocked it out. We recorded Roy's vocal on a C-12 mic."

The soundtrack's release proved to be a boon not just for the artists — from Roy Orbison to LL Cool J — but for all parties involved. Rubin proved he could produce platinum results for any genre of music and Def Jam expanded its mainstream audience. For the legendary Roy Orbison, Rubin helped him achieve a final peak in his recording career before he passed away a few short years later; his rendition of "Life Fades Away" closed the film.

CHAPTER 8

The Cult

Electric

RUBIN TOOK THE SUCCESS of *Less Than Zero* as an opportunity to veer away from hip hop; his next act was The Cult. Seeking to break from their alt-rock beginnings into something more mainstream, The Cult had already had a hit in their native U.K. with "She Sells Sanctuary." Rubin would later describe *Electric* as "the first rock 'n' roll record I made." The production proved as cutting edge and influential in the late '80s world of rock as his rap productions had been in the first half of the decade.

Rubin would produce a razor-sharp rock album that didn't just cut edges but the fat from the bloated rock productions popular at the time, the height of hair bands. Drawing sonic inspiration from the power of AC/DC's *Highway to Hell*, Rubin explained in *Rolling Stone*, "Whether it's The Cult or the Red Hot Chili Peppers, I apply the same basic formula [to producing a rock record]: keep it sparse. Make the guitar parts more rhythmic. It sounds simple, but what AC/DC did is almost impossible to duplicate." With that goal in mind, Rubin chipped away at the band's outer alt-rock shell until he had sculpted a record that showcased The Cult's true sound, revealing a classic hard rock band in the tradition of AC/DC, Aerosmith, and the Rolling Stones.

Before meeting with Rubin, The Cult had already tracked *Electric*'s basic instrumentals with *Love* producer Steve Brown. Lead singer Ian Astbury recalled, "The initial *Electric* album was recorded in more of that psychedelic fashion, the atmosphere was more like what was going on when we recorded *Love*. I mean, the *Electric* album still had those 'fairy realm' aspects to it." These "Manor Sessions" recordings were scrapped, but nine eventually showed up as B-sides and on *Rare Cult*. In an interview with *Kerrang* in 1987, Astbury explained how the switch in producers was made: "We were going to stick with Steve's stuff because we were happy with the performances, but what ended up happening was when we got to New York and set up to re-record 'Love Removal Machine,' we actually started jamming 'Peace Dog.' And we ended up recording it. It sounded incredible." Lead guitarist Billy Duffy felt a shift when the band began working with Rubin. "When we were sitting in New York City with Rick, in America, the ultimate rock nation, the change in scenery certainly played its part that our musical direction has changed."

After his initial session re-recording "Love Removal Machine," Rubin and The Cult realized a common aspiration for the band's next LP — to strip down the sound to something straightforward but powerful. Astbury described the creative direction of the recording sessions: "*Electric* was really our garage album. It was our way of exorcising the peer pressure that existed in the U.K., the subconscious pandering that everybody is prone to. We had to go to New York City with Rick Rubin to blow away the cobwebs. There was a blatant rock side to us and we wanted to exploit it to the hilt. It was a good exercise because it made us realize the strength of what we do, which is Billy's guitar playing and my vocals. We did it naked, we said, 'This is it.' . . . It was very much plug in and go. We wanted a noisy 'in your face' record . . . We enjoyed it. . . . It sounded incredible and was what we really wanted to be like. It taught us a lot about attitude, and not getting too hung up on the art. We just wanted to rock out and rage, and the three singles taken from the record ['Love Removal Machine,' 'Lil' Devil,' and 'Wild Flower'] sum it up."

Duffy explained to *Kerrang* in 1989, "It was brilliant to work in an environment where it's perfectly normal and acceptable to make a loud, obnoxious, ballsy rock record, where if it's good enough it will sell. In Britain, producers would always be saying things like, 'Isn't this a bit too heavy for radio?' Well, I'm sorry, but that's rather an irrelevant issue. To us, because of the experience we had with that album, it's given us a whole new depth to our career." The guitarist felt the album marked a distinct shift in the band's direction: "*Electric* was a complete exorcism from the Positive Punk movement. *Electric* left no doubt that we were a rock band. . . . We made an album that sounded like it was made in 1971. It was very abrasive and Spartan, which was what Rick Rubin was totally into."

Recording began at Chung King, the same studio that spawned the Beastie Boys' *Licensed to Ill* and Run-DMC's *Raising Hell*, before moving to more posh digs. Assistant producer George Drakoulias remembered Rubin was relying on raw instinct over experience, being new to recording a band like The Cult. "We learned to set up for the first time with a live drummer with The Cult; it was a mystery. The whole thing was so new. That happened sort of by accident too. They came to Rick to do a remix, and he told them it was no good and they needed to re-record the whole thing. So they were supposed to be there for a week, and ended up staying, like, four months and re-cut the record. Rick had never done a rock record, and he was a little nervous, but he had the lexicon of AC/DC down, and Led Zeppelin was more of the touchstone for me, so we combined some of those things to try to make the record better.

"We recorded the drum tracks at Electric Ladyland, Jimi Hendrix's studio, which was decent sized, but wasn't huge. We got the drum sounds for that record pretty fast and pretty easy. There was nothing too tricky on that. The kick drum was miked with 47/87 overhead mics, an SM-7 on the snare drum, and 421s on the toms. We did trigger a sample, an early version, which was really fantastic. And one time Rick gated a tom-tom, and got this very bizarre effect that I was very impressed with. When we were tracking, no one really got too obsessive about things. We cut everything live, and overdubbed the guitars, but once we got a good drum track, we'd cut the tape together, make the best pieces, and it was pretty easygoing. Our routine with The Cult was usually that the band came, tracked the song, then we took it apart, put it into the AC/DC rock mold, then tried to make it a little more interesting. That was most of my function — suggesting different things. For instance, I remember working with Billy Duffy a lot on the guitar solos, even though they are out of tune on the record, trying to get him to abandon his older style that he was used to from the *Love* album, and turn off the effects. He had some kind of crazy pedal board, and I was like, 'Let's just bypass it, and play the solo,' and I remember that was a big step for him. He took encouragement, he was great. He had a couple Marshalls and a Les Paul, and I brought in my Les Paul that he used on a couple tracks. We miked Billy's rig with an 87 or 57 on the cabinet."

Billy Duffy had to adapt quickly to the Rubin method. "On *Love*, I was using this Gretsch [guitar], I had a lot of delays and chorus. The songs were more melody-oriented: there wasn't a lot of rhythm guitar, which was clear in focus on *Electric*. It was a bit of a shock to learn Rick's method. Right on the spot, he'd say, 'Play it clean, man; use a Les Paul, no effects.' . . . There are no effects on *Electric*. I used the wah-wah sound on one song. I switched between the rhythm pickup and the treble pickup, and that's it. It went straight into an amp, out of the speaker, and onto tape." Getting back to playing in a style he hadn't used in years, Duffy explained, "I had to get rid of the Gretsch, the chorus pedal, the delay, and just go back to a totally dry sound. . . . I wish I'd had six months to work on it before I did *Electric*, but I had to learn on the run."

When tracking the album's vocals, Rubin dealt exclusively with notoriously moody frontman Ian Astbury. Drakoulias explained, "Ian and Billy are two of the most opposite people you're ever gonna meet, because Ian is from outer space. He just lives in a parallel universe, and Rick dealt with Ian a lot more than I did on that record." Astbury, for his part, felt satisfied with the results he and Rubin achieved: "What was in our hearts came out on *Electric* and we've never looked back since." While the sessions were focused, Drakoulias also recalled, "We were having a lot of fun. It was really fun being in this really pro recording studio, which we didn't get to do much since we usually worked downtown out of Chung King. And The Cult had this really huge food budget, so every other band on Def Jam ate off our catering budget. The Beasties would come down, and we'd say, 'Hey we're ordering dinner. What do you want?' And at one point, we were spending $500 or $600 a day on food."

Once recording and mixing were completed, both the group and the producer felt satisfied they had achieved the stylistic goals they set for the album. Bassist Jamie Stewart summed up the experience: "On *Electric*, we stripped off all the surface clutter and got down to what we're really all about. . . . That LP taught us the reality of what we were built on." Ian Astbury was equally pleased. "Rick concentrated on the hard rock elements — we call them the sonic side — and he did a good job of portraying that sound on the *Electric* album, and producing a minimalist sound accordingly. . . . *Electric* was the first album statement that this band made that I felt satisfied with."

Critics responded well to The Cult's successful reinvention, hailing them as one of the first credible purist rock bands of the '80s, with high caliber songwriting and performances. Consider *Rolling Stone*'s observation that "[*Electric*] swaggers, crunches and howls, all right, but it does so with irreverence (not surprising with raunch expert Rick Rubin behind the board). . . . This record could have been unbearably heavy-handed . . . but this album isn't The Cult raising ghosts; it's just The Cult raising a little Cain." By April 1987, when the LP was released, Rubin had clearly moved on from rap to rock. The stylistic shift was an indication of the growing distance between partners Rubin and Russell Simmons.

CHAPTER 9

From Rock to Metal

Slayer and Danzig

CAPITALIZING ON HIS SUCCESS with The Cult's *Electric* LP, Rubin turned his attention to Slayer and Danzig, projects which had been put on hold while Rubin completed his other production commitments. Rubin's work with both groups would cement his reputation as one of rock/metal's most sought-after producers.

Long before *Rolling Stone* had placed Slayer "on the shortlist of the most crucial metal bands ever," no mainstream label would go near the speed/thrash metal group. When Rubin first discovered them, it was arguably the first time anyone in the industry had questioned his A&R instincts. The group had been signed to independent Metal Blade Records when Rubin first took note of the band in 1985 and "thought their stuff was incredible." Seeing the band live, he was blown away. "The first time I saw them, I'd never heard of them. This was at the time they were playing so fast you couldn't even tell what they were playing, it was just a blur . . . The command they had of the audience, I'd never seen anything like it. [There was] something there I'd never heard of! They had such an arrogant presence on stage, and they had this sold-out place of kids killing themselves, into the music — jumping around, stage-diving, everything — the band so . . . arrogant and not caring. They knew. They knew that it was right. Do you know what I'm saying? They weren't smiling, it wasn't like that. . . . They did not care what was going on, because they knew that they were good. And the audience respected it and were 100 percent with them." After freeing them from their contract with Metal Blade, the band became Def Jam's first and only metal signee, with Russell Simmons going along with the deal because "it was something [Rick] wanted to do . . . I trusted him." For Rubin, signing Slayer "made perfect sense. When I heard Slayer I just thought that I had to sign them because they were just as extreme and relevant as, say, Public Enemy."

Rubin had first entered the studio with Slayer to work on their debut LP, *Reign in Blood*, in spring 1986, well before he established himself as a commercially credible rock producer. An impressive gamble, lead guitarist Kerry King recalled to *Metal Hammer*, "That album was a lot of things coming together at the same time. In '86, no one was gonna bother actually putting in some work to produce a thrash album. Rick did. He really took care over it and at the time we had some fucking awesome songs we wanted to record." For his part, singer Tom Araya recalled Rubin "really liked what he heard . . . He took our sound and kind of fine-tuned it: that Slayer sound we could never really capture in the studio. We kind of realized, 'Oh my God, this guy, he's got the touch of gold.'" Rubin's approach to the production changed the genre, and for the better. "It was a change in sound," said Araya to *Kerrang*. "In thrash metal at that time, no one had ever heard good production on a record like that." The singer credits Rubin with developing the "Slayer sound" first heard on *Reign in Blood*: "He cleaned up and established . . . that very raw sound, very minimal. Anything we do in the studio, if we can't do it live, we're not going to do it. The only tape we run is an intro tape."

King explained, "With [*Reign in Blood*], that was the best songs we had. They were the 10, which is why it was so short. At that time, Rick told us if we had 10 songs we had an album, so that's what we had." The songs were written collaboratively. "From the beginning we've always divided up the writing duties on the albums just to make things less boring for the listener and for us. *Reign in Blood* is where that really came to the fore — we were all writing different kinds of songs but they all came together with this definitive Slayer sound. People ask us if we've been trying to top it ever since." It's hard to top something that defines a genre, which is what King believes is partly responsible for the high esteem that album is held in. "That record was all about . . . taking your production, getting your reverb out of it, and hitting you square between the eyes with it. I think that was the first time people heard thrash music with clarity, and I think that's why it stands out in people's minds as one of the best."

Once the band had entered the studio with Rubin, the producer helped Tom Araya hone in on a singing style that would become his trademark. "In the early days, I wasn't literally trying to sing so you wouldn't understand what the fuck I was saying. We didn't grunt and growl and say those were our words. Over the years, I've tried to get more away from that, if anything. When we first started singing our songs, the other guys kept asking me to be more aggressive. Then I hit a perfect note with *Reign in Blood*. From then on, I said to myself, 'This is what I'm gonna do. I'm gonna sing, not growl, but in my own way.'" Co-lead guitarist Jeff Hanneman explained his experience working with Rubin, "That album was stamped into my memory because things were really starting to change for us and things were starting to get professional and serious, and that's the first time we had a tour bus and a real record label. And we put that album down . . . I don't know how long it took us, but everything was done, everything was fast, everything was good. In fact, you've probably heard this, but our biggest scare on that record is that once we got finished with it, we checked the time and it was, like, 28 minutes. We were like, 'Holy shit. Too short!' So we sat there with Rubin and thought, 'Does it sound great? Yes. Do we all like it? Yes. Fuck it!'"

Upon completion, Def Jam Records' distributor CBS Records refused to release the album due to its Satanist themes. CBS's decision forced Rubin to seek an alternative distribution deal for the album, and he launched Def American in the process. Rubin took *Reign in Blood* to

Geffen Records. Araya saw that move as "Rubin [taking] it upon himself not to fuck us over, and the deal that he had with the band." Going gold on word-of-mouth without any support from radio or MTV, *Reign in Blood* shaped the speed-metal genre (along with Metallica's *Ride the Lightning* and *Master of Puppets*), a fact that became clear as the decade carried on. Araya felt that "the heaviness wasn't there until we came around — the same with Metallica, Anthrax, Exodus, and us. I think we've had a big impact on the sound. We took music and made it really heavy and I think it's affected a lot of music from then on." Looking back on the album when it was re-released, Araya said, "*Reign in Blood* is our signature record and if people think that it helped set the path for that genre of music, that's great. It's a record that means a lot to all of us in the band." Kerry King, for his part, feels that "People are always going to look back at *Reign in Blood* and look at how groundbreaking it was." Calling it "the album of their lives [and] of that genre," Rubin felt the band "was on the highest level."

Flourishing independently of industry trends, Slayer continued to lead the speed/thrash metal pack with their sophomore project, 1988's *South of Heaven*. The band decided to vary its formula, mixing in slower metal. Kerry King explained, "Every album for us is a refinement of what we do. Obviously you want to grow musically, you want to move things on. It's just that many bands feel guilty if they aren't trying new things and try and overcompensate by 'progressing' or some bullshit like that. 'Progressing' normally means doing things you're not good at — we're not gonna suddenly do an album of ballads just to progress. We know that what we're best at and what we love is incredibly aggressive, fast, heavy music. . . . Basically it was the only album we did that we thought about before we did it. We actually sat down and said: 'Right. This album's gonna be slower than the last one.' I guess we didn't want to get fenced in and the album suffered because of that. We tried things that didn't necessarily work." Tom Araya reasoned that the "album was a late bloomer — it wasn't really received well, but it kind of grew on everybody later." Upon release in July 1988, the

Rubin-produced LP debuted at #44 on Billboard's Top 200 Album Chart and went over well enough with fans to again go gold. In the meanwhile, Rubin had turned his attention to Danzig, whose talents the producer had first showcased on the *Less Than Zero* soundtrack.

* * *

Glenn Danzig was best known as the lead singer and songwriter for legendary punk band the Misfits, but the sound of his new band, Samhain, drew from blues, metal, and rock-a-billy. Metallica bassist the late Cliff Burton was a friend of Rubin's and recommended he check out Danzig. Rubin admitted he "was never a Misfits fan. I didn't like them and I actually thought they were terrible. But I always knew that Glenn was a great singer and that he had great songwriting potential that hadn't been fully realized." The singer's voice has been compared to Elvis Presley and Roy Orbison.

Glenn Danzig recalled to *Spin* how he and Rubin came to work together on Danzig's first album: "Rick Rubin came down to see us [Samhain] at the New Music Seminar in '86 and he came running backstage and said, 'You guys are great! The best band I've ever seen, blah, blah, blah.' He gives me his card, and I think he's a freak. I didn't know who the fuck he was. But he seemed sincere. . . . So I went down to his offices, right off Houston [Street] in New York City, and I hear this loud music blaring. And it isn't even a fucking record company office, but a fucking loft apartment. Records all over the place, phones ringing, people calling, Rick screaming, 'What? What? What? Fuck you,' and sticking the phone into the speaker and then hanging up." Rubin wasn't the only record producer looking to sign Glenn Danzig and his band, which included former members of punk bands the Circle Jerks, D.O.A., and Black Flag. Elektra, Epic, and Profile were talking to them as well. For the meeting with Rubin, recalled Danzig, "We went out, had some pizza, walked around town. He told me he saw us as a real band, not a trendy band, and though we could get a little more focused, he thought we had more to say than some groups. I liked that."

Danzig elaborated on how the partnership began to *Metal Mania*. "We started talking about what he wanted to do if we decided to go with Def Jam. A lot of his ideas and my ideas were the same. What he saw in the band is exactly the same things I saw in the band: the aggressiveness, the attitude, the whole deal. So it worked out very well. He's to the point. I don't like people who beat around the bush. He tells you exactly right up front. You don't have to mince words." Deciding to go with Rubin because of his approach to the music and his commitment to the band, Danzig and the producer found common ground. "The thing with Rick was that we needed to see if we could work together before we decided if he was gonna produce us. We said this needs this and he added stuff. . . . He likes bands for the reasons that I like bands. Music that's aggressive and violent. Not that he looks for violence. It's usually accompanied by aggressiveness."

As the band and Rick Rubin began discussing the band's debut LP, "aggressive" was definitely part of the direction. Glenn Danzig was not interested in making a commercial record. "Rick and I approached it as 'Let's just make a great record and work on the band.' When I first talked to Rick, I told him that any band that's worth its weight didn't make it on their first record. I mean, it took AC/DC four albums before anyone even knew who they were. When we talked with all the different labels, we decided to go with Rick because of the long-term commitment. We told him that it was gonna take two or three albums before he's gonna see any real amount of sales, and he was cool about it. That's what we were looking for, someone who was into us. . . . The deal we set was we didn't care about advances, we just wanted as much money as we needed to make a great record . . . Rick Rubin was the best deal we could get, he understands exactly what we're doing." Speaking to *Metal Hammer* in 1989, Danzig said, "Rick Rubin is a really good producer, probably one of the best at the moment. He understood exactly what we were all about. It was really difficult for me to find a suitable producer, because I've always produced my own material until now."

Prior to entering the studio, the band, now called Danzig, underwent some line-up changes, which Danzig and Rubin made together. "When I signed with Def Jam, Rick and I put the band together. That was the original concept, to play with different guys for every record," explained Danzig. From the band's previous incarnation as Samhain, Danzig would feature Eerie Von on bass. "When we decided to dump our other drummer, Rick asked me who were my two favorite drummers. I said Philthy Phil and Chuck Biscuits. Philthy, we decided, might be kind of old and set in his ways. He might not listen if you said, 'Play that this way.' I'm real picky and so is Rick. And Chuck Biscuits was available. We tried him out and he worked out good. The chemistry was right. . . . We did auditions for six months for a guitar player. [John Christ] came in and we had 10 minutes left. He was waiting all night so we said, 'You got 10 minutes.' He came on like blazes. He beat out all the competition so he got it. Rick really liked him. I liked his leads better than anyone else's. We wanted to be able to put them in where we need them."

As a creative team, Glenn Danzig and Rubin worked well, finishing each other's sentences with the artist respecting the producer's opinions and intelligence. "[He was] pretty influential," recalled Danzig. "I'd say about 25 percent of the album is Rick Rubin. I wanted a producer, I wanted that other voice. Originally when we signed, we wanted to see if we could work together, if he was open to my suggestions, and if I could listen to what he was saying about stuff other than songwriting, like how the band was handled, cover art, the whole direction of the band. And it just turned out that we had a lot in common, that we were on the same wavelength, and it was really good." The first thing the pair agreed on was to strip Danzig's song arrangements down to their most basic instrumentally. As guitarist John Christ explained, the sound of the album is "very dry . . . Rick Rubin played a big part in pulling everybody together and making it sound like a band. Rick, at that point, was trying to make everything sound like *Back in Black*. He did that with The Cult record — a really flat drum sound and clean, punchy guitars that were really tight-sounding, a minimal amount of reverb, and a good loud vocal. That's pretty much what he did with us."

Def American Records' official press release introducing Danzig described them as "a new band that creates new music even as it preserves those qualities that made classic rock great. In other words, it's both timely and timeless. This music will sound as good 10 years from now as it does today. . . . It is every bit as voluminous as heavy metal, but this is also introspective music you can reflect upon and think about. The power without the plastics. A thinking man's band . . . Danzig was formed to realize Glenn's personal vision; a vision that in the past has been marred by others. Bands like the Misfits and Samhain garnered a solid cult following due almost entirely to Glenn's melodic sense and charismatic voice. Tired of being just a cult phenomenon, Glenn decided to create a band that would be the ultimate evolution of his ideas . . . music and lyrics . . . that often reflect his fascination with the study of pagan religions such as Celtic and Black Satanic Catholicism. Danzig is the result."

In spite of Glenn Danzig's desire to remain off the commercial metal map, mainstream critics were eager to show respect for the artist and highlight his credibility. The *Washington Post* pointed out his punk heritage and the key role Rubin played in crafting the album: "Metallica's hyperspeed hammering couldn't have existed without hard-core punk's oratory experiments in six-string velocity. Glenn Danzig, however, actually was a punk, with a cult band called the Misfits. Under the watchful eye of Rick Rubin, the rap/metal auteur who put the Led into the Cult, Danzig has been reborn as a metal man, albeit a punky one, with a band and an album that bear his last name.

The band might better be called Rubin." Rick Rubin's role in creating *Danzig*'s "10 perfectly presentable pounders" was lost on no one.

Kerrang noted, "Danzig now sounds as true a rocker and as hard a roller as he ever did before, channeling the aggression of the Misfits and Samhain into more than just speed or stage shock. Whilst Danzig the man has always displayed the ability to perform as such, it's been a rare occasion in the past and one can't help feeling that Rubin has helped focus Danzig properly, leaving the diminutive frontman with a clearer objective and a sharper view of his own music." Britain's *Melody Maker* called Danzig's voice "impressive" and complimented the album as "disquietingly inviting," noting that "Danzig can change moods faster than the cracking of skulls. From the teaspoonful of meekness accidentally revealed in 'Soul on Fire,' complete with the ghost of Jim Morrison, to the pressing heart attack of 'Am I Demon' they come close to giving The Night a decent voice." Riff heavy and packing enough heavy meal credibility, the album was picked by Metallica's James Hetfield and Kirk Hammett as their favorite album of 1988 in *Guitar Magazine*.

Rubin and Danzig's collaboration became an instant critic favorite, and Glenn Danzig was pleased with his decision to sign with Def American. "We stay as outside of the record industry as we can. That's one of the reasons we're on Def American. We don't get any of that from Rick Rubin. I think people are finally catching on and we'll see what happens. Maybe things can change. We're one of the bands that is saying 'enough is enough, we're not doing that crap and we don't care if we sell a couple of million records.' We're just coming from a different area, we're coming from a musical area." Further to that point, Danzig revealed his feelings about the band's biggest hit, "Mother." "I remember calling Rick Rubin in the middle of the night and telling him that I wrote an incredible song — probably the best song I'd ever written. It was the song I always wanted to write. The first time we played it, people went crazy. I never wrote that song to make it a hit — I never wrote that way, and I still don't. But I write songs so that they say something and do something, and if people like 'em, great — and if they don't, they don't."

In 1989, Rubin and Danzig re-teamed for the band's sophomore LP, *Danzig II: Lucifuge*, which would eventually go platinum. ("Lucifuge" means "sleep of light.") Guitarist John Christ described Glenn Danzig's demo process for that album to *Musician*: "The way he did it, he'd have a song on one of those little microcassette recorders, just his voice going duhnn-duhnn-duhduh-duh-DUHNN-duhnn-duh-duhduh — you know, stuff like that. Then he and I would sit there [with] guitars; once we got one or two guitar parts, Eerie and Chuck would come in, and they'd kinda start jamming to it. We do a lot of mid-tempo songs . . . Danzig likes to go from really soft to really loud. We like the big power that comes when everything is crashing in." Christ also talked about the band's songwriting process. "As far as songs go, Glenn sometimes has an entire song in his head, or he has a chorus or a riff. Rubin also makes suggestions. Unless the whole thing is already done, we all mess around with it and see where it goes. Usually, we give Glenn options to choose from. If it makes it to the record, that's the way it stays. When we play live, the songs changes a little bit. We've gotten used to working with each other, so things come out fast. For instance, there are certain chords that we never use."

The band's lead singer and chief songwriter, Glenn Danzig said, "[I] always know beforehand what kind of record I want to make. Those ideas dictate how the songs will sound. And sometimes it's not always easy to execute the ideas. For example, writing 'Her Black Wings' was a laborious and tedious experience — but that's the way it had to be for the song to come out right. But sometimes I'll just start playing and get an idea and write a song. There are songs on this record that I wrote in five minutes — and some of them are my favorite songs because they were so spontaneous. So it varies."

For drummer Chuck Biscuits, this album presented an opportunity to push further with the sound. "I've had problems with the drum sounds on previous records. They've been too flat, too controlled. In the past, Rick has been into that dry, tight AC/DC sound. This one was looser, with more spaces, more noise — all the good shit I like." Glenn Danzig also had some artistic muscle

to flex on this sophomore album, telling *Kerrang*, "One of the problems I sometimes have with Rick is that he wants me to rhyme my lyrics. It's not that big a deal at all, he'll just tell me that this or that should rhyme and I'll tell him that no, it shouldn't. He has no idea what I'm trying to say here." Pushing back on some of Rubin's ideas was one of the lessons Danzig took from the creative experience. "Working with a producer like Rick . . . taught me that if something is important enough, then people can fight for it; if not, then let me try it my way."

A successful gamble, *Rolling Stone*'s review of *Danzig II: Lucifuge* praised Danzig's artistic knack for "bizarre realism" and the stylistic consistency of "[carrying] on in the tradition that made their debut so heady. Here again, Sabbath often rings in as an influence," and noted the band's musical growth in "the '50s rock 'n' roll of 'Blood and Tears' or the guitar-fueled cabaret of 'Killer Wolf.'" Danzig's first two albums helped shape a sub-genre of metal, and Glenn Danzig and Rubin continued to work together until 1994, a seven-year partnership that persisted even as the demand for Rubin's producing skills continued to rise.

* * *

By the end of the 1980s, only four years into his career as a producer and record executive, Rick Rubin was responsible for co-founding a new generation of hip hop, bringing it unprecedented commercial success, and for popularizing a stripped-down style of rock production that would influence the early 1990s grunge explosion. Despite these successes with Def Jam, Rick Rubin and Russell Simmons knew that their partnership had become strained to a breaking point. "Russell and I were going in different directions, both musically and business-wise. And I thought that being as we were good friends, it would be better for us to break off and still be able to be friends, instead of some day hating each other — being in business together and it being a big, ugly mess. So I said, 'Do you want to leave?' And he said, 'No,' and I said, 'Okay, fine, I'll leave.' And we're still friends." Elaborating to *AV Club*, Rubin said, "If I would have stayed, it would have been completely different. I don't know if it would have been the same successful thing that it is. I can't imagine what it would have been like, had I stayed . . . The reason I left Def Jam . . . had to do with mine and Russell's vision of our company growing apart, and wanting to maintain our friendship. It felt like if we were no longer partners, we'd be able to remain friends, and everything would be good, and that's exactly what happened." Simmons, for his part, recalled that the departure made sense commercially and artistically. "[Rick] was in L.A. making a bunch of rock 'n' roll records that had nothing to do with Def Jam . . . and I was making a bunch of R&B records."

Said Rubin, he and Simmons "had been stepping on each other's toes a lot, kind of growing apart creatively, no communication. I felt like my vision was being compromised and I was sure he felt like his was. It just made sense." The split was not acrimonious because "business never came first . . . Our focus was on doing good work and moving forward, not looking back and signing documents and arguing." Reflecting on his time with Def Jam and the label's influence on the hip hop scene, Rubin said, "It really was a wave. We just happened to be in a good spot on the wave. The wave was coming." Rubin's heyday at Def Jam as hip hop's most influential, pioneering producer had come to a definitive conclusion — albeit a happy one for Rubin and Simmons both personally and professionally.

"One of Rick's favorite phrases is 'metaphor deficient.' If people write things that are metaphor deficient, even he can't help them."

— CHRIS ROCK

The Early 1990s

CHAPTER 10

Building
Def American

IN 1988, RICK RUBIN BEGAN the new era of his career by relocating. The headquarters of Def American would be in California, because as Rick reasoned, "I got a deal with Geffen and I wanted to be right across the street. Also, musically there are a lot of clubs. For the kinds of records I'm making, there's a rock 'n' roll community in L.A. that doesn't exist in New York." New York had been hip hop's epicenter in the '80s and Rubin had been in the thick of it; L.A. was where Rubin needed to be in the '90s. "It's nice to be able to make a record and turn on the radio so you can hear it. In New York, it's like making records in a vacuum," said the producer. "You never hear your records on the radio, because radio is all Top 40, there's no rock 'n' roll station. . . . It's nice, when you're doing any kind of art, to be able to see the effect. It helps you do it. It's just the fact that the community exists feels good, makes you want to do it. In New York, all it is is numbers on a page."

Under the terms of the Def American deal with Geffen Records, the major which would serve as the independent label's distributor, the producer retained ownership of the master tapes and the freedom to release any genre of band he wished. That freedom was something Def Jam with its rap-dominant roster couldn't offer. Russell Simmons explained, "Slayer and Oran Jones had nothing in common. If we'd been a huge label with many divisions, it would have been fine. But at a small company like Def Jam, it was apparent that a real cultural and creative separation [had taken] place." In his separation agreement with Def Jam, Rubin took Danzig and Slayer to Def American, while Simmons kept control of the bulk of the Def Jam artists.

As soon as Rubin's spin-off label was green lit, he signed some controversial acts, like comedian Andrew Dice Clay, as well as some with mainstream marketability, like pop-friendly Seattle rapper Sir-Mix-a-Lot. Rubin explained to *Rolling Stone*, "I think Mix-a-Lot is a tremendous artist. He's a great entertainer. From the first time I ever heard him, I just loved him." America did too; in 1992 "Baby Got Back" became a smash hit, going double platinum and winning a Grammy. But it was the wildly controversial Houston rap act the Geto Boys who brought Rubin the most heat with their explicit lyrics and violent image, rivaled only by N.W.A.

While Dr. Dre and Death Row Records would go on to dominate gangsta rap, the Geto Boys are widely recognized as one of its pioneering acts. In spite of N.W.A's success with 1988's *Straight Outta Compton*, Rubin had to wage a fierce battle to get the Geto Boys' first major LP released, with mainstream record industry executives reluctant to go near such controversial music. Rubin had gone beyond just signing the group; he offered their parent label, the independent Rap-A-Lot Records, a distribution deal at a time when no one else would touch them. Rap-A-Lot Records' James Smith said, "This rap shit is the biggest challenge to the government in a long-ass time. It's bigger than Martin Luther King and all them." Years later, Rick Rubin still stood by his decision, saying to the *New York Times*, "I thought the art was good. As a fan, the Geto Boys were thrilling in the same way that a horror movie might be thrilling."

When Geffen balked at distributing 1990's *The Geto Boys*, Rubin took it to an alternate distributor to guarantee retail coverage. The move soon became permanent when Rubin left Geffen for Warner

Rick Rubin and George Drakoulias in the early '90s.
(© Jay Blakesberg)

Bros., which had a more solid history of standing behind even their most controversial artists. David Geffen recalled years later to the *New York Times* that he "just couldn't put out a record about sex with dead bodies and cutting off women's breasts. I begged Rick not to put out the Geto Boys. In the end, I lost. He left and went to Warner Brothers." Rubin had always been drawn to controversial artists and found the Geto Boys were no less commercially viable than rock acts in terms of record sales. "Edgy things tend to get my attention," he told the *Washington Post*. "But it wasn't the fact that it was offensive that made me like it. There were other offensive records that came out that I didn't like and wouldn't support, like 2 Live Crew.

The music is what drives me; I just like great art and music, even if it's great and ordinary. But if it's great and it happens to be offensive, too, then that makes it even more exciting."

One safe bet on Def American's roster came with Atlanta-based blues-rock act The Black Crowes. George Drakoulias, who had followed Rubin from Def Jam out to California, was Def American's in-house A&R man. Drakoulias discovered the band and brought them to Rubin's attention. Released in late 1990, The Black Crowes' debut LP, *Shake Your Money Maker*, was executive-produced by Rubin with all in-studio production duties in the hands of Drakoulias. The album would almost single-handedly modernize the southern-rock genre. Selling in excess of five million copies and producing the hit singles "Hard to Handle," "Jealous Again," "Seeing Things," "Twice as Hard," and "She Talks to Angels," the success of The Black Crowes' debut established Def American as one of the leading independent rock labels.

Rubin was back in the studio with Slayer for the band's third LP, 1990's commercial breakout *Seasons in the Abyss*. The album's reception validated the long climb Rubin had made with Slayer to the top of the thrash-metal scene. MTV, which had virtually ignored the group's first two albums, put the video for "Seasons in the Abyss" into heavy rotation. *Kerrang* named *Seasons in the Abyss* the top album of the year, while *Entertainment Weekly* commented: "Slayer piles on the grim vocals, the frenetic guitar work, and the gore . . . the band pulls it off, thanks to its relentless musical drive. The guitars of Kerry King and Jeff Hanneman don't just blare; they slice through the speakers."

Another repeat act for Rubin, Danzig was heading into the 1990s as one of metal's top draws after the success of their sophomore album. Released in 1992, *Danzig III: How the Gods Kill* was Danzig's most relevant and commercial album to date. *Rolling Stone* described the band as one that "embodies the best in contemporary hard rock while displaying an originality that transcends genres. . . . Rock is alarmingly short of visionaries these days; Danzig is the genuine article." As Glenn Danzig explained to *Hit Parader* at the time of the album's release, "We've never tried to fit into any particular musical slot. We're certainly not your typical heavy metal band that doesn't have anything to say. We say anything we feel like saying, and if that causes some within the establishment to cringe, that's great. Most of the music you hear today is just pre-processed garbage designed to appeal to as many people as possible. It's not very dangerous . . . but we are."

While that album was well received, Danzig would achieve its biggest success with a song already years old. "We wanted to put out an EP after *Danzig III*," said Glenn Danzig, "but the record company told us we were crazy because EPs don't sell. As far as I was concerned, it was too soon to do another studio album or record a live album, so I thought an EP with four live tracks and three studio tracks would be the best thing to do. So we went into the studio and recorded 'It's Coming Down,' 'Violet Fire,' and 'Trouble' in one day. We put them together with some live tracks, and put it out as *Thrall-Demonsweatlive*. 'Mother' was one of the live songs, and it just started getting airplay. So we decided to shoot a live video for it. MTV had to play it because it was doing so well on radio. It was kinda cool because no one called us a 'sell-out' since 'Mother' was already six years old when it became a hit." Rick Rubin described Glenn Danzig's vision to *Rolling Stone* as "very dark, apocalyptic, and beautiful in its own way. But that's how he really sees the world. He's a brutally honest guy."

Gaining early momentum with his Def American artists, Rubin expanded his roster with bands like The Jayhawks, Skinny Puppy, Love and Rockets, and MC 900 Ft. Jesus. Rubin also took a gamble on The Jesus and Mary Chain, earning indie credibility while continuing to post major-label numbers. But it was his next studio project for

Warner Bros., with funk-rock founders the Red Hot Chili Peppers, which was the start of a fruitful musical pairing that still thrives nearly 20 years later.

CHAPTER 11

Red Hot Chili Peppers
Blood Sugar Sex Magik

THE MASTERS OF MELDING MELODY with madness, the Red Hot Chili Peppers blend funk with rock 'n' roll and are never afraid to explore new musical styles. Bassist Flea declared that the Red Hot Chili Peppers have "never been a part of any movement or any collective thing or any existing category. We just try to create our own categories." Together the Chili Peppers play with passion and expertise, a band comprised of talented musicians and songwriters. As Rick Rubin told *Q*, "They're very different individuals. Each has their own world." Beginning with 1991's *Blood Sugar Sex Magik*, Rubin worked with the band on 1995's *One Hot Minute*, 1999's *Californication*, 2002's *By the Way*, and 2006's *Stadium Arcadium*.

Alternative rock at the start of the 1990s was at the center of American pop culture with the rise of grunge and bands like Jane's Addiction, whose 1990 album *Ritual de lo Habitual* spawned the smash single "Been Caught Stealing." For their fifth studio album, the Red Hot Chili Peppers would create the breakthrough *Blood Sugar Sex Magik* and the biggest alt-rock single of 1991, "Under the Bridge," which peaked at #2 on the Billboard Hot 100. *Blood Sugar Sex Magik* marked the Chili Peppers' arrival in the mainstream.

Heading into this album, the stars seemed aligned; guitarist John Frusciante, bassist Flea, drummer Chad Smith, and lead vocalist Anthony Kiedis working with Rick Rubin was a natural pairing. Both Rubin and the Chili Peppers drew from a multitude of musical influences. "Working with Rick was something that turned out to be a magical experience," said Kiedis in a promotional interview for the album. "At first we had a lot of reservations about working with the man because we didn't know him and he seemed more on the demonic side of life than the explosion of positive energy that the Red Hot Chili Peppers have always been perpetrators of. We didn't know if he would be able to blend in well, what with Slayer and the boiling goat heads of Danzig and all. But he turned out to be a completely open-minded, free-flowing, comforting spirit. If Baron Von Munchausen were able to ejaculate the Red Hot Chili Peppers onto a chess board, Rick Rubin would be the perfect player for that game."

The band first met the producer a few years before they worked together. As Flea explained to VH1, "We met Rick Rubin when we were getting ready to make *Uplift Mofo Party Plan* in 1987. He came by our rehearsal studio with the Beastie Boys. We had a dark drug cloud over us, so they got uncomfortable and left." From Rubin's perspective, the Chili Peppers "were always incredible musicians, but that doesn't necessarily make a great band." Fortunately, the producer kept his eye on RHCP and approached them a few years later. "Rick came up after the last show of the Mother's Milk tour and said, 'You guys were phenomenal,'" recalled Flea. "We were in a much healthier situation. I talked to him about producing our record and he said he would love to do it. He wanted to capture who we really were, whereas the producers we worked with in the past were trying to control us. Up until then I was being as wild as I could with my bass. Rick said, 'Be yourself. But it's not about being fancy. It's about serving the song.' I started looking at the song's big picture instead of trying to make fancy bass art pieces." Rubin's challenge in working with the band as a whole was analogous to the barriers the bassist had to overcome. "My job was to break down those boundaries," said Rubin to the *New York Times*. "No band has to fit into a little box. I saw the Chili Peppers as being like the Beach Boys in some ways. They represented Los Angeles, a place of dreams." As Flea told *Guitar World* as he looked back in 2002, "*Blood Sugar* is the first time that we got down on tape what we really do. We'd never done that before. In the past, we'd always been intimidated by the studio. It would be a tense and alien environment. But that album was more about creating a vibe for us to jam and do our thing in." Flea has great respect for the producer: "Rick is a really smart guy. He's very clear-headed and has a good, open-minded view of pop music. Our music is very multi-cultural, and he has many cultural influences himself. After all, he's produced Run-DMC, LL Cool J, Slayer, the Beastie Boys, and The Bangles. And he just seems to have a natural understanding of what kids like."

Rubin pushed each band member to a more mature place. No greater example of the success of this strategy exists on *Blood Sugar Sex Magik* than "Under the Bridge," the first ballad Anthony Kiedis wrote and sang. "When you're using drugs, life is pretty lonely. I got clean, but the loneliness didn't go away. I was driving in my car, feeling that loneliness, and started singing the song to myself. I liked what I was singing, so when I got home I taped part of it and started finishing this poem," Kiedis recalled to VH1. The words may have stayed a poem if it hadn't been for Rick Rubin's encouragement. "He would visit me at home where I did my lyric writing, sit with me on this old '50s couch and say, 'Let's see what you have.' That's where I first sang, 'Under the Bridge.' It was almost completely written — the arrangement, the verse, the chorus — as this poem. I had a little melody for each part." Rubin felt "Under the Bridge" was "something that cried for singing, not rapping, and for a melody, not just a funk beat, and I said, 'What's this?' and he said, 'Oh, that's not for the Chili Peppers, it's not what we do.'" But the producer convinced Kiedis to take the song to the band's rehearsal. "I was so nervous that my voice cracked when I tried to sing it," said Kiedis. "The band listened to every last word with a very intense look on their faces. I was about to say, 'We don't have to do this,' when they walked over to their instruments and started finding what they wanted to do with that song."

Flea recalled, "John and Anthony had a melody and Chad and me added what we could to it. John's mom came in with her church group and sang the background vocals at the end. It was trippy seeing all these women up there singing, 'Under the bridge downtown.' John and I were playing together at the end and had one of those great moments when you're looking at each other and the music's just flowing through you. We both made a little random fill like, 'boo boo da loop' at exactly the same time. The odds of that happening were 10 zillion to one. We were like, 'How the fuck did that happen?' We knew that was the take. So I never thought that would be a hit, but I knew that it was good." "Under the Bridge" became the band's biggest hit, a testament to the band's ability to break through its own boundaries and to Rick Rubin's ability to spot greatness in a song's earliest incarnation. Anthony Kiedis praised Rubin for "[letting] us reveal our music's other sides."

Pre-production for the album, as Kiedis told VH1, occurred at "this amazing rehearsal space called Alleyway. It was run by this biker/hippie couple and decorated with '70s artifacts. We would start playing and every time I heard something that I could relate to, I would say, 'Let's play that again.' John is perfectly non-judgmental when it comes to creative ideas. He believes that anything that comes to you is meant to be. Our brains work differently, but if you put them together it's like the idiot and the savant. Every time we broke out a guitar or a notebook, we came up with a great song. Then the producer Rick Rubin started coming to rehearsal. He would lay down on the couch with his big-ass beard and appear to take a nap. But he absorbed every note and arrangement and lyrical concept like a sponge." Rubin joining rehearsals about halfway through pre-production was an arrangement that carried over to future albums. Kiedis explained the general process to *Fader*: "We write for two or three months, then Rick comes and sits through rehearsal for another month or two, and then we go into the studio. . . . His participation is incredibly nonchalant. He just comes by and chills out, sometimes horizontally. He's got a pen and paper and is somewhere between a nap and a meditation. Or sometimes he's on the phone and sometimes he isn't. He notices things about colors and melodies and textures. He's listening to not only the drumbeat itself, but also how it's relating to the bass part. He has an incredible head for arrangement." *Blood Sugar Sex Magik* was rehearsed for nine months. "We wanted to cut [the album] very quickly," said Rubin, "but it was that advance time that really made the record what it was. It's more about working out the details, the transitions, and the arrangements. This way you have a very good draft before you go into the studio, so you're not trying to write the song in the studio." Rubin, as he explained to *Guitar Player*, "was involved in songwriting and arranging. A lot of what I do is structural, having to do with turnarounds, getting in and out of choruses, putting in space — whatever it takes to make a song sound like it's not just parts strung together." For Anthony Kiedis, the length of time they took in rehearsal "was a luxury that we never really had in the past. There was nothing forced about making this record. We were completely relaxed, which in our opinion, is the key to creative success. The more relaxed you are, the more freely your beautiful spirit can come into the music. When we made our last album, we had been together with this line-up for about three months. This time we were able to develop a fluid musical conversation. We really got to know each other this time."

Once rehearsals were complete and the band was ready to record, the Red Hot Chili Peppers didn't go into a traditional studio but a haunted mansion in the Laurel Canyon neighborhood of the Hollywood Hills. The off-the-wall idea was Rubin's: "They had made four or five albums in traditional recording environments prior to working with me. I wanted to make our first record together in a completely different environment. So we rented a big house and put a studio into the house, and the band lived in the house while we made the record. This was an entirely different experience for them. The chance of something magical happening was much greater because it felt special. From the time that we were there, the vibe was totally different and really conducive to making great music. You need to come up with different ways to inspire that special feeling that makes a record unique."

Kiedis remembered that when the idea was first raised by "The Bearded Wonder," the Chili Peppers were "totally gung-ho."

Recording in the house allowed the band to set up their ideal recording atmosphere. "When you go to a house like that you can create your own environment," said Flea. "You can make it whatever you want . . . living, working, eating, having sex, all in the same place, untouched by the outside forces of the world which can really be a distraction when you're trying to focus purely on making music. We could establish the vibe as opposed to a studio where a vibe already exists, with secretaries and owners and lots of extraneous undesirable individuals strolling around the premises." John Frusciante agreed with his bandmate: "We sleep here, eat here, and every day we just wake up and start recording. It's a chance not many artists get — to not have to think about bills, answering phones, or shaking hands we don't feel like shaking."

For Anthony Kiedis, the process of making *Blood Sugar Sex Magik* was "really good fun and a really productive, creative growth spurt for the band as well as for me. There was a lot of growth in the making of that record. For some reason we were in the middle of a record company contract dispute, so we had this extra six months to write music, and there was no pressure of having to make a record since we were in limbo. We kept doing the blue-collar thing and going into the studio and making music. There weren't a lot of changes taking place. It wasn't torturous or destructive. It was a natural evolution. Even the making of it was pretty fun — all under the same roof together." Flea agreed: "The whole house was really just a big, warm, beautiful, peaceful place. Not for one minute did we feel any negative energy. Even living together, which could really create tension, turned out perfectly."

In that old Hollywood mansion, the band used old equipment, like a Neve board from the '50s. Their recording setup was less than traditional, as Frusciante explained at the time. "We all play together facing each other downstairs in the living room. The board is in the next room over, and we mic all our amps down in the basement. . . . [On one song] we ran cables up [the hillside beside the house], and Chad played drums with his hands. . . . I recorded the acoustic guitars [in my bedroom], and Anthony does all his vocals from his bedroom. Instead of looking through a window at three sweaty guys frowning in the control room, we're looking out at trees and flowers." With a conducive environment, months of rehearsal, and years of playing together, Flea felt the Chili Peppers had "an intense telepathic thing going musically, anticipating what's going to happen next and being able to really listen to what someone was doing and understand where it was coming from. Playing together and writing together has so much to do with improvisation and that can't happen unless we get inside each other's heads. Our ability to do that has been fully developed." Looking back years later, Flea described it as a "very peaceful time."

On working with Rick Rubin, Kiedis felt they had found the best possible producer for the band. "He's very intelligent, very emotionally in tune with hardcore, soulful music," Kiedis reflected to *NME* in 2001. "He knows how to extrapolate the best and most relaxed natural performance of a band without changing them. . . . He makes subtle, little, well-focused, well-thought out changes in the arrangement in songs and basically lays there and lets you do your thing." Part of that thing for Rubin was recording in a "natural" way. Speaking to *Guitar Player* in 1991, Rubin described his approach: "We've mixed 15 Chili Peppers songs so far, and I don't think we've used any reverb yet. It's amazing how dry and personal this record is. What you hear is what you get — there's not a lot of trickery. A lot of people want the biggest sound, with a wall of guitar and huge drums. But I don't think those things matter . . . the 'newest sounds' have a tendency to sound old when the next new sound comes along. But a grand piano sounded great 50 years ago and will sound great 50 years from now. AC/DC's *Highway to Hell* came out 12 years ago but could have been recorded yesterday. Same with the Zeppelin stuff. I try to make records that have that timeless quality. And as time goes on, I find that I like the organic sound of everyone playing together in the same room, facing each other. If you don't worry about the perfection of individual parts or perfection of sound, you get the best performance."

Frusciante felt that recording at the haunted mansion provided the right atmosphere. "'Womb' is a very good word. We didn't ever leave the place — you just woke up, relaxed, took a few deep breaths, put a grape in your ear, and started making music. Very easy. Very beautiful. Concentrating on doing nothing. I don't really care about my own creativity. I didn't even pay attention to my own playing. I just care about my life. I wasn't even listening to the guitar or how I was making it sound during the recording sessions. I just enjoy playing music with people I love. You don't pay attention to what you're playing, you just look into the other guy's eyes, or at his hands, or his knee, or whatever." Recording *Blood Sugar Sex Magik* was a landmark experience for Frusciante. As he said to *Guitar Player*, "Our music is so much more colorful than in the past, and I'm so happy about it. I never took anything so seriously in my life . . . It's an entity made by the four of us jumping out of our bodies into a cosmic swell. We've all grown out of love and admiration for each other."

To VH1, Flea described how they recorded the Robert Johnson cover "They're Red Hot," which took place "up on a hill behind the house up at, like, two in the morning. It was a hot summer night. We had chairs set up and all our acoustic guitars out there. Chad was playing with his hands. We started playing and it felt so fucking good. Right at the end of the track these people drove down the street in Laurel Canyon. You can hear them if you've got headphones. They're like, 'Wee-hoo!' reveling in their party-ness. We thought we were in a haunted house when we were making this record. Noises like that just added to the whole ambience. . . . There were times when I thought that I felt something. These ghost experts did a séance and said there were ghosts all over the place. I liked the idea that there were ghosts. One time this big plant leaf started waving up and down, even though there wasn't any breeze. John thought he could hear a woman making sexual noises. It freaked him out."

Kiedis said, "There were ghosts everywhere. They came out on about four of the photos we took for an album cover session — these floating nebulous shapes. The pictures were taken with a red filter and anytime ectoplasm experts are attempting to photograph ghosts they always do it with infrared. The photographer, Gus Van Sant, did it and he wasn't even trying to capture a ghost. Keep in mind that the house was built in 1917. It had been owned by gangsters, the Beatles had taken LSD there as a foursome, Jimi Hendrix stayed there, people were born and died there . . . it's deeply saturated with history. It's obvious to us that there's a real world of spirits that people just aren't tuned into. We were accepting of the fact that we were living among them. We weren't there to be obtrusive. We were there to make music and to coexist in what was really their house more than ours."

Blood Sugar Sex Magik marked a change in the Chili Peppers' sound to include slower songs like "Breaking the Girl." As Flea explained, that song "started off with John Frusciante getting these chords together with his acoustic guitar in his house in Mount Olympus. Anthony wrote those words and sang a beautiful melody. When we got to the studio, the drummer Chad Smith started doing that really loose, beautiful beat on it. We went to the junkyard and got a bunch of stuff to play the rhythm on. I always wanted to do that because when our ex-drummer Cliff Martinez was in Captain Beefheart's band, he would go get car hoods and metal pipes and buckets to play on. It was really fun." John Frusciante was listening to a lot of Led Zeppelin while working on "Breaking the Girl": "I especially liked 'Friends.' I also played a 12-string back them. That's where the idea to 'Breaking the Girl' came from. I took the chords of the chorus from the book on Duke Ellington. I tried to learn one song from this book and played three chords of a song, which has at least 50 chords. Based on these three chords and some additional stuff I wrote our song . . . I did draw a lot of inspiration from other music and imagined to comprise the style of some of my favorite guitarists in my work."

Not only making room for more mellow tracks on the album, Rubin's trademark stripped-down production style allowed the band to showcase its musical personality. Flea outlined the difference in sound on *Blood Sugar* from some of its contemporaries: "On the majority of rock records you don't hear a guitar or drums or bass. You hear a bunch of processed synthesized shit. That's all because it's a wall of sound . . . a recording studio creation. This record is very minimal and it's very live. When I hear it, I get a picture of a hand hitting a guitar, a string vibrating. This is four guys playing music. That took us awhile to learn to do. There are so many options in the studio, you've got to know what you want. We were real careful not to do anything unless it helped the song, which meant keeping that 'band feel' all the time."

A lot of the Chili Peppers' songs are born in jam sessions, with the roots of a song often growing in the relationship between bassist Flea and guitarist John Frusciante. "I remember a good exercise we did during the time of *Blood Sugar* to practice playing together," Frusciante told *Guitar*. "While Flea played a complex funky and syncopated rhythm I tried to fill the holes with chords and to kind of play in between Flea. I think it is important to create new rhythms. If someone plays something and you want to join the jam, you should try to find a different rhythm, one that is part of what the other plays and that supports whatever he started out with. This way you create something completely new. Sometimes we play harmonies that suit each other and sometimes we play stuff that is totally apart."

As Frusciante says, "you can't force inspiration," it just happens — as it did on a hot summer day in the rehearsal studio with "Give It Away." Kiedis explained that song's origin to VH1: "Flea started hitting that big heavy slide bass line. I had been thinking about this concept Nina Hagen planted in my mind. She was my girlfriend when I was 20 years old and believed that the more she gave, the more she received. When I got sober, I realized that sobriety revolved around giving something away in order to maintain it. So this idea of 'give it away' was tornado-ing in my head for a while. When Flea started hitting that bass line, that tornado just came out of my mouth." Rick Rubin liked the band's fluid songwriting style, praising the Chili Peppers' "love and appreciation of music, and the musicianship between the players in that band, the level of interactivity in their playing — I don't think there are any other big bands that do that, that really *jam*. They really do. They can play anything, and they *listen* to each other, which is so rare. A lot of bands, people just play their parts, but the Chili Peppers are truly an interactive band, kind of in the way that musicians might have been in the '60s. That's one of the reasons that there were so many bands back then; it was a different kind of musicianship. It was about playing together, playing off each other, complementing each other. Really, John Frusciante and Flea have this kind of magical interaction, almost like a psychic relationship."

Though his playing on the album was sophisticated, while recording John Frusciante set aside the goal of creating a technically proficient performance, deciding to feel the music rather than think it through. "Around the time we started writing *Blood Sugar* . . . I thought, for example, that Keith Richards makes music that connects with so many people and he plays in such a simple way, so why don't I pick a variety of people along those lines who play simple but do something that makes a beautiful sound that affects people emotionally? For me that was a new way of thinking that took a while adjusting to. So by the time we recorded *Blood Sugar,* I still felt as though I was doing a balancing act and I didn't really feel comfortable with what I was doing, which is probably a good thing." Flea saw the change in his bandmate's style. "John is playing much freer and thinking less," he said to *Guitar Player.* "I loved John's playing on *Mother's Milk,* but now he's so pure and spontaneous. He never considers doing something again and again — he'll just record maybe one overdub. He likes capturing the natural feeling on tape." On *Blood Sugar,* "almost all the solos are first takes and some of them were cut along with the basics, like 'My Lovely Man' and the first solo on 'Funky Monks,'" said Frusciante. "On 'Funky Monks' I played everything without a pick, even the solo. I've been playing that way more and more lately — in fact, I haven't used a pick in weeks now . . . I was thinking 'rubber band.' I've gotten more into those kinds of rhythms, because they sound more natural than really straight stuff. The second part of the solo is one of the few fast parts on the album. I though of it as a parody of a rock star solo. The intro has electric guitars not plugged in, just miked acoustically. It's the same thing Dave Navarro of Jane's Addiction does on 'Been Caught Stealing,' though Snakefinger did it first."

When it comes to equipment, Frusciante likes to keep it simple as well. "Those Mesa/Boogie amps were too hard for me to understand. For most of the basics, I used two Marshalls: a guitar head for edge and a bass head for punch and low end. I split the signal with a DOD stereo chorus pedal. For some overdubs I used a Fender H.O.T. practice amp, but for a lot of parts, even solos, I just went straight into the board. You can get amazing, funky tones that way. In fact, a lot of my distortion is from overdriving the board [which he did for the 'Suck My Kiss' solo]. My main guitar was a '58 Strat, though I used a Les Paul reissue on a couple of things. I also have a '57 Strat, which someone had screwed up by putting on those big stupid frets that everyone uses these days. I vomited and told them to make it fretless. . . . Some people think those big frets help your vibrato, but I make a point of using as little vibrato as possible, though I might do it more if I had long, pretty black hair. And I didn't use any whammy bar."

For "Blood Sugar Sex Magik," Frusciante used a Coral Electric sitar and "an old Gibson lap steel for the solo at the beginning of 'The Righteous and The Wicked.' My acoustic is a newish Martin steel-string. But my favorite guitar in the world is my old, fucked-up Fender Jaguar. The strings are all crusty, and the notes crap out when you bend them. I used it to write most of the music, and I became really attached to it. My only effects were an Electro-Harmonix Big Muff and an Ibanez Wah. I like the Ibanez because you can make adjustments without taking it apart, and it has a bass setting that sounds more like an envelope filter than a wah. I used that on 'Naked in the Rain.'"

As Frusciante refined his playing style so did acclaimed bassist Flea, whose performance on *Blood Sugar Sex Magik* was his most poetic and sophisticated to date. Rubin described the evolution that occurred: "Up until that time, Flea's bass playing was a particular style. He was famous for it, considered one of the best bass players in the world because of it. But when we started working together, that bass playing that made him one of the best didn't necessarily serve the songs in the best way. It was more about the bass being great. And the song is more important than the bass. I think, starting with that record, he changed the way he played. Not that it was so different stylistically, but it was more about playing the parts that supported the song. Instead of playing the parts that he liked the best or that were the coolest. It was a very interesting part of the change in the Chili Peppers' sound, from being a, let's say, 'traditional' funk band to being more of a songwriting band." Both the bassist and guitarist decided to serve the song, rather than grandstand. Frusciante made a conscious decision to "aim at playing behind Flea, keeping my sound clean and using my distortion pedal only for solos. I wanted to keep my solos as minimal as possible and wanted to play in a more spatial way. I wanted to create more room. The guitarists that I then considered to be good models were Matthew Ashman of Bow Wow Wow, who's also playing with a rather 'busy' bass guitarist, and Andy Summers of The Police. I considered myself more and more as support for Flea and Chad. This way I discovered exactly what I'm good at. And the most fascinating thing about it was this: since I began to retreat from the foreground, creativity simply started to pour out of me, thus automatically putting me into the fore at the same time however in a deeper way. Flea on the other hand also became more simple, more delicate, and useful for me to play with. Somehow everyone in the band suddenly took off into this direction."

Flea said to *Guitar Player* that on *Blood Sugar Sex Magik*, "I consciously avoided anything busy or fancy. I tried to get small enough to get inside the song, as opposed to stepping out and saying, 'Hey, I'm Flea, the bitchin' bass player.' I can play fast things that make bass players say, 'Wow!' but it's better to imply your technique with something simple . . . I hardly slap at all on the new record, aside from 'Naked in the Rain.'" The bassist went on to detail the gear he used while tracking the landmark album: "I started using Music Man basses because they're good and inexpensive. When I could afford one, I got a Spector, but it kept shorting out. I went back to the Music Mans because they're so simple and pure, but I've had problems keeping their necks straight — I had to constantly adjust them on tour. For this record I wanted something really good for the studio with a variety of sounds, so I got a WAL, which I used for most of the four-string songs, though I used the Music Man for five-string and fretless stuff. I still think Music Man basses look coolest. Every amp I've ever had breaks. For this album I used a Gallien-Krueger head with Mesa/Boogie cabinets. I'm not especially into them — they're just the shit I happen to

play through now. There's no effects except for an old Mu-Tron on 'Sir Psycho Sexy' and some envelope filter on a couple of things. I used a combination of mic and direct for most of the album, though I used direct only on a few things."

The critical and commercial success of the Red Hot Chili Peppers' fifth studio album would rocket them into worldwide stardom and prove highly influential. As Anthony Kiedis put it, "We weren't just communicating to a small circle of friends in Los Angeles and New York anymore. It might not swim with the current, but it's out there — putting something beautiful into a stream that gets a little stagnant at times." Unfortunately, the band's growth on *Blood Sugar Sex Magik* would be temporarily stunted when guitarist John Frusciante abruptly quit the band in 1993, at the height of the band's successful world tour in support of the album. Three years later, the remaining Chili Peppers enlisted Dave Navarro to fill Frusciante's spot and headed back to the studio with Rick Rubin to create *One Hot Minute*.

In the meantime, Rick Rubin produced Tom Petty and the Heartbreakers' biggest hit of the early 1990s — "Mary Jane's Last Dance" — on the rock legend's greatest hits LP. That collaboration would lead to a decade-long relationship.

CHAPTER 12

A Tug-of-War Album

Mick Jagger's *Wandering Spirit*

IN 1993 DANZIG AND RICK RUBIN joined forces for their final collaboration: *Danzig IV*. Said Glenn Danzig to *Flux*, "I like to do things different ways to stay fresh. It's the same with our albums — if I had to do the same album over and over again, it would be too boring for me, and I wouldn't do it. Once you find a certain way to say something, you then have to find a different way to say it. And there's a certain percentage of people who like it when bands try new things — but there are way more people who just want the same thing over and over again." For this album, Danzig and Rubin produced the album together. Two years later, Danzig was ready to produce his own work, a confidence built on the seven years and four studio albums he and Rubin had done together.

But not all of Rubin's partnerships were as successful. Legendary Rolling Stones' frontman Mick Jagger collaborated with Rick Rubin on his third solo album, the only one he released in the 1990s. Rubin had turned down a project with Jagger in the late '80s, remarking, "I don't think our schedules are going to work out. I don't even own a

Stones record." But by the summer of 1992, Rubin had signed on to produce Jagger's next solo LP. Rumors swirled during the recording sessions for *Wandering Spirit* that there was a fundamental disagreement between the two. Said Rubin, "I could tell early on . . . it was going to be an ego-driven project, not a music-driven project."

Trouble had begun during pre-production when Rubin brought the same brutal directness to Jagger that he does to all of his artists. When he voiced his opinion that some songs were not up to par for the album, Rubin recalled Jagger's "face fell. . . . It was probably the first time someone criticized his work in 30 years. . . . I don't think Mick's used to people telling him what they really think." In addition to having different taste, Rubin recalled he and Mick Jagger "were both going in different musical directions a lot of the time. There was some tension." To *AV Club*, Rubin outlined what he felt was the main crux of their creative difference: "I think he very much wanted to make a Mick Jagger solo record that was not like the Stones. And I think there's just a Stonesiness around him that comes naturally. If he writes a song that sounds like it could sound like a Stones song, it wouldn't feel good to change it just for the sake of changing it. I would say it was a little bit of a tug of war, that album."

In the studio, Rubin and Jagger had different styles as well, with the producer running into more disagreements than usual. A tense atmosphere when recording, said Rubin, "to him it was normal. To me, it was kinda weird." The working relationship was rife with tension with both men to blame for it. "Certain things that he'd wanna do that I didn't like, I'd really make it obvious that I didn't like it, and get all cranky," recalled Rubin. "And he said 'Look, if you don't like something that I wanna do, just go out and get a veggie burger or something. But don't make everyone feel uncomfortable.' So I started getting a lot of veggie burgers." Rubin declared *Wandering Spirit* was "probably one of the more difficult works [I've done]." Session guitarist Smokey Hormel had more positive memories of the atmosphere Rubin created. "He runs a real democracy. He's still the only producer that does that. [He] asked, 'How can I make guitars sound better?' That was a first."

In 1993, Rick Rubin held a funeral for the word "def" after it appeared in a dictionary, losing its original street meaning with that mainstream validation. Rubin changed the name of his company from "Def American" to "American Recordings." Reverend Al Sharpton is on Rubin's right. (© Kevin Estrada)

The collaboration between Jagger and Rubin produced some tracks that didn't fit the style of *Wandering Spirit,* but one found its way into the world 12 years later. In 2007, a song from the Jagger/Rubin sessions showed up on a greatest hits compilation, *The Very Best of Mick Jagger.* "Checking Up on My Baby" was recorded with the Los Angeles blues ensemble The Red Devils in 1992. Said Jagger, "The difficult decision I was faced with when listening to the tracks I recorded with The Red Devils, and having to choose only one, reminded me what a great band they were."

Despite their in-studio difficulties, Mick Jagger and Rick Rubin created *Wandering Spirit,* an album that was well received, and Rubin felt it "came out, in my opinion, 70 percent or 75 percent as good as it could have been, which I think is really good." While Jagger may have had problems with the direction Rubin pushed him in, the critics loved it and looking back, Rubin felt "really proud" of *Wandering Spirit.*

"So much of my work is trying to be critical without being judgmental. I try to make criticisms in a very, very specific way. The more specific it is — if someone can really understand where you're coming from and what you're suggesting — the more it will actually help them."

— RICK RUBIN

PART IV

The Mid-to-Late '90s

CHAPTER 13

The Man in Black
American Recordings

THOUGH HE LOGGED STUDIO TIME with other artists, in 1994 Rick Rubin was focused on a great challenge: resurrecting the career of country music legend Johnny Cash. First offering the dark side of rock 'n' roll 30 years earlier, Johnny Cash could be called the founding father of alternative rock, though his career began alongside the likes of Elvis Presley and Jerry Lee Lewis before it transitioned onto a more traditional country music path. The partnership between Johnny Cash and Rick Rubin brought Cash's sound and sensibility — his artistic persona as an elder statesman of music with a haunting voice from years of untold hardship — to covers of alt-rock songs as well as traditional songs and original compositions. With Rubin's trademark "production by reduction" approach, the albums would bring the legendary Johnny Cash his first platinum success in years and showcased a more raw side to him.

Rubin explained to *AV Club* how he came to work with Johnny Cash: "I felt like between Def Jam and American, I had only ever really signed new artists, and only really worked with young people on their first albums. It seemed like it would be a fun challenge to work with an established artist." But the producer wasn't interested in working with a legend at the top of his game. "I'd been thinking about who was really great but not making really great records; what great artists are not in a great place right now. And Johnny was the first and the greatest that came to mind. A unique character, kind of his own force of nature." Rubin described him to *USA Today* as "someone without peer, still capable of good work. He felt lost artistically." Rubin saw potential in himself to assist Cash, to help him be prolific again. "I just thought that he was clearly one of the greatest artists of all time and wasn't doing his best work and it seemed like with the right support he could be doing his best work and that would be great." When Rubin approached Cash, the producer told *Music Angle*, "I don't think he knew who I was. He was receptive, I think, because I think he was surprised that anyone cared at that point."

Cash recalled being initially skeptical of working with Rubin. "Rick heard that my contract was running out with Mercury. For some reason he wanted me on his label. He came down to see my show at San Juan Capistrano; he came to a fair in California to see me, he came to about three or four shows. Backstage at the first show, he said he wanted to sign me, and I said, 'What would you like to do with me?' And he said, 'I would like for you to do whatever feels right to you.' That sounded pretty good to me. I didn't know his track record, the music he had recorded, until a little later. I asked who else he had on the label that he'd produced, and you know, it's kinda like, I was on the same label with Mitch Miller, but I didn't do what Mitch did. That is the silliest thing that's going around now; people are talking about how Johnny Cash's producer is the same producer who did Slayer and Red Hot Chili Peppers and all these people. But that's got nothing to do with me. Rick made me know that I could maintain my musical integrity, that I could do what felt right, and we would take plenty of time and all the money it took to do the album we wanted to do, and that the promotion budget was unlimited. And all of this sounded really good to me, after coming off several dry years where the record company just did not put up what it took. Jack Clement did a great job

Rick Rubin and Johnny Cash at work in the studio. (© Kevin Estrada)

on me with what he had to work with. Mercury/PolyGram Nashville did the best job they could do with what they had to work with, too. And I understand about demographics; I don't have to be told about demographics anymore, but I'm happy to be doing what I do and I'm comfortable with it."

Of their first proper meeting, Rubin recalled to *AV Club*: "I liked him very much. I would say we hit it off, though we didn't say much at our first meeting. We were both pretty quiet. But it felt strong, and it felt like there was potential for really good work to be done. I think he was almost at the point of giving up. I think he'd probably made a hundred albums, and making an album wasn't a big deal to him. It wasn't important to him. It was just another one: 'Eighteen months roll by, put out another one, doesn't really matter, no one really cares. I'll either do it or not, it doesn't make a difference.' I think that's where he was at, where the record-making part of his artistry didn't matter so much to him after being not treated so well, after being dropped from Columbia, his longtime label, and then being at Mercury, where he was not really cared for very much. I think he may have still been going through the motions, but I don't think he was emotionally invested in the record-making process. I think the idea of doing something new appealed to him, but I don't think it was that big of a deal. Until we started having some success, I don't know that he cared that much about his recording career, again, only because of the way he had been treated. It was almost beaten out of him in some way."

In his autobiography *Cash*, Johnny Cash wrote, "I thought it all pretty unlikely. He was the ultimate hippie, bald on top but with hair down over his shoulders, a beard that looked as if it had never been trimmed, and clothes that would have done a wino proud." Cash described to *Livewire* one of their first formal meetings: "I auditioned in his house, in his living room, with his dogs running around at my feet, and we made our first record right there. When I first started recording with Rick, word got out that I was 'happening,' whatever that meant. But I really felt it was — like something really was happening. It felt really good to know that there was a possibility that I had an audience among the young people out there." Having Rubin interested in him and his work provided Cash with the most creative freedom he'd had since starting with Sun Records. Said Cash, "Working with Rick has been a really joyful period of growth artistically for me." Rubin was pleasantly surprised to find an abundance of common ground, telling *USA Today*, "We both loved music and the history of music. We were interested in spirituality." Setting out to put together an album, Rubin had a simple plan: "Wherever the magic is, [we will] follow. That's how the first Johnny Cash CD came about. We didn't set out to make an acoustic album. We tried a lot of things and we always hear stories of people who do demos and then they make the album, the demo was great and the album was not so good. If you really pay attention there's no way that can happen. Ultimately you'd record a whole lotta stuff and then you listen back and whatever sounds best is what your record is! Not well, 'We recorded this at home so that's the demo and we recorded this in the studio so that's the record,' that's ridiculous. The first Cash album was really demo recordings recorded in my living room in my old house."

In the course of choosing material for Cash's album, "I guess I thought of the legendary image of the Man in Black," said Rubin to *AV Club*, "and thought that we could find material, or write material, and kind of use that imagery as a framework for the kind of songs that we were going to do. Make sure that whatever he sang suited the mythic character, that was really maybe a caricature of himself. There was probably some of him in it. That's probably where it came from. But we were trying to find, from a content point of view, what someone who loved what Johnny Cash was would want to hear him sing. Sometimes we would pick songs that you wouldn't think of him singing, like a Beck song, something you wouldn't think a Johnny Cash fan would want, or a Soundgarden song. But it's less where it came from, and more the actual content of the material. I always tried to pick material that really suited him, that when you heard him singing the words, it made sense, and you feel it. You feel the truth in what he's singing, whether [he] wrote the song or not."

Recorded digitally on ADATs in Rick Rubin's living room, Cash recalled there was "no echo, no slap-back, no overdubbing, no mixing. Just me playing my guitar and singing. I didn't even use a pick; every guitar note on the album came from my thumb." The album featured songs by legendary figures like Kris Kristofferson, Leonard Cohen, Tom Waits, and Loudon Wainwright III. For the aptly titled album *American Recordings*, the singer explained, "I learned the songs one day and recorded them the next day." The producer explained how the song selection took place: "We recorded songs first for the idea of which ones should be on our album and then we recorded other songs, maybe not even thinking about the album. [Cash] would say, 'Do you know this song?' and he would play it to me, so I got to learn his taste. And then I would suggest songs that I liked that I thought would fit that same world." The singer and producer were astoundingly prolific. Said Cash, "I did something like 110 tracks in all. Every time I got a good cut on a song, Rick would say, 'Now what else do you want to do?' He always asked me what I wanted to do, and I appreciated that. But he had his own ideas too. He would lay songs before me, or mail songs to me. Some I liked and some I didn't. I did some and some are on the album. We tried a few other things too. Tom Petty's guitar player was on a couple sessions, but playing country acoustic. We also experimented with some other rhythm sections, but it didn't work, and we never really expected it to; we just wanted to experiment.

"I've never spent this much time on an album, and probably an average of two sessions a day for about 30 days, at least — I'd need a calculator. Good new songs kept coming in, and the old classics kept popping up from the different people saying, 'Why don't you do this one and that one,' and I'd run right out then and cut it. And then I'd do them over and over and over, until we got that right attitude, that right mood. I'll be in a different mood tomorrow than I am right now, and it's got nothing to do with drugs; it's just that that's the way we are. I'd get a cut of a song and say, 'Maybe that sounds pretty good right now, but let's try again tomorrow night, later, see how a late evening performance of that song might sound.' They may be subtle differences, but they are differences, and we kept going for that one final performance that was the one that had all the feeling and emotion that we wanted. That's what took a lot of time. Whereas with a lot of musicians you'd take a lot of time to get everybody sounding right and doing the right licks, I had to get all the emotional licks right. . . . And it's pretty scary to sit down in front of a DAT recorder, just me and my guitar, 'cause I'm not a musician, I just accompany myself on my guitar, just me and my thumb, no pick. There'd be little things I didn't like about my voice that we'd do over, and then there'd be this new one I wanted to try, and it's just a lot of work to get 110 songs right. But we did it because we were going for the best we could come up with. . . . We did blues, we did gospel, we did country, we did Appalachian, we did Carter Family, we did Jimmie Rodgers, we did Gene Autry. I did songs by people really active and hot on the music scene today . . . What fans will hear is 13 songs from the gut and from the heart, and they will feel, I think, the emotions I felt when I recorded it. . . . I think with all the heavy stuff on the album they'll appreciate me sharing a little humor with them. . . . I think they'll know the real me, whatever that's worth."

Of all those different styles and songs, Rubin explained to Gibson.com, "Many of those experiments are actually on the *Unearthed* boxed set — those songs that were recorded prior to the first American album. We were just trying to find our way. The first thing we did were acoustic demos, in my living room. And then we went into different studios, with different players, and tried songs in different ways. Ultimately, after many experiments, we kind of looked at each other and decided that we liked the acoustic stuff — those first demos — better than any of the other experiments we tried. . . . I think [Cash] had mixed feelings about that. I know there was a part of him that was excited about it, and that always wanted to do it. And there was another part of him that was insecure about it, and felt, 'Well, if they don't like this, I'm really in trouble, because this is really me.'"

The final track listing for *American Recordings* was a blend of covers and original compositions. "I wrote five of them, and I wrote four within the last year: 'Let the Train Blow the Whistle' and 'Drive On' was my Vietnam veterans song; 'Redemption' is a gospel song about the plan of salvation through the blood. 'Like a Soldier' is a love song. The other is the new lyrics to 'Delia's Gone,' which is a really old traditional song. I cut it before, but this is a newer version. I couldn't remember enough verses of the old one to sing it, so I wrote some new ones. I sing that one a lot in concert, and fans are always asking for it, so I thought I'd cut a new version and try to get it before a new audience. 'Drive On' came from what I remembered about Vietnam, from being there in '69 plus a lot of books I read, and talking to a lot of veterans. 'Drive on, it don't mean nothing' is an expression they used a lot in Vietnam. 'Tennessee Stud' is a song I always wanted to record. A rock artist named Glenn Danzig wrote a song for me called 'Thirteen.' My ex-son-in-law Nick Lowe wrote 'The Beast in Me' in 1979, and I've just been able to record it. 'The Man Who Couldn't Cry' is an old novelty song by Loudon Wainwright III. . . . I haven't been writing all that much, but I'm beginning to. I picked up a song that I started a year ago that I really like that I'm going to finish. I don't write if I can't sing it a little bit, because I have to hear what I've written down. I still don't read music — maybe that's been a help, maybe a hindrance. When I'm writing, I have my guitar, and I sing the lyrics and work on them until they feel right to me. . . . I've never recorded a lot of my own songs on an album. I've always had an open mind and tried to be objective about every song that I remotely considered doing, you know? And, usually, they're songs by other people that I love. Then I have to rack my brain to go, 'Now, what did I write that I like?' You know? Well, I've come up with a couple, maybe, for this next album."

To launch *American Recordings*, Rick Rubin suggested something similar to the format of the album itself: Johnny Cash alone on stage with his guitar at the legendary L.A. club The Viper Room. "It was an incredible night," recalled Rubin to *Being There*. "Dead silent. You could hear a pin drop. People couldn't believe that it was Johnny Cash there in the Viper Room. He started playing, and I could see how nervous he was, but by the middle of the first song, or the beginning of the second song, all of the fear was gone. He was in the music and it was beautiful. People who were there that night still talk about it as one of the greatest things they've ever seen." The way Cash seemed to view it, he had nothing to lose, and everything to gain in wearing his heart on his sleeve. "I know I'm 62 years old. And I've been around twice, and it looks now like I might have a third shot at a new audience. If I don't, I can still get work."

But he found that new audience; MTV put the video for Cash's first single, "Delia's Gone," into heavy rotation, which featured supermodel Kate Moss as its star alongside Cash. *American Recordings* garnered critical popularity as well. *Rolling Stone*, in its four-star review, called Rubin's production "tougher than leather" and highlighted the "stark guitar and Cash's wise-as-Isaiah vocal delivery." The album won a Grammy for Best Contemporary Folk Album in 1995. For both artist and producer, the reception of the album helped them realize the significance of it. Said Rubin, "I think he knew the music was good while we were doing it, but it wasn't until it came out and got the kind of critical praise it received that it really sank in. And when young people started coming up to him, telling him how much they liked the album, that's when he really knew. It had more to do with other people's reactions." For Rubin's part, he told *Music Angle*, "I knew we could make great music but I had no idea what the acceptance would be."

Cash reckoned that to the younger generation the album looked "like I'm doing something new. But this is the most comfortable way to do it for me, just me and my guitar. It's an album I always wanted to do. Twenty-five years ago Marty Robbins and I were at a show, and we were talking about things we wanted to do, record-wise. And I told him that I always wanted to do an album called Johnny Cash Alone, with just my guitar, singing one on one, just me to you. He did an album like that, after that, and I always wanted to do mine, but I never had any record company until now interested in supporting a project like that. But with this new record company, Rick Rubin wanted to get the 'real,' whatever that is, Johnny Cash."

More important to Cash than his commercial and critical success was the kinship he'd found in Rubin. After *American Recordings*, "Rick immediately asked what I wanted to do next," said Cash to the *LA Times*. "I mentioned [an album of] black gospel, and then I mentioned an album of songs that would show my musical roots, and Rick said, 'Let's do them both.' I was dumbfounded. I thought I might finally be at the point where I would only be singing for myself. . . . Most important, Rick made me have faith in myself again. He made me believe in myself and my music, which I thought was gone forever."

Rubin felt they had achieved what they had set out to do, reaching "really noble goals. We both wanted to do the best work we could, and there was very little in the way of 'commercial' thoughts. It was really about the art, and about the love of great songs." Describing the nature of their relationship to *Music Angle*, Rubin said, "We collaborated. I would inspire him to bring out the best in him and refocus. . . . I think that this rhythm of what it is to be an artist takes over and it's not necessarily conducive to making the best music. So the first thing I had to do with Johnny was reframe the record-making experience back to 'We're going to take as long as it takes, we're gonna try a lot of different things, we're in no hurry to ever put out a record, all that matters is that this next record you make is the best record of your life. It's all that matters. Nothing else matters.' That's a radical difference for a guy

that's made 100 albums. . . . It just took a little time, and it took trust on his part because it definitely went against his programming for the last 30 years. But once we made the breakthrough and once he heard it, and then once it came out and people liked it as much as they did, he knew everything was different from now on." Following the album's release in 1994, *Rolling Stone* named Johnny Cash the Best Country Artist and the Comeback of the Year, concluding that *American Recordings* was "a spare beauty that reintroduced the Man in Black to a new generation of fans who identified with the pain and loneliness at the core of his music."

CHAPTER 14

Tom Petty and the Heartbreakers

Wildflowers

AFTER WORKING WITH TOM PETTY on "Mary Jane's Last Dance" for the artist's greatest hits album, Rubin returned to produce a new, full-length studio LP with him in 1994 for Warner Bros. Tom Petty was arguably the rootsiest rock project Rubin had undertaken up to that point in his career, aside from his brief collaboration with Roy Orbison on the *Less than Zero* soundtrack. Rubin sought to draw upon what had been Petty's greatest currency, his songwriting. "If you look at his body of work, there are so many great songs. He's an incredible songwriter and when it comes to record making, he's a true craftsman. There are just not a lot of people that can do that. It's somewhat of a lost art."

For *Wildflowers*, Tom Petty surprised even his producer. Said Rubin, "At the time I thought 'this is good,' and it was really successful and I was surprised by how successful it was at the time . . . because I thought it was good but I didn't think it was amazing at the time. I really love it now. . . . I thought of all of his contemporaries and it was much better than anything his contemporaries were doing. Even the late '60s artists at that time — Paul Simon wasn't making great records — the great artists, Paul Simon, Paul McCartney, their new albums weren't so great. For grown people Petty's record was a milestone album in that respect because his contemporaries weren't doing anything that was par with it." *Rolling Stone* sought to give Rubin the appropriate credit for his role in boosting Petty, saying Rubin "had successfully revitalized the career of the legendary country star Johnny Cash with a set of stripped-down folk music. He does the same for Petty, whose new folk and country-style songs on *Wildflowers,* are well served by Rubin's simple production." Rubin shrugged off the credit given to him, instead suggesting the success of *Wildflowers* rested on the shoulders of the musicians, saying to *Billboard* that it was working with Tom Petty and the Heartbreakers, "arguably the best American rock band, so you have a great band, with great songs, who make great records. It's really hard to beat."

Tom Petty recalled the atmosphere in the studio while recording *Wildflowers* lent itself to those magically accidental musical moments that can lead to a song like "Girl on LSD" (a B-side to "You Don't Know How It Feels"): "I think I was just trying to entertain George Drakoulias! He frequently came to the *Wildflowers* sessions, and I remember that night I was really singing that to George, just trying to make him laugh, and Rick Rubin said, 'We've really got to put that down!' And I was like, 'Are you serious?' He said, 'Yeah, come on, come on!' I think it's one of the first psychedelic folk songs."

Rubin saw Petty's songwriting craft as one on par with the best who can draw on "ideas that are of the moment. There's a sphere of influence almost that great artists can just tap into. For example, in working with Tom Petty, he tells me that sometimes he'll be sitting there with his guitar, and a whole song will just come out, beginning to end, lyrics, the whole thing. Tom will just sit down and play a song that he's never heard before, thought about, or written. Three minutes later, there's a whole song, with all the lyrics, and about something he doesn't know anything about." Speaking to *Mix*, Rubin praised Tom Petty as "a record-making craftsman . . . in that he hears the whole thing. Some of the things I'm most proud of are things I've done with Tom. Like the *Wildflowers* album. I really like it a lot; it sounds like it was made on a weekend. Of course, it took us two years to make it sound like it was made on a weekend — the right weekend!"

Wildflowers produced a hit first single, "You Don't Know How It Feels," as well as the follow-up hit "You Wreck Me." But for Rick Rubin, neither single stood out as his favorite song from the album, instead "there's a song on *Wildflowers* that really moves me called 'Hard on Me.' It's one of the very first things we cut together, so it's got some emotional relevance to me personally. Both the song is good, the tone of it is great, and the mood of the performance just captures the song perfectly. It's a perfect moment in time. It sounds really real, really live, personal, and intimate, and of a moment. It's personally revelatory lyrically, open and honest. It's just a beautiful song." For Tom Petty, he and the Heartbreakers "felt like we had a really good little rock and roll band, and we said we ought to make a record like we were a rock and roll band."

CHAPTER 15

Ballbreaker and
One Hot Minute

WORKING WITH AC/DC was a career-long dream that came true for Rick Rubin when he stepped into the studio with the legendary hard rock band. He first worked with the band on a track for the *Last Action Hero* soundtrack ("Big Gun") before getting a chance to produce a full-length album. AC/DC's style of rock 'n' roll had long been Rubin's archetype for producing rock bands. The result of Rubin and his idols working together to produce 1995's *Ballbreaker* was, according to *Rolling Stone*, "tighter and slightly cleaner sounding than the group's last studio album, the muddy and plodding *Razor's Edge*. The boys seem to be going for a bluesier feel."

One fundamental change that helped account for the group's tighter sound was the return of original drummer Phil Rudd. Rubin felt he was ideal for recapturing the band's classic sound. Describing his drumming style in *Rolling Stone*, Rubin wrote, "You can hear it in how he drags behind the beat. It's that same rhythm that first drew me to them in junior high. . . . The best thing was the return of Phil Rudd, who had left the band in 1982. To me, that made them AC/DC again."

The rhythm section, as Rubin pointed out, was a huge part of what made the band stand out from its contemporaries: "The thing that separates AC/DC as a hard-rock band is that you can dance to their music. They didn't play funk, but everything they played was funky. And that beat could really get a crowd going." Bassist Cliff Williams agreed, "We wanted to do a good album . . . and that's what we did. Now we've found our rhythmical section from our beginning back, AC/DC is a real group." But that didn't mean the recording of the album was without its challenges. "The making of the album was really hard," said Williams. "We started to record [at] the Record Plant Studios, in New York, but we didn't enjoy the [sound] we had. Many musicians told us, 'It's an excellent studio to record drum parts.' But we tried the drums in each of the rooms of those studios and haven't been able to have a decent sound. So, we fixed carpets on the walls, we put a tent onto the kit too, to obtain a more live [sound]. Result: we lost two months. . . . The only positive thing [was] we knew perfectly every new song. Then, we chose the Ocean Way studios in Los Angeles."

Phil Rudd elaborated on the rocky start the album had to *Rhythm*: "When we started doing *Ballbreaker*, there was a bit of a difference of opinion in the studio about drum sounds and we were working with a new producer. So we went through this big rigmarole where we couldn't play together because of the sound reflecting off the wall. It was bizarre! We tried playing on risers and even had a marquee built over the riser to contain the room sound. This was before we got started. Then they brought in a 'drum doctor' from Europe and he had cases full of bass drums and snare drums, but at the end of the day we sent him packing because I knew that the problem wasn't down to the sound of my gear. It's a very personal thing and I always do things the best way. That's how it is. In the end we went to another studio."

Once the group had settled into Ocean Way with Rubin at the production helm, Williams described being put through a recording regimen wherein "Rick Rubin made us record every track about 50 times each to obtain the good dynamics and we kept those who got the best feelings." For basic tracking, as Williams explained to *Hard Rock*, AC/DC has "always recorded live playing, all four of us, together. As

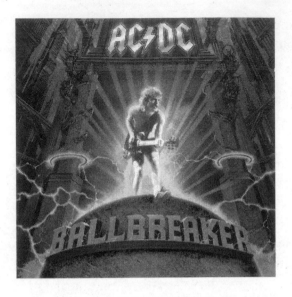

time's gone by, we tried to record with a click but, with Phil, it's totally useless. We record basic tracks, tracks' bones, then Angus adds his guitar parts. . . . Malcolm, Angus, and me played in a small room with glass, to enable ourselves to see Phil [who] was still in the main room." Rick Rubin recalled to *Rolling Stone*, "The first day we worked together Malcolm Young told me that before he came into the studio he tested 100 different Marshall heads before he selected the one that was right for him."

Guitarist Angus Young said of *Ballbreaker*, "The plan was we wanted to do a stripped-down record, a bit hard and tough. Yet again, I think what was being played on the radio at the time was dance things, mostly the disco-type dance. We felt we should get in and do a nice tough rock record, maybe a bit more hard-edged. You can hear it on the 'Ballbreaker' track, you can hear it on 'Hail Caesar,' and especially 'Hard as a Rock.'" Upon release, the album peaked at #4 on the Billboard 200 and produced three hit singles with "Hard as a Rock," "Hail Caesar," and "Cover You in Oil." *Ballbreaker*, which heralded the return of four of rock's favorite sons, was embraced by fans. But *Rolling Stone*'s review of the album was not much more than tepid: "AC/DC deliver the same goods they've delivered for 21 years: fist-pumpin' riffs, the dual-guitar assault of brothers Angus and Malcolm Young. . . . They deliver guilty-pleasure metal like no other hard-rock band." For Rubin, the album was his best effort at creating "a tribute to how great they were."

* * *

Turning his attention back to the Red Hot Chili Peppers, Rubin entered the studio with the band to record the highly anticipated follow-up to *Blood Sugar Sex Magik*. Following John Frusciante's departure in 1993, the band had tided over fans with one last song featuring the guitarist, "Soul to Squeeze," as well as a retrospective album from their first decade together, 1992's *What Hits!?*. With the benefit of hindsight, Frusciante said his departure had been fueled in part by "a certain amount of tension between me and Anthony then that isn't there now.... That was a big part of my reason for quitting the band. Anthony and I just couldn't see eye to eye. Back then we were both the kind of people who tend to blame anyone other than themselves for what's wrong." After their guitarist had quit, the Red Hot Chili Peppers did not perform publicly until the summer of 1994, debuting the new line-up with guitarist Dave Navarro at Woodstock.

In the minds of Chili Peppers fans, Navarro's tenure with the band lasted, figuratively speaking, as long as the title of the album they made together. But it was a fitting pairing. Jane's Addiction was no more, and Kurt Cobain was dead; the Chili Peppers were one of only a handful of superstar bands keeping alternative rock alive commercially. Dave Navarro described to *iMusic* how he fit in with the Chili Peppers: "Everything that encompasses who I am and who I've been in my life has been brought to this band in an amicable way. I think that I come from a slightly different place, musically speaking. These guys are percussive and sharp edged, to use an expression that Flea has come up with, and I'm into melodic and ethereal sounds. And I think that the combination has really worked and given birth to something really new." Anthony Kiedis saw the benefit of bringing Navarro into the fold quite simply: "Dave had something that nobody else had and that was Dave."

With Navarro, the band's first order of business, according to Anthony Kiedis, was "getting to know each other and hanging out together and working on music. No one told us when [the album] was finished because we knew when it was finished. If it takes 10 years to make a record, then that's how long it takes. This record took us a year to make and it's a good thing that it took that long, because if it would have taken less time, it wouldn't be what it is now. There's a natural flow of creative unity and that doesn't happen according to a schedule or a deadline." Flea agreed, "The commercial success of a record is really not our concern. Our concern is trying to make the most honest music that we can. We're really proud of this record. We think we've grown a lot and made an album that sounds different than anything we've ever done. And whatever the world wants to do with it is fine." For Navarro, the focus seemed to be on fitting into the band's sound without compromising his own, explaining the writing and recording process as one that was "different for me because for the past 13 years I've worked by myself and now I have the input of these guys. But it works to the fullest potential and we've come up with something really exciting and new and we hope everyone loves it."

One Hot Minute is a complicated, emotional record, but Flea felt his role was to keep his playing simple. As he said to *Bass Player*, "When you play less, it's more exciting — there's more room for everything. If I do play something busy, it stands out, instead of the bass being a constant onslaught of notes. Space is good. I think my playing on *One Hot Minute* is even more simple [than on *Blood Sugar*]; I just wanted to play shit that sounded good. I thrashed through the recording and didn't care about the parts being perfect. . . . I'm thinking less as a bass player and more as a songwriter."

The bassist took a more central role in songwriting on *One Hot Minute*. "I wrote the chords and the melody and most of the words. I wrote a lot of the lyrics on 'Deep Kick' and 'Transcending,' for example." Flea described the writing process for this album: "Mostly I'd play acoustic guitar and come up with the chords and melody, and Dave would take my simple guitar part and play it in his magical Navarro way. Or, I would have a bass line, and Dave would think of a guitar part to go with it." Flea playing an acoustic guitar to help with songwriting came at the suggestion of the album's producer. Said Flea, "I started a couple of months before we began making this record. Rick Rubin gave me a Martin acoustic, and I bought a Neil Young songbook to learn chords. Playing guitar has definitely helped me as a songwriter; instead of thinking in terms of bass lines and grooves, which is an amazing way to think, I now think about chord progressions and melodies. It's another musical dimension for me."

There was some adjusting required when the band took to the studio for *One Hot Minute*. "Dave Navarro is intensely different from John Frusciante," said Flea to *Bass Player*. "When we recorded *Blood Sugar*, John played all his tracks once and maybe overdubbed a few solos, so the whole record was very spontaneous. Dave is really into the studio; he would spend weeks on every song, put something like 15 tracks of guitar on every tune, and weed through it in the mix. Dave's sound is more layered and 'effecty' than John's, which was like, boom — play it dry and leave it alone. Also, Dave and I are very different musically. He'll often play some '70s rock song, and most of the time I don't even know who did it, but I'll start playing along — and to me it's ridiculous. But our differences create our music."

Anthony Kiedis was eager to avoid over-analyzing the band's creative process, because describing it "takes all the fun out of it, it takes the mystery and the beauty out of it. We work on songs and we record them for people to hear and it isn't our place to sit there and try to give detailed explanations of how a song came to be or what it's about. . . . There's no formula. No song is ever written the same way twice. It happens with a bass line. It happens with a guitar part. It happens with a drum part. It happens with a vocal part. It happens when we get together and work and there is no secret to it. It's just an intangible factor." Flea was much more vocal about his development as a musician and songwriting. "My dynamic has changed — I really want to improve as a bass player. . . . Plenty of bass players have fancy chops, but they don't make you feel any emotions. You don't feel anger, fear, or love. That's what I call 'all flash and no smash.'"

While *Blood Sugar Sex Magik* had been an album created in large part through rehearsal and jam sessions, *One Hot Minute* was, from Flea's perspective, "the least jam-oriented record we've made. I mean, we definitely jammed on the ideas, but there's only one groove on the whole album that came from a jam, 'Deep Kick.' The rest of it came from my sitting down with a guitar or bass and saying, 'Check this out, guys.'" For "Aeroplane," the album's third single, Flea explained:

"I was sitting in my garage with a bass Louis Johnson gave me — a Treker Louis Johnson Signature four-string — and I started playing that '70s funk line. The bass had light strings on it and had that whacka-whackita sound. It's kind of a 'been done' groove, but it's nice and Anthony liked it. The chorus part was one of those things where we were stuck; sometimes when we're looking for another part, I'll have no idea what I'm going to do, but I'll say, 'What about this?' . . . It's all sliding on the E string. Actually, 'Aeroplane' was the only song I was worried about — I thought it sounded like another stupid white boy trying to be funky! I put it out anyway, but it's the one thing I'd go back and fix. When I played it live in the studio with the band, the bass didn't record right for some reason, so it was one of the few things I had to overdub. The part kept feeling stiff to me, as if it wasn't my day; I wasn't flowing with the drums. I wanted to redo it, but Rick said, 'It's cool.'"

Said Flea, "'Coffee Shop' is chock full of bass stuff, including a solo. It's funny — 'Coffee Shop' would never have been a song if it weren't for this effect called the BassBalls." Playing with the effect while in Hawaii, Flea found that it had stopped working by the time he was back in L.A. to record. "I almost didn't even want to record the song, because to me, it was all about that bass sound. I ended up using a Boss Dynamic Filter on the record. In the solo, it sounds as if you're ripping the strings off the fingerboard. We didn't know what to do at the end, so I said, 'I'll solo.' I played the track once, and I wanted to fix it later because I thought it sucked, but I never did." On "Pea," the bass-and-vocals solo song, Flea used a Sigma acoustic bass guitar.

To capture his bass sound, Flea used "an Alembic for most of the record. . . . It was the bass I had in the studio, so I was like, 'Let's record, let's rock.' The Alembic isn't as in-my-face as the Music Man, but the high notes are as loud as the low ones, from the bottom of the neck to the top, which is a problem on the Music Man. I probably could have used the StingRay for the entire album, but when we go to record, I always think I need the best bass for recording. . . . [For my rig,] I used an 800RB head with a Mesa/Boogie 2x15; I like the way they sound together. I'm not picky when it comes to equipment. . . . I've tried a bunch of different stuff, but I haven't found anything else as good."

Instead of trying to replicate the setting for *Blood Sugar Sex Magik* and heading back to a haunted mansion, the Red Hot Chili Peppers had a new idea. "I think it would be pretty stupid to try to recreate something we did a long time ago," said Kiedis to *iMusic*, "so we tried to do something new this time. We went to Hawaii for three months and lived and wrote songs and played around together." Kiedis and company took great comfort in having Rick Rubin back behind the recording console. "He was with us the whole time and his influence was greatly appreciated," said Kiedis. "He's our friend as well as our producer, so we have a great rapport and it was a rewarding experience as always to work with him."

Asked to choose standout tracks from the album, Anthony Kiedis couldn't. "My favorite track is different every day. It depends on the mood that I'm in because all of these tracks are very meaningful to me. They were born and grew out of honest experiences, sad experiences, happy experiences. And because those experiences are expressed in these songs."

As the long awaited follow-up to the universally acclaimed *Blood Sugar Sex Magik*, it was not surprising the album garnered mixed reviews. *Rolling Stone* praised it ("*One Hot Minute* is a ferociously eclectic and imaginative disc that also presents the band members as more thoughtful, spiritual — even grown-up. After a 10 plus–year career, they're realizing their potential at last") while other critics were less kind. But it was all the new music from the band critics or fans would get until John Frusciante returned to the Red Hot Chili Peppers for 1999's *Californication*.

CHAPTER 16

Three Legends

Tom Petty, Donovan, and Johnny Cash

IN 1996, RICK RUBIN WOULD WORK together once again with Tom Petty and the Heartbreakers, putting together a soundtrack to the Ed Burns film *She's the One*. *Entertainment Weekly* celebrated the soundtrack saying "Petty sounds like he's having the time of his life. . . . *She's the One* may not be the most serious album Tom Petty has ever made, but, in a way, that makes it one of his most enjoyable."

Rick Rubin headed away from the mainstream for his next project, working with Donovan. A relic of the 1960s folk-pop movement, Donovan may not have sounded much like the artists Rubin had worked with in the past, but the artist and producer had much in common personally. "When I met Rick Rubin . . . I was looking for a producer with sympathy, and I found someone who was very sympathetic," said Donovan to *New Renaissance*. "His interests are yoga, vegan diet, Kundalini yoga. He also has a library of mystical books. So the most popular producer in the world met me and we had these spiritual feelings."

With that connection, the two felt they could work together on Donovan's new album — but what kind of album to make? To the producer's query, Donovan replied, "'One we like.' As the album progressed, it became clear that we should make this kind of album. Not rock 'n' roll, jazz, folk, ethnic, classical or world music; not go for the pop chart. So we made this album *Sutras* and shocked everybody." *Rolling Stone* described the album as dominated by "quiet ballads, crafted to the point of preciousness." In the album, Donovan put new melodies to ancient Chinese and Buddhist texts, Irish blessings, and quotations from Sappho and Edgar Allan Poe. The collaboration between Rubin and Donovan was of course compared to Rubin's with Johnny Cash, and the process of building and choosing the album's tracks was similar.

The same amount of creative freedom and time was granted to *Sutras* as it had been to *American Recordings*. As Donovan said to *Grip*, "What you hear is 14 songs, so there's 86 songs that you haven't heard. . . . Once the project began, I started writing daily. I wrote 100 songs over a period of a year and a half. . . . It was basically the same process of songwriting as I've always used. So, the songwriting revolved around the same themes as I've always been concerned with." One difference emerged from the writing process as Donovan felt Rubin was focused on making "a mature voice of me, the now me." Rubin enlisted an all-star modern-rock backing band to flesh out Donovan's songs, which included Dave Navarro and members of the Heartbreakers. "When Rick asked who I wanted to play with I said, 'Danny' [acclaimed bass player Danny Thompson] and he said, 'Right,' so we had Danny on seven songs. Then it became difficult for Rick, because we tried playing with an ensemble he put together, but he felt when I played these songs by myself, acoustically, they were much more powerful. He liked it 'in your face' as he called it. So we recorded umpteen versions of many different songs in this personal, solo way, and then we would add things. He brought in [the Heartbreakers'] Benmont Tench, and when I heard him I thought, 'He knows how to play with a singer-songwriter.' And of course he had, with Tom Petty and Dylan and others. He plays just the right amount of notes, which is difficult. Then, when Dave Navarro put in the electric sitar and the backup vocal, I was very happy with that.

And I was very comfortable with the two musicians from the band Spain we worked with. Those guys play in this low-key tempo, which is kind of Leonard Cohen or J.J. Cale on downers. So they were great to have on the three songs we used them on. And the two cellists and Tom Petty's drummer — they were all great."

Donovan had nothing but praise for the producer. "I rate Rick with the greats. With Phil Spector, with George Martin, with Mickie Most. All the great producers that love songs. And Rick Rubin gives me the impression that he's more like a '50s or '60s producer than an '80s or '90s producer. He's not really high-tech, or [into] digital. He likes tape. In fact, he's played my records to his other artists through his whole career, saying, 'That's how a voice should sound. That's how a guitar and a bass and drums should sound.' So, here was a guy who impressed me immensely with his attention to the songs." A true journey of rediscovery and reawakening for Donovan, Rick Rubin felt their work together allowed the singer to find "his voice, and it's a kind of grown-up, deep spiritual recording. . . . I think if you were ever a fan of Donovan, you'll relate to the recent album but at the same time, he's not rehashing what he did before. I'm proud of it . . . [and] really pleased with it." Perhaps Rubin's greatest accomplishment with the album was to re-establish Donovan's confidence as a recording artist, something he had done for Johnny Cash.

* * *

That same year, Rick Rubin and Johnny Cash began working on their sophomore album together, *Unchained*. Whereas Cash's first album with Rubin had principally featured the singer alone with his guitar, Rubin enlisted none other than Tom Petty and the Heartbreakers as Cash's backing band for *Unchained*. Recalled Rubin to *Music Angle*, after finishing the first album, Cash "became obsessed with wanting to do great work as opposed to before, just about continuing on the process, and now it was about everything being great and whatever it took." Finding the right songs was the first step. "I would send Johnny cds that contained 30 songs, sometimes, and other times it might be one song. It was just whatever I could find that I thought he might like,

Tom Petty, Rick Rubin, and Johnny Cash in the studio to record *Unchained*.
(© Kevin Estrada)

or that I thought might be appropriate. And then he might call me back and say, 'Well, I like four of these,' or 'I like this one a lot.' And he would send me songs, and I would tell him which ones I liked, and why, and which ones I didn't like, and why. It was a matter of finding common ground."

Backing player Tom Petty recalled fondly the time recording that album. "I still think that's the best Heartbreakers record: Johnny Cash *Unchained*. It's the best playing we ever did. I *love* that record. And I'm so proud that we did it, and did it so well. . . . There was one night when Carl Perkins was there. And we were recording with Johnny Cash and Carl Perkins. And we had the best time, it was just a million laughs, till your ribs hurt. We were just so in awe of these guys, Carl Perkins and Johnny Cash, and I felt so great when I was reading the liner notes, and Johnny wrote, 'That was one of the greatest nights of my life.' That made me feel so good because it was really one of mine too. And I didn't know John felt that way about it." Seeing Cash work hard to overcome any physical limitation he had was inspiring for Tom Petty. "He was pretty healthy. He would get sick at times. He would get very tired. But he was so determined. I know there would be times when he would stop for an hour, and take a nap. He'd stop for an hour, then

he'd come back and hit it again. He was determined. . . . That really inspired me because I kind of struggle in the world with the fact that I'm getting older. . . . So that kind of inspired me: look at this guy. He went much longer and was really relevant all the way out."

One of the album's biggest singles was a completely re-imagined rendition of Soundgarden's "Rusty Cage." Cash could not wrap his head around covering that song. "At first I said, 'That's not my kind of song.' Rick Rubin said, 'Listen to the lyrics. If we can get an arrangement you're comfortable with, would you try it?' I said, 'I'll try anything, but I don't think I'll ever do this song.' I heard the arrangement and it felt so comfortable that it's one of my favorite songs." Rubin's selection was based on the lyrical content of a song rather than the style of its original recording. "Everything else could change but the lyrics were always what made a song suitable," explained Rubin. "Hopefully the tune would be one that would make sense with him singing, but it was really about the words. I remember I played him the Soundgarden song 'Rusty Cage,' and he looked at me like I was insane, because if you've ever heard it, it's a fully heavy metal record with Chris Cornell singing it with crazy, high vocals. It just didn't seem like anything that Johnny could ever do. And then I did a demo of the song, I think with Dave Navarro just playing guitar and me singing it, just to show Johnny the vision of the song and how he would do it. I played that for him and he was like, 'Oh, I like that song, I'll do that one.'"

"Rusty Cage" got major airplay on college radio and alternative rock stations upon its release, but no love from traditional country radio. The rest of America loved the album, with *Entertainment Weekly* saying "Cash still sounds like the Voice of the Ages, with his bass baritone wobbling on pitch as it hasn't in years." Ironically, the album won a Grammy Award for Best Country Album. Celebrating the achievement in fuck-the-system fashion, American Recordings ran a full-page ad in *Billboard* featuring the classic photo of Johnny Cash, middle finger aimed at the camera, with a caption that read: "American Recordings and Johnny Cash would like to acknowledge the Nashville music establishment and country radio for your support."

CHAPTER 17

Slayer and System of a Down

AS AN EXAMPLE OF HIS CONTINUED DIVERSITY, in 1997 Rubin worked on the soundtrack *Chef Aid: The South Park Album*, as well as studio work with Rancid and Lucinda Williams. The following year saw him back working with longtime American Recordings' artist Slayer. Rubin had executive produced 1994's *Divine Intervention* and 1996's *Undisputed Attitude*, but for the band's next album, *Diabolus in Musica*, the producer was back in the studio, hands on. Said Kerry King to *Hardforce*, "I think that [Rubin] chooses the people with whom he wants to work. When he has collaborated with Trouble or Danzig, those bands were very important. They merited that he spend time with them. Nowadays, how many metal bands merit that we spend time on them? Two or three, not more. I wasn't preoccupied by his implication in the production, because he knows us from *Reign in Blood*. . . . When he's more implicated, he is more interested, like this time. When he was working, [he] nuanced the tones and that's why we have got this sound."

Slayer wasn't looking to reinvent itself for the new album. Kerry King told *Metro*, "When we started out it was all kids into us. Now those kids have kids. We're a lucky band with a regenerating fan base. . . . We've always been Slayer. We never tried or claimed to be anything different." Guitarist Jeff Hanneman echoed his bandmate, "We stay ourselves. When we started writing this kind of music we did not think [anyone] was going to be into it because it was so extreme. Over the years our fan base has just kept growing and growing. Now we do it for us and the fans. The main reason we have not changed our style is that the fans don't want us to change."

The band's songwriting process hadn't changed much for the better part of 12 years, as Hanneman explained it: "I just sit down and start fucking around with the guitar and come up with a riff or chord pattern, then make it as heavy and evil as possible." Speaking to *Sonic*, Hanneman said, "Lyrics are always the last thing to get done. . . . Every now and then we will change the song to the lyrics. But we don't really plan out our records ahead of time. Whatever riff we are doing at the time we see what the lyrics are like, but they're not going to be wimpy." The lyrics always follow the music for Slayer. "I'll come up with [some music] at home, or Kerry will come up with something. And eventually — you know, because I can do my stuff at home because I have a new 24-track and a drum machine, so if I get an idea I can run with it as far as I can get it. Then I'll bring it to these guys and play it, see what they think, and Kerry will add a riff or Dave will say something about 'change it here' or 'change it there' and Kerry does the same thing. And then when we get together we try to get the basic structure of the song done, and then we kinda know where the lyrics go and where the leads go. That's when the lyrics start falling into place, and the song will change here and there; but it's all done spontaneously, it's not like — we don't sit down around a table before the album comes out and have a meeting on what the album is going to sound like. It's whatever we're into."

Diabolus in Musica peaked at #31 on the Billboard Top 200 Album Chart, and *All Music Guide* called "an album that will certainly please fans. . . . The music is still the same old Slayer, and that's pretty much what sellout-wary diehards want to hear."

* * *

Rick Rubin with Slayer. (© Lester Cohen/WireImage/Getty Images)

While Rick Rubin had taken to working with the same artists repeatedly and older artists he felt could use a career restart, he was also still interested in new acts. In 1997, Rubin signed System of a Down. The band's bassist, Shavo Odadjian, explained to *Hard Radio* how the group hooked up with the producer: "We had offers from other labels, and Rubin had heard about us through Guy Oseary at Maverick. He brought Rick down to see us at The Viper Room. There were several labels at that show who had been checking us out for a while but never really made us an offer; but as soon as Rick came into the picture, all the labels started coming to us with offers. The thing about Rick, even when we had doubts about signing with American, he still came to our shows as a fan; in fact, he even came to our show in NY [at the CMJ convention] when we were falsely labeled as Universal/Cherry recording artists. Rick really believed in us and seemed to have a special interest in our music." Lead guitarist and songwriter Daron Malakian, whose favorite album was the Rubin-

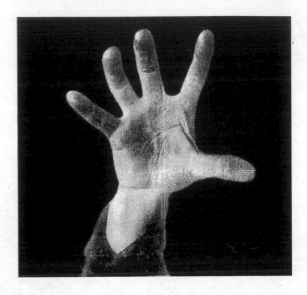

produced *Reign in Blood*, explained to *LiveDaily* the qualities that made System of a Down ultimately choose to sign with Rubin: "He brings a lot to the table. He's got an amazing ear for music, in harmony, in what works or what doesn't work. He's got great taste, which is why I think he can produce different genres of music so successfully. He's not a genre producer."

Beginning with the band's 1998 self-titled debut, Rubin and System of a Down would work on four albums together over the next seven years. Said Malakian, "Production with Rick doesn't mean you're going to sit in a studio. It might mean you go to a record store or to the beach. Or you go for a drive. You bond as people first. And then you get these songs, and Rick's like the song doctor. . . . If you play something for him, it's like going in for a checkup. He's like, 'Here, take a couple of these vitamins and see how you feel.' And the songs always feel better after his suggestions. And so do you. He's just so easy to be around. That's why people keep going back to him."

CHAPTER 18

Dream of *Californication*

RUBIN REUNITED WITH THE RED HOT CHILI PEPPERS for the disarming and brutally beautiful *Californication*. Guitarist John Frusciante was back. To *NY Rock,* he described the album as "a second chance for all of us. There is a weird chemistry between us. The way I play guitar, it only works when Flea is the bassist, and Flea only can write songs the way he does when Anthony sings. In a way, we're all co-dependant and we know it, but we also trust each other." The longest road back was Frusciante's. "The only reason that I make music now is because Flea and Anthony had the belief in me that they had when I rejoined the band. Because I'd play with other people around that time, like Perry Farrell, but he couldn't see it as the future. He had no belief in me. He just knew what I was at one time, and what I was now, which was significantly less than what I had been. Whereas Flea and Anthony saw what I could be. They had a vision. I don't even know that they knew what I could be. To them, they just thought I was great right then. They just thought the sound of us playing together is the greatest thing in the world. It's just a chemistry that's there. I don't think they were thinking, 'Oh, in five months he'll be good.' They were thinking, 'This is the greatest thing in the world right now.'" Said Frusciante to the *LA Times*, "It didn't matter that my fingers were very weak and my guitar playing didn't sound the way it used to sound, and that I couldn't think as quickly musically. They didn't see any of that stuff. They saw in me what I was capable of, and for that I'll always feel indebted to them. . . . It's the best thing anybody ever did for me."

With Frusciante back in the band, the Chili Peppers were able to return to their natural songwriting process — jamming. "We don't talk much about songs or how songs should be constructed," said Flea. "We just start to play and see what happens, how they develop. We improvise a lot. We find a groove. We experiment and somehow it turns into music. With Dave, it wasn't possible to work like this. With him it was more like a long thought process, endless discussions, and it took a long time. We talked about what riff should be played and all that. With John it's completely different. We just play. I don't mean to dis Dave in any way. He is a great person and he's a great guitarist, but the way we work is just different. You never know why it happens with some people and not with others. It's pointless. It's like asking why you fall in love. There is no real reason, nothing that can be explained or that would make sense."

Echoing Flea's sentiment, drummer Chad Smith reasoned to *Guitar World*, "With bands that have been around for 20 or 25 years, you get a kind of musical telepathy. You can't manufacture that. It can only happen from just doing it — being connected and wanting to be connected. That's why I love going to see a band like Cheap Trick or Aerosmith — they're just regular rock bands, where it's been the same guys in the band all along. Musicians who have been playing together for 20 years or more have definitely got their own thing." At the suggestion of Rubin, the band embraced the practice of transcendental meditation, which Flea says helps him "to just be in the moment and not be scared of pain and anxiety."

Though Kiedis had been devastated by Frusciante leaving the band, losing both a bandmate and friend, once the guitarist was back, he felt the pieces of the Chili Peppers fit back together in a way they hadn't in years. "Chemistry is beautiful and important to any musical endeavor, and it's also impossible to figure out or force it. And the first time we came together with John Frusciante, that kind of elusive and abstract chemistry was there. But then when he left, I realized that it was harder to write songs and feel spiritually connected to art and music as a band. When he came back I felt it again, instantaneously." The friendships were rebuilt as well, and as importantly. "Just the feeling of us hanging out was really great and cool in a way that it had never been before," said Frusciante to *Addicted*. "The way we were getting along together as people was the most important element in my being comfortable with being in the band again and knowing that it was gonna work out. We were getting along and speaking to each other." Said Kiedis, "Now that we're together again it makes perfect sense that we all had to go through some difficulties, some learning, some changing. Now we're all very close friends and in love with what we're doing, whereas when John quit the band we weren't so friendly with one another and we had stopped enjoying what we were doing together. Right now it's just so good I can't really bum out on the past or worry about what's gonna happen next." As much as the Chili Peppers had matured as individuals, their music had grown with them. Like Flea put it to *Guitar World*, "I guess people's perceptions of us was no longer as these lunatics with socks on their dicks but as guys who were really taking care with writing music and playing the best they could."

Frusciante felt somewhat rusty coming back to the Red Hot Chili Peppers. "I hadn't spent too much time playing guitar over the last few years, so my hands were kind of weak. They didn't really get extremely strong until we had almost finished recording. I had a really strong right wrist right from the start, but that was kind of cool because that was like a lot of punk rock guitarists — they have incredibly strong right wrists, you know, from doing really fast down strokes. So that had an effect on my style of guitar playing during the recording. Which was great because I really wanted to approach my guitar playing from a non-musician's standpoint, because that's the kind of guitar playing that never eats itself up, as you sometimes do if you focus too much on the technical aspect. But I worked really hard during the recording of this album. I was playing guitar constantly when we were writing it, and when we were recording, I would go home and play for five hours after a 10-hour recording session." The guitarist drew inspiration from "new wave guitarists and punk guitarists for the style that I wanted to do on this album. People like Matthew Ashman from Bow Wow Wow, Ricky Wilson from the B-52s, Bernard Sumner from New Order and Joy Division, Robert Smith from The Cure, Ian MacKaye and Guy Picciotto from Fugazi, Greg Ginn from Black Flag, Pat Smear from the Germs, the guys in Echo and the Bunnymen, Johnny Ramone — people who developed guitar styles not from years of playing, but from years of loving music and then all of a sudden getting freed up by realizing there was no 'technique' that was necessary to express something. People who weren't really technically great guitar players, but were great guitar players because they made up original styles that were their own. I've gone through so much inside the last few years that I wanted to approach the guitar — being in this band — from that standpoint. I just thought it would be interesting and fun if I made that the direction of my playing for this album, and that's what I did." In an interview with *Total Guitar*, the guitarist said, "I like *Californication*, because I feel like it's the result of all that searching." Modest as ever, when Frusciante listens to the album, "I hear someone trying to [be the] best they can at that time."

Frusciante explained how the band writes its music. "Everybody just writes their part, I don't write any of the lyrics, sometimes I write melodies, but definitely on the last album Anthony wrote pretty much all those melodies himself aside from the ones that had something to do with the guitar part." The lyrics were the domain of Anthony Kiedis. "Some songs come from jams, and some come from parts that someone writes on their own. In my case, I write a million things that I throw away before I stumble upon something that ends up on the record. Certain things are only good at the moment you write them. Others are good for a while, and then lose something. Some ideas keep getting more magical vibrations attached to them — they sound better and better the more everybody hears them. Those are the things that become songs." On *Californication*, songs that were derived from those jam sessions included "Parallel Universe," "Scar Tissue," "I Like Dirt," and "This Velvet Glove." The album was built in a period of approximately eight months, with four spent rehearsing and writing, before Flea had a sojourn in Australia. The actual in-studio recording time took only three weeks.

Speaking to *Addicted*, Kiedis said of the time spent creating *Californication*, "It didn't feel like plowing because we spent a lot of time just playing together and writing songs. We practiced from late spring through summer with the idea that when we got into the studio we wanted to know what we were gonna do." During pre-production, said Flea, the Chili Peppers "wrote a lot of songs, 30 or 40. It was us in the garage, jamming and hanging out and playing grooves and putting them together until we felt like we had enough songs to go and make a record. It was quick compared to how most rock bands worked and how we have worked. But we did put a lot of time and effort into making them what they are."

With the band members all sober, Kiedis found Frusciante's dedication to his craft highly inspiring. "He's blowing my mind. I feel as good as I possibly could about our future. John is a really incredible person, and right now all he cares about is putting good energy into the universe, and the way he does that is through music. So basically he's doing one of three things: he's either playing live, or he's listening and playing along with music, or he's writing music 24/7. Call John at midnight, and he'll be playing along with an Ornette Coleman record. Call him up at two in the afternoon and he'll be working on a couple of songs that will be good for us. Call him up at 10 at night, and he's just finished a mystery novel and is going to go listen to an acoustic Jimmy Page solo that he wants to learn. That type of dedication is heavily contagious stuff, and it just makes us want to write more music and make more records and play more shows and just create more beauty for the world. You know, art is a good thing like that. No matter what's happening in the world, there's always room for some more beauty, so we're just kind of along for his cosmic ride right now."

The theme of the album revolved around "the act of the world being affected and saturated by the art and the culture being born and raised in California," said Kiedis. "Traveling around the world, no matter how far I go, I see the effect that California has on the world. It's about that good and bad, beautiful and ugly." For "Around the World," Frusciante "thought of that guitar part at my house, and I said to everyone, 'You gotta hear this, but I can't play it by myself, or you'll hear one in the wrong place because it has a really deceptive downbeat.' I had Chad keep time on the hi-hat while I played the lick. Everybody dug it, so I just kept playing it over and over until Flea came up with his bass part." Said Frusciante, Flea composed the song's bass line in "maybe 15 minutes. Flea is the best bass player in the world. His sense of timing and the way he thinks is so crazy. I mean, the way that bass line goes with my guitar part is amazing. When we play them without the drums, they don't make any sense. But with drums, they really lock in. Our styles complement each other, and we really love playing together." Frusciante's inspiration for "Get on Top" came from "listening to Public Enemy one morning, and I came up with that rhythm on the way to rehearsal — just tapping it out with my foot. In fact, that's me working Flea's wah pedal with that rhythm at the end of the song."

As with other Rubin-produced albums, the pre-production time helped cut down on actual in-studio time. The Chili Peppers were primed to record once they entered the studio. Frusciante told *LA Weekly*, "Analog sounds the best to me, and I feel that's how my music should be recorded. I'm not gonna go on a big tirade against computers, because a lot of music I really love is done on them. I would point out, though, that somehow, as convenient as computers make things, albums take longer to record now than they did in the '50s or the '70s. So I don't know if the convenience is actually convenient; I think it's just the illusion of convenience, and in actuality it makes things more complicated. . . . You have to work with [analog], and it brings the best out of you. Magnetic tape is the way I like doing it; it's really fun for me. I like doing first takes, I don't like doing multiple takes, I don't like comping, I don't like doing all that bullshit. For me, the first take has a special excitement to it."

Frusciante catalogued the gear he used on *Californication* to *Guitar One*: "I used a real old '65 Marshall. I also used a 200-watt bass head that I used on *Blood Sugar*, I use a bass head and a guitar head at the same time; that's how I play. I had a good sound for this album, but Louie [the band's right-hand man] doesn't want me to take the heads on tour because he thinks they'll break. As far as guitars, I used a '66 Jaguar on 'Around the World,' one of the guitar parts on 'This Velvet Glove,' and the odd guitar part here and there. I used a '56 Stratocaster for most of the basic tracks, and a '62 Stratocaster, the sunburst one, on some stuff. I also used this '55 Gretsch White Falcon, it's the kind of guitar that Matthew Ashman used in Bow Wow Wow and Malcolm used to use in AC/DC, for 'Californication' and 'Otherside.' I have .012-gauge strings on it. I'd like to go more into that, developing a guitar style using thick strings like that. It's fun. I also had a '61 Gibson SG, and I used a Telecaster on some things too, like 'Easily' and 'Scar Tissue.' [Filmmaker/actor] Vincent Gallo helped me find a lot of those guitars that are old, collectors' kinds of pieces. He knows more about guitars than anybody who lives in Los Angeles." Frusciante's style of playing had a lot to do with what kind of instrument he was using, as he told *Australian Guitar*: "I play differently on different guitars. On the album *Californication* I mostly play a Fender Stratocaster from 1956, or '55 or something. It has a maple neck and it's really a great guitar." On "Scar Tissue," Frusciante used his 1955 maple-necked Strat ("I think I ran it through the Showman because the Marshall wasn't clean enough") and a 1965 Telecaster for the slide parts into a Fender Showman amp.

"For 'Get on Top' I wanted to play something that would create a contrast between the solo and the background. . . . [On 'Savior'] that heavy delay tone is my '55 Strat into an Electro-Harmonix Micro Synth and a 16 Second Delay. Even though it's a weird sound, it's inspired directly by Eric Clapton's playing in Cream. If you listen to the actual notes, they're like a Clapton solo — they just don't sound like it because of the effects." Of all Frusciante's playing on *Californication*, two of Kiedis's favorite pieces are "Road Trippin'," and "This Velvet Glove": "[They mean] a lot to me, because John plays two guitar parts; it's one of the few songs that has an acoustic rhythm track happening. That's

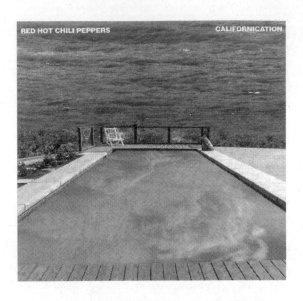

important, because I'm a terrible guitar player and could never play that part."

Working with the producer for the first time since *Blood Sugar Sex Magik*, Frusciante described Rick Rubin as "the perfect producer" for the Chili Peppers. "He's not exactly involved in the writing, but he plays a big part in the construction of the songs. He'll tell us if a song needs a section or a part, and he helps us balance the songs so we don't have sections that are too long or too short." In a *Cousin Creep* interview, Frusciante elaborated: "We've found that for us we need a producer to be like pretty much devoted [to us for] a few months. That's what Rick Rubin does when he works with us, if he's doing something else it stops at least a couple weeks before we go into the studio. We need to feel we've got somebody's undivided attention.... He doesn't do any disciplining but that we do ourselves. I love making music and I love writing music and nobody needs to push me to do that. But Rick has a real mellow type of a vibe that he generates when he listens to our music. We know that that's the only thing going on in the world for him when it's happening. He's not the kind of person that gets distracted or comes to the rehearsal studio with something else on his mind or carrying his personal life into the studio. He's very focused and not a big party guy, he's a real focused centered person. And that's why he's the perfect person for us because we can trust him that way. No matter how off center any of us are we know that he's got a clear head about everything." Said Frusciante to *Musikexpress*, "The harmony vocals weren't even my idea, but Rick Rubin's. He led me there, at first even against my will."

Californication became the Chili Peppers most successful album to date, peaking at #3 on the Billboard Top 200 and selling over 15 million albums worldwide. Said *Rolling Stone*, "While all previous Chili Peppers projects have been highly spirited, *Californication* dares to be spiritual and epiphanal, proposing that these evolved RHCP furthermuckers are now moving toward funk's real Holy Grail: that salty marriage of esoteric mythology and insatiable musicality that salvages souls, binds communities, and heals the sick." The album's writing and recording had healed the band, and reveling in its success, Kiedis said to *Q Magazine*, "Who would have thought that *Californication*, 18 years into our career as a rock band, would have been our biggest album? With this album we had so much stuff. We never felt we were hitting writer's block or feeling the pressure in any way. Nobody talked about sales and there's nobody punching cards when it comes to working. We do it all in our own time." The band seemed finally at peace, and with the success of *Californication*, they would enter the new millennium as one of its most critically respected and culturally relevant bands.

CHAPTER 19

"We'll Meet Again"

American III: Solitary Man and

American IV: The Man Comes Around

AMERICAN III: SOLITARY MAN, Rubin's third project with Johnny Cash, came out three years after the successful *Unchained*. This was in large part due to Cash's deteriorating health; he was forced to stop touring when he was diagnosed with the neurodegenerative disease Shy-Drager syndrome. (His diagnosis was later altered to autonomic neuropathy, which can be associated with diabetes.) But Cash continued to record with Rubin. Said Rubin to *Independent Mail*, "He wanted to be able to do more than he was physically able to do. He couldn't understand why one day he would come in and be able to sing great, and feel good, and then the next day he would come in and not be able to catch his breath, or would have to lie down between takes. He was suffering a lot. Actually he had suffered a lot for years, and yet he could still get the job done whenever he wanted to. But now, for the first time, he was experiencing times when he wanted to be working, and the frustration of either physically not being able to do it, or mentally not being able to stay focused, or voice-wise not being of strong voice. This was all new to him, and it was very difficult for him to deal with. . . . I know there were times when he wished his voice was better. Sometimes he felt embarrassed, and it really took the people around him to say, 'This is beautiful, and we love it.' And again, he trusted the people who were saying that, because we really did feel that way. But there were times, I know, when he felt a little insecure about his voice, and wished he sounded stronger."

The manner in which this album was put together followed the model of the previous two. "The common theme I see in these albums is they weren't made by a committee," said Cash to *All Star*. "They were made by Rick Rubin and I, with my son's help in Tennessee. These things are very personal. . . . Each of the songs has some personal meaning to me. I have a personal affinity and a feeling for it, or I wouldn't have released it. I try a lot of songs to see if I feel like I can make the song my own. If I can't, I drop it. I don't think anymore about it. . . . One of the purposes of the album, to stretch as far as we could for a variety of themes and songs and beats and tunes, but to be sure that I could feel them personally, that they belonged to me when I did them." The work Cash had done with Rubin was intensely personal. "These are the things that my heart has been into, in the last three albums. That is where my heart is, these albums. . . . I'm sure that's going to stay where it is, because [Rubin] has told me that I can record one album after another, so long as the demand is out there and so long as I feel like doing it."

The collection chosen was diverse, covering a wide range of eras and sung in ways which completely reinvented the songs. One song Cash had always wanted to record was "Mary of the Wild Moor": "I was probably three years old when I heard that the first time, and I always knew someday I would record it. I guess I must have thought about it at every session I ever had, and, finally, I just went ahead and did it. 'Wayfaring Stranger,' I have the same feeling for. It's an old Southern spiritual that I always wanted to record. It's a far stretch from there to [Nick Cave's] 'The Mercy Seat' and to Bono's song, 'One.'" The album became another critical favorite, with *Rolling Stone* singling out "The Mercy Seat," for its "layered production, with organ, regular and tack piano, and accordion swelling and receding under Cash's onrushing, Leonard Cohen–like delivery. It's the moment of the greatest artistic risk." Notice was taken of the effects Cash's declining health had on his artistry, and critics complimented his ability to use the weakening of his voice to grow in a new direction. Including the album in its top 10 of the year, *Entertainment Weekly* highlighted the perfect marriage between the songs, Cash's performance, and Rubin's production: "Producer Rick Rubin frames that deep-sea voice with harmonies and churchy organs, making for a dark-angel beauty of an album that's austere but welcoming." The magazine went on to say, "[These songs] have rarely sounded so authentic, thanks to arrangements that are spare but never colorless and a voice that's deep in more ways than one."

* * *

It wasn't long before the pair were working on the next album, 2002's *American IV: The Man Comes Around*, which drew thematically on Cash's declining health and channeled his deep religious convictions. With his mortality undeniable, Cash made the most of his time left, recording tirelessly in a prolific but brutal period. "I worked on this album in spite of everything. I found strength to work just to spite this disease. Sometimes I came to the studio and I couldn't sing — I came in with no voice when I could have stayed at home and pouted in my room and cried in my beer or my milk, but I didn't let that happen. I came in and opened up my mouth and tried to let something come out. There are tracks I recorded when that was the last thing in the world I thought I could do, and those are the ones that have the feeling and the fire and the fervor and the passion — a great deal of strength came out of that weakness." His battles would become the main theme of the album. "The theme is spirit," said Cash to Concertlivewire.com, "the human spirit more than the spiritual or godly spirit, the human spirit fighting for survival. It probably reflects a little of the maturity that I've experienced with the pain that I've suffered with the illnesses that brought me so close to death."

Cash wrote "The Man Comes Around," the album's title track, inspired by a dream he had "about seven years ago, in Nottingham, England. I dreamed I was in Buckingham Palace and Queen Elizabeth said, 'Johnny Cash, you're just like a thorn tree in a whirlwind.' I couldn't figure out what that meant, and I couldn't get it out of my head." Evenutally, Cash decided to look it up in the Bible and found that "the whirlwind is always symbolic of God, and the thorn tree is symbolic of man's obstinacy, and arrogance. So there you have it: me and my arrogance standing against God. I don't know why Queen Elizabeth felt she had to preach to me, but she did." Cash "wrote dozens and dozens of verses — I thought it was just going to be one of my weird poems but I started seeing a song forming. I never had a writing project that I put in as much time and as much writing, as I did that song. I knew I was overwriting, but I had to get it out." He called it his "song of the apocalypse, it comes from the Book of Revelation, I love the language there. It's astonishing and it's scary, but there's so much love and kindness in it at times that you wouldn't think that's what it's all about."

For the songs on the album he didn't write himself, Cash tried to make the collection as personal as possible. "I think he tried to make them all his own," said Rubin to Gibson.com. "I don't think he was especially concerned with what the writer's original intention was. It was a question of, 'How does this song hit me, and how can I convey that mood, or the emotion that I feel, in my version of the song?'" Cash described his process for selecting material to Concertlivewire.com: "I listen to everything that people bring me. I get my coffee early in the morning and I listen to some music, usually to songs that were submitted to me the day before. I start recording the songs that I couldn't get over — the ones I just had to get out. I brought a pocketful of songs to every session, and if I couldn't sing this one, I'd sing that one. In the middle of taping something that wasn't quite working, I'd just start a new song. And that always worked — to alternate, to go to something that I could do. We wound up with about 32 songs that I liked and wanted to record, and then came the painful process of weeding them out to the ones that made the final cut."

His covers of songs were so evocative because, from Rubin's perspective, Cash "was really a master at taking a song — even a song you might've heard many times in your life — and imbuing it with a kind of storyteller mentality. Again, even if you had heard a particular song your whole life, when he sang it, all of a sudden you understood it, or thought about the words in a different way, or you took the song more seriously." Cash took a certain ownership of the material in his performance of it. "The way I approach a song, I have to love the song up front first. But I knew that with those songs, I couldn't sing them the way they were recorded — and I didn't want to sing them that way, I wanted to sing them my way. I wanted to make them my songs. And if I'm recording and it doesn't begin to feel that way, I just throw it out." Once the collection of songs had been chosen, Cash saw that "as it turned out, the album took a very sad theme in a lot of ways. But it has its humor too — like 'We'll Meet Again' and 'Sam Hall.'"

So successful were Cash's interpretations of songs, in some cases he completely reinvented the song — most notably in the case of the single "Hurt," his cover of the Nine Inch Nails hit. Said Cash to *Time* of including the song, "It was Rick Rubin's idea. We were looking for a song that we felt had an impact. He found this one, and he asked me what I thought of it. I said, 'I think it's probably the best antidrug song I ever heard, but I don't think it's for me.' And he said, 'Why?' I said, 'Because it's not my style, it's not the way I do it.' And he said, 'What if it were?' And I said, 'Well, I could give it a try.' So I went out and recorded it. When I listened to it, I felt it came out all right. . . . I would just get down and do it until I felt like I was doing it with feeling. I probably sang the song 100 times before I went in and recorded it, because I had to make it mine." To Johnny Cash, "Hurt" was a song about "a man's pain and what we're capable of doing to ourselves and the possibility that we don't have to do that anymore. I could relate to that from the very beginning."

The Depeche Mode classic "Personal Jesus" was a much easier song for Cash to conceptualize in his own way. "That's probably the most evangelical gospel song I ever recorded. I don't know that the writer meant it to be that, but that's what it is," said Cash to *Livewire*. "It's where do you find your comfort, your counsel," he told NPR, "your shoulder to lean on, your hand to hold to, your personal Jesus." Rubin enlisted Red Hot Chili Peppers' guitarist John Frusciante to play guitar on the song, who told *Paper Magazine*, "I recorded it in the amount of time it takes to play the song, and I sent it to Rick. And Johnny sang along with the scratch vocal. I never met him!" Frusciante felt that it was destiny he should work on this song. "Rick Rubin knew very well that I'm a fanatic of Depeche Mode because he is also working with the Peppers. Rubin had kind of a slow, dark blues in mind but he couldn't convince Johnny. As I knew Martin Gore's original concept for the song by chance, it was pretty easy for me in the end to suggest him a corresponding version on the acoustic guitar."

On some of the more traditional selections for the album, Cash noted, "I recorded ['Streets of Laredo'] in the '60s but wasn't happy with the recording, not at all. This time we made it the song I really wanted to record. 'Give My Love to Rose' came up on the spur of the moment in the studio, and I think it's also better than the original recording. . . . We recorded ['Danny Boy'] in the Episcopal church in Los Angeles. The session lasted about two hours and it was over — just exactly the way we had hoped and planned and prayed it would be. It really adds an element that I've never had on record before, never had anything like that."

Upon completion, Cash was satisfied with the album he and Rubin had put together. "I firmly believe that it's the best record I've done for American. We put more blood, sweat, and tears and love into this one than anything we've ever done. It reaches out even farther and in more directions than the others did — the simplicity of Nick Cave and singing 'I'm So Lonesome I Could Cry' with just a couple of guitars, and some of the pop songs that no one would ever in a hundred years think of me singing, me included, until I heard myself singing it. It goes in so many different directions but they all come together in a one-ness with me, that I could make these songs my own. They come together in being my songs." For Rubin, it was difficult to single out a song more poignant for him than the rest but felt that "Bridge Over Troubled Water" was one track that Cash managed to make completely new. "I've heard that song my whole life, but until Johnny sang it, I never thought about what it meant. All of a sudden the words took on a whole new seriousness, when he sang them. Some people have said they felt that way about 'One' — the U2 song. They've said that

when Johnny sang it, the words rang true in a way that was different from what they had heard before."

Less than a year after *The Man Comes Around* was released and just a few months after his wife, June Carter Cash, passed away, Johnny Cash died on September 12, 2003, at the age of 71. It was the *New York Times* that best described the closeness of Rubin and Cash's relationship in an article published after Cash's death, writing that Rubin had been "much more involved with every aspect of the production — from the choice of songs to the arrangements to the videos — than he had been with any other artist. Rubin and Cash also had a deep spiritual kinship: during the final months of Cash's life, they took communion together every day, even though Rubin, who was born Jewish and now sees himself as not having any specific religious orientation, should not be eligible for the holy sacraments. Even after Cash's death, Rubin would close his eyes and hear Cash's voice as he said the benediction."

"When all else fails, call Rick Rubin."

— LARS ULRICH

PART V

The 2000s

CHAPTER 20

The Rise of the Supergroup

Audioslave

BETWEEN HIS WORK WITH JOHNNY CASH on 2000's *Solitary Man* and 2002's *The Man Comes Around,* Rubin returned to the studio with System of a Down, who were working on their sophomore LP. During the lengthy pre-production process, Rubin said to MTV, "It's hard to know where it's gonna end up, but I heard a lot of things that were really wild and exciting." The band was hyped to be back at work with Rubin. Besides being the head of their label, Rubin had done "a great job with the last [album]," said guitarist Daron Malakian. Drummer John Dolmayan said of the producer, "He's just a cool guy who brings out the best in people." *Toxicity* was recorded in February and March 2001 at Cello Studios and released on September 4, 2001. The album debuted on the top of the Billboard Top 200 Album Chart and won the band a Grammy nomination for the single "Chop Suey!"

After Rage Against the Machine frontman Zack de la Rocha left the group in 2000, the remaining three members wanted to keep making vital music. Rick Rubin suggested they meet with former Soundgarden singer Chris Cornell. The musicians found common ground and chemistry, and supergroup Audioslave was born. So grateful to Rubin was bassist Tim Commerford that he called the producer "the angel at the crossroads because if it wasn't for him I wouldn't be here today. Rick Rubin was the one who said, 'You guys should jam with Chris Cornell.' That was a great piece of advice, and Rick opened up his house to us and we had meetings there with a therapist, and we hammered out [musical] ideas at Rick's house."

Guitarist Tom Morello recalled to Axis of Justice that he and Rubin first met while working on a song with the legendary frontman of the Clash: "A couple years ago, I had the opportunity to play on a Joe Strummer record. He was doing a song for the *South Park* soundtrack, and Rick Rubin asked me to come down and play guitar, because the guy that they had doing it just couldn't cut it. I had never been more nervous in my life as I drove up in my 1971 muscle car to the studio and was introduced to the great Joe Strummer. Joe did not disappoint. While the song was not the best, he certainly was. At the studio, [Joe] would disappear for hours at a time into his ancient Cadillac, where he would work on lyrics for the song, and listen to the latest mixes that were coming out of the control room. Rick Rubin and I would sit in the control room waiting as a gofer would shuttle notes back and forth from Joe." Rubin and Morello had worked together again on the final Rage Against the Machine album, *Renegades*, in 2000. Rubin had also been in discussions with Chris Cornell about the singer's next solo LP when the idea arose to bring the musicians together.

Chris Cornell was confident it would be a great musical pairing: "We knew that me singing over Tom [Morello's guitar] and Tim [Commerford's bass] and Brad [Wilk's drums] doing whatever they want to do — whether it's riff-oriented or kind of funk rock — it would sound great. And when we first started playing, just in ad-lib situations, when we were doing that, it was great. So we went there and it was a comfortable place to go, and we had never done it as a group." The biggest issue in getting the band together was not creative, but "just the way the organizations had different managers," said Rubin. "It was an odd start. But, musically, it was always really solid."

Rick Rubin and Tom Morello in 2000. (© Jay Blakeberg/Retna Ltd. USA)

Speaking to MTV, Morello had high praise for Rubin calling him "the fifth Beatle.... He's a great collaborative partner. He has a big-picture way of looking at music, which only tends to bring out the best with the artists he's working with."

Said Cornell in an interview with *Rockline*, "The songwriting process was the part that really blew me away, I mean, we seemed to be so prolific. I think all four of us at one point would get nervous here and there like, 'We, ah, are we missing something here? Is this awful and we just don't know it?' Because we felt like the music was coming out and we were just loving it. It seemed effortless. To me it was kind of a dream record, where I always think, the next record I make hopefully is going to be one of those moments where the music comes together really quickly and the energy's great.... We wrote songs so fast that sometimes we'd have to go back to a rehearsal tape from a week before to remember what it was. And sometimes I would have to take home tapes and [when I'd] wake up the next morning — and the song had come together so quickly and completely — that when I put it on I didn't remember any of it and then it was like listening to somebody else. So it had, like, a freshness always. I could be a fan of the music while we were making it. Instead of — often rock bands, or any bands, you get too up into it, playing it too much, and thinking about it too much in the studio, and thinking about the mixing too much, and the mastering too much and when the records done you don't even want to hear it. And this was not that." Quipped Morello, "We wrote and recorded more new music in eight months with Chris than we did in the previous eight years with Rage Against the Machine."

Morello explained the band's songwriting process to *Ultimate Guitar*: "The initial germ of the song comes very quickly. We write about a song a day, that's the pace; the first record, we wrote 21 songs in 19 days. It's very easy for us to assemble verse/chorus/bridge/heroic outro with a complete vocal melody in the course of one hour to five hours in a day's rehearsal. That's very easy to do. . . . there is so much more mutual support in the process [with Audioslave than with Rage]. If someone initially came up with an idea, I might cock an eyebrow and think, 'Hmm, I'm not so sure. But let's see what happens.' And after a while, you kinda go, 'You know what? That turned out to be a damn fine song' and you get that energy back. So it's a process of everyone continuing exploring and making musical discoveries as opposed to tenaciously fighting for ideas. . . . Sometimes the big hook of the song or parts of the lyrics will come on the day of the songwriting. The lyrics are fleshed out once all the basic tracks are recorded but sometimes the style of music and style of lyric are felt on that day when we're writing that song." Morello felt Rick Rubin was a very crucial partner in the pre-production: "Once we've written the songs and rehearsed the songs, we will come in and discuss every song. How can it be made better? And sometimes it can be the most subtle changes that can really help to make the chorus explode. Or he might even suggest trying it a half-step up and those kind of changes can make a huge difference. Sometimes there are more dramatic changes than that, but little changes can make a big difference. And then in the actual recording studio, he's great at giving us perspective on when we've got the take, which is harder to do when you're kind of in your own world of recording."

Their pre-production process was smooth and prolific, but once they entered the studio to begin principal tracking, there were some bumps. Drummer Brad Wilk explained, "Recording was actually the challenge because the first time that we had went in and didn't have any set directions for the songs so we would try all day, we would have different versions of the songs and by the time, by the end of the night, we would decide on one different version and record that and that's really challenging actually in the studio, it's not something we were used to doing. It seemed to work out alright." Rubin helped the band slim down the mountain of songs to the final track listing for the album. Joked Commerford to *Flagpole* of Rick Rubin's seemingly magical ability to create hit albums: "One thing that people don't realize is that he doesn't wash his beard and that he keeps a lot of treasures in there. If you know him close enough, he'll actually allow you into his beard to pull things out. If you're that lucky, then you're assured that you'll have a hit because there's more than one hit in his beard. He let us all go in there a few times and just hang out and we came out of there with a bunch of hits."

Rubin spent the greatest amount of time focused on Morello's guitar sound, saying "in many ways Tom Morello is the Jimmy Page of today." Morello described his technical setup: "I'd set the guitar, amp, and pedals up, then the techs would put mics in front of the cab. There was no constant tweaking, basically, what I set up went straight to tape. Sometimes with overdubs, there were a couple of little amps I'd use for cleaner tones. Otherwise, I'd just use the same amp as normal and turn my guitar's volume down to clean up the amp sound." To *Ultimate Guitar*, Morello got deeper into the technical nitty-gritty: "I've had the same setup now for over 15 years. It's identical. It's unchanged, for every RATM album, every Audioslave song, every show.

It's a Marshall 2205 head, a Peavey 4x12 cabinet, which is embarrassing to admit but it's true and it sounds alright. Which of course I had to ratchet the Peavey [logo] off the second that I bought it to keep my shame to a minimum. The pedals are an MXR Phase-90; a DOD EQ pedal set for a boost for solos; a DOD digital delay pedal; the original Digitech Whammy pedal, not the remake original Digitech but the original Whammy pedal. And there's a CryBaby wah and sometimes a DOD tremolo pedal. . . . That's what I bring into the studio."

Not surprisingly, Rubin referenced his rock archetype for Audioslave's guitar sound. Said Morello, "[He] would like every guitar solo to sound like Angus Young; the more it sounds like Angus Young it's a good solo, the less it sounds like Angus Young it's a poor solo." Rubin demanded the best performance from the player he knew to be great. "To be honest, kid gloves were never an option with Rick," Morello admitted. "He was so hard to please." That high standard for excellence extended to the entire band. "We'd be in the studio just finishing a take that felt really awesome," recalled Morello. "But just as the last cymbal crash dies away, we look up at the control room to see Rick showing us a big thumbs down. Actually, that would happen a lot, and we'd be like, 'Oh no, you're killing us!'"

To achieve the "very dry drum sound," Brad Wilk used vintage Gretsch kicks and toms, but he needed a few lessons from the master producer. "[He] always complained that we didn't have a clue how to play a slow song, so we had to learn it. It was pretty tough, but I think we all grew with it. With Audioslave, I feel much more of a musician than I did with RATM." Wilk first played softer on songs like "Getaway Car," "Like a Stone," and "The Last Remaining Light," but "Rick said, 'When you play those harder, they sound better. The dynamics are still gonna be there. Trust me.' I did, and he was right. So we have slower songs that are in a more ethereal light, but it's still a solid block of a record."

As with many of his past band productions, Rubin recorded Audioslave's basic tracks live off the floor, which worked for Wilk. "It was the first time I've ever done a record where I actually had the vocalist there doing his thing. That's important, because what's going on vocally has a lot to do with [what] you're accenting. On 'What You Are,' for instance, the hi-hat and vocals are attached to each other in a way that's simple but really hypnotic. And 'Cochise,' I feel like that's the sluttiest groove I've ever played. I don't know how else to describe it. I don't think I could've played those songs like that had Chris not been there." Morello also loved recording live.

"If somebody makes a horrendous mistake, we'll fix it, but we've always recorded to try and get that. It's playing to our strengths; what we do best is we play as a rock band together.... The overdubbing process this time was pretty extensive; mixing the guitar tones and stuff to get it right. But, yeah, it's everybody in a room rockin', Chris too; he's singing along with the track while we're rockin' it."

Chris Cornell approached the Audioslave album differently than he had Soundgarden albums, taking a less hands-on approach to the overall production. "With Audioslave, I was away from the producing side of it. [I just wanted] the producer to do their job. Soundgarden never allowed that. We would just shut them down. I just wanted to see what [not producing] was like. I was working with Rick Rubin.... It was comfortable to let that go. I was very into the singing, lyrics, and the songwriting process but I didn't go in when Tom was recording his guitar parts or anything like that."

Upon completion, the group was thoroughly satisfied with the record they had created. "When Timmy and I sat in his garage the first time and listened to the whole record I was knocked over by it," said Cornell to *Rockline*, "and that's more than any other record I've made. It's great." Fans old and new agreed, sending the album to a

Top 10 debut on the Billboard Top 200 Album Chart in November 2002. The group and its self-titled debut were nominated for multiple Grammy Awards in 2003, including Best Rock Album and Best Hard Rock Performance.

CHAPTER 21

Red Hot Chili Peppers
By the Way

"IT TURNS OUT *Californication* was only foreplay," said *Rolling Stone* in its review of the Red Hot Chili Peppers' 2002 album *By the Way*. Even though this was his fourth album with the band, Rick Rubin continued to be astonished by their creative output. On John Frusciante, Rubin said, "He's brimming with ideas, and he lives and breathes music more than anyone I've ever seen in my life," while Anthony Kiedis "really outdid himself" with his lyrics and performance.

Reflecting on his evolution as a lyricist, Kiedis said, "I've never felt comfortable writing 'love songs' or 'relationship songs,' but it's sneaking in there and certainly not in a typical way." The way he approached his lyrics was from a more emotionally honest place on *By the Way*. "I put less sexual aggression into the songs and try to give them more soul. I don't feel like I have to hide behind an image anymore. I am who I am. I'm not a sex machine. I'm human, a spiritual being and there is nothing wrong with showing emotions. Things change and people change. Now, I see being able to be emotional not as a weakness. I see it as strength. Even my lyrics are far more personal and, of course, due to that, more emotional." Kiedis felt the album as a whole had a lot to do, thematically, with "either being in love or the desire to be in love. It's definitely what I've been feeling for the last year. A profound sense of wanting love in my daily experience."

The writing of *By the Way* began, as Kiedis recalled to *Guitar World*, when "John and I got together in his room at the Chateau Marmont, where he was living at the time and we worked on some more obscure pieces together. Like the song 'Cabron,' which sounded almost like he'd written it to be a flamenco guitar instrumental. I just loved it because there was energy in there like crazy. I took home a rough copy of it from a low-tech tape recorder and started thinking of vocal lines to go with this music. John and I are both very much in love with doo-wop — vocal music from the '50s. I was feeling that kind of energy, but with a Mexican flavor, 'cause the soul of Los Angeles is largely fueled by our Mexican population here. So I started singing kind of a doo-wop melody to this really wild acoustic guitar instrumental. I brought that into the band, and it took Chad and Flea awhile to find their places in it — because it was so different and weird for us, coming from left field."

Early on, the idea of a wider range of vocals piqued Frusciante's interest, as he related to MTV. "I remember Anthony coming over during one of the first songs we were writing, and I asked him, 'What do you think about backing vocals being a bigger part of the album this time?' So, when we'd be working on a song, I'd be listening for a part that would be good to have a backing vocal. I was really inspired by a lot of doo-wop music from the '50s and a lot of '60s pop music and Queen." The lyrics remained the sole territory of Kiedis. About "By the Way," the lyricist explained, "It's a landscape of L.A. — an evening that happens simultaneously across the entire city, and the feeling of anticipation and hope and joy of going out into the fray. Maybe you're going to meet some magical adventure partner that's going to warm the cockles of your soul and sing you songs and hold your hand and take you to places to go dancing. But it's also about people getting beat up, and drug deals happening, and prostitution going on, and car crashes and people playing dice. It's about all of this stuff happening at the same time." The spiritual "Don't Forget Me" took the band in new directions lyrically. Kiedis called the track "a cornerstone of our record, because no one's ever heard us play anything like this. This song is my ideal of what God is, and what life is, and what this whole picture's all about, and how it's just everything and everywhere, and the good and bad and the in between, and the experiences of a lifetime. . . . I think it will be our opening song for the next three years or so because it puts us in such a good mood."

Frusciante continued to find joy in working and writing with the Chili Peppers. "Like *Californication*, writing *By the Way* has been one of the happiest times in my life," said Frusciante to *Total Guitar*. "It's been a chance to just keep on writing better songs and improving my guitar playing. . . . The time when I was working on new songs for the band every day was the best time in my life." Once an idea for a song has entered his mind, the guitarist typically prefers to write on either acoustic guitar or "sometimes I write on an unamplified electric guitar. I have a few old Martins, two small-bodied O-15s and an O-18, at my house that date from the '40s. I usually write songs on one of those. And I always bring a couple of acoustic guitars on the road with me to write with. Writing songs on an un-amplified electric has its drawbacks. The guitar is so quiet that I sometimes sing in a high falsetto voice that doesn't really work when I do the final recording. So I've learned to write on the acoustic and actually sing in the style that I want to use on the final recording."

For *By the Way*, Frusciante tried to emulate the sound of The Durutti Column's guitarist Vini Reilly. "The main thing about his guitar playing is that it's really textural. There's lots of really interesting chords and shapes and you can't really tell what's going on. It's a combination of his Les Paul plus some echo, flanger, chorus, and phaser and not using distortion. You can't tell what you're hearing . . . I have to really sit down and listen carefully to find out what's going on. He's just a great guitar player, full stop. I wanted to listen to these people who weren't just about technique but more about textures. People like Johnny Marr [The Smiths], John McGeoch [Magazine, Siouxsie & the Banshees], and Andy Partridge [XTC]. People who used good chords."

Beyond guitar players, Frusciante had other influences while composing. "I learned all Gary Numan's synthesizer parts on the guitar because that was very much in the way that I wanted my guitar playing to be. I was spending a lot of time learning parts from Kraftwerk and Depeche Mode, Human League and Orchestral Manoeuvres in the Dark, because I was finding that people who were programming synthesizers in this early electronic music were playing in a very minimal way, where every single note means something new and every note builds on what the last notes were doing." Frusciante combined that minimalism with a density in chord construction, as he outlined to *Guitar World*. "I was thinking of writing chords that are dense — that have more to them than just a root, third, and fifth. These chords have 9ths and 11ths and 13ths. I tried to make the guitar pretty impossible to figure out correctly. I learned a lot throughout the making of this album from studying Charles Mingus and learning his chord progressions. I studied a lot of music books, and learned about the way different people, like the Beatles and Burt Bacharach, construct chord progressions — just things that I would never have been able to figure out by ear. It started changing the way that I play guitar."

His personal evolution as a musician mirrored what he saw happening in a broader way among music creators. "I think that in each era, period of time, there are the same energies which make it possible to create good music. But all of this is a question of being impartial in such sense that you see that those energies take on different shapes in different periods of time. For me those energies that once made Jimi Hendrix create new sounds are the same energies that come over Depeche Mode when [they] recorded *Violator*; an album that does sound like no other rock album before. Well, you know, there was a time in my life when I was a little child and I thought: music was at its best in the '60s. But I don't feel this way anymore. The more I opened myself to all varieties of electronic music of the past 20 years, the more I had to realize that some of this stuff is at least as guiding and exciting as the music before it."

Frusciante described to Germany's *Guitar* how the songs on *By the Way* grew from ideas to fully formed compositions: "Sometimes I bring the entire guitar parts for a song along and the others add their parts. We did this, for example, with 'Venice Queen,' 'Cabron,' or 'I Could Die for You.' Things such as duration or arrangement are of course developed by all of us together. 'This Is the Place' and 'Don't Forget Me' are jam session songs and do sound like the sessions during which they came around. During those jams Flea played the same bass line for over half an hour and I tried various guitar parts on top of it. Flea loves it to put himself into a hypnotic groove. I join in and as soon as he has caught me I will play one part after the other, each one giving Flea's bass line a completely different flavor."

Together Frusciante and Rick Rubin explored another genre of music to find inspiration for the orchestral parts and colorful vocal harmonies. "Me and Rick Rubin would get together every day, and he's got these CDs of AM radio hits from the '60s. And they'd have stuff by the the Mamas and Papas and songs like 'Cherish' by The Association and 'Georgy Girl' [by The Seekers]. Those songs are all about harmonies."

The Chili Peppers explored their new musical interests on *By the Way*, an evolution in sound that Rubin discussed with *LA Weekly*. "I think for a band that's been making albums for a long time finding new ways to express themselves keeps it interesting. And on this album there were lots of lush vocals and an orchestra, which we'd never used before, and that just took it a new way. Maybe the next album will be much more sparse. I don't know the direction it will go, but I know that evolution and change is a good thing." Chad Smith felt Frusciante's role as musical motivator was even stronger on *By the Way* than it had been on *Californication*. "John really inspired us to take it to the next level on this album. On *Californication* he had just rejoined us, and he started writing music right away. But we hadn't really had time to reconnect, personally and musically, through touring, traveling together, and spending time back at home. The chemistry of our band is so important. And now John is a really key, integral part of this new music that we have."

With praise from his bandmates, Frusciante remained humble. "I know what Anthony and Chad and Flea have said but I think of it more as a band effort. I do put a lot of energy into everything, sure, but I don't underestimate that the real energy comes from the four of us." Describing their songwriting process as "completely democratic and selfless," Frusciante felt the Chili Peppers' whole was greater than the sum of its parts. "Now each of us appreciates the other. In the BSSM era everyone believed he was the most important member of the band, while now we are aware that individually we don't count. We know it's important to create together. We think the world is what others make, not what we make singularly." And by no means did *By the Way* mark the end of the musical journey or the height of possibility for the band, from the guitarist's perspective. "I feel that there is still more territory to cover musically," he said to *On the Record*. "I feel like we're getting better. I see Flea growing as a musician; I see Anthony growing as a singer and songwriter. I feel like there's a lot more to do within the context of this group that is of interest to me."

Once the band had entered the studio, as always, Rick Rubin became the group's unofficial fifth member. "Rick is so incorporated into what we do in the band that it's hard to pinpoint exactly what he does, but he definitely infiltrates," said Frusciante to the *Austin Chronicle*. Rubin's involvement meant some of the guitarist's ideas wouldn't end up in the final mix. "I definitely contribute production-type ideas, but a lot of things end up being compromised. I might record a ton of different sounds and things like that for a song, but Rick is always going to favor the lead vocal in the mix." But Frusciante was grateful for the producer's insights. "I mean he's as much a part of the record as any of us. It's just in a more ethereal, kind of feminine way. You can't say, 'Oh, there's Rick.' Brian Eno produces records where you can tell he treated the guitar, so you know it's an Eno-produced record. There's nothing like that with Rick, but he's all over the record just in terms of his ideas. The fact that the record is as concise as it is has a lot to do with Rick." As Frusciante explained, the band prefers to capture the live feel performance, opting to "use click tracks as little as possible. Sometimes Rick suggests it, and we'll do it just to feel what it would be like to play exactly in time. But we never like the way it sounds when something's recorded with a click, and usually switch it off when we go for a take." The band tracked most of the album live off the floor, but, as the guitarist explains, in certain instances, "we were doing it separately, like I would be in one place, doing my backing vocals, and Anthony would be in another place, doing his lead vocals." Once principal tracking was completed, Frusciante recalled to *Total Guitar*, there were "28 songs in the end, some of which will be B-sides. There was definitely a lot of good stuff, but we didn't have time to work on everything we wrote."

On the track "Cabron," Flea used a Höfner bass with a capo on it. "That song was a little frustrating for me; it took me awhile to find the right bass line. Basically, I had a bass line that I love, but everyone else didn't like it. Then John said, 'Use a capo, it'll make it sound completely different.'" On the tracks "Throw Away Your Television" and "Don't Forget Me," Frusciante played "16th notes [on a DigiTech digital delay] . . . but the echo is set to where it's doing triplets. That whole song, by the way, is played on only the high E and B strings." The riff for "Can't Stop" was inspired by "Ricky Wilson, the B-52s' guitarist," said Frusciante. "He died around 1985, one of my heroes. He took off the D and G strings and tuned the upper strings to the same note. He considered the low and the high strings as two separate things and often played them simultaneously into two opposite directions. It's a simple way for him to give the impression of using two guitars. This is exactly what I tried on 'Can't Stop.' The high notes move back and forth while the lower ones change chords." The song "On Mercury" had a ska sound; as Flea explained, the Chili Peppers "always listen to ska, but we never, ever had a ska sound on one of our records. But John came in with this great guitar part, and we just did it. It had a natural, free-flowing feeling that just worked." Frusciante didn't think of it as a ska groove while writing, "but everyone called it that. I think what made it more ska in my eyes was when Flea played the melodica."

Another new element to Frusciante's guitar work on the album was the presence of reverb. "That's one of the main differences in the guitar sound. I was really influenced by all the surf music I've been listening to. I had an old Fender spring reverb. Toward the end of the project, for a couple of overdubs, I started using the Holy Grail [digital reverb] pedal by Electro-Harmonix. . . . I was playing a lot bigger, denser chords than just your standard triads or whatever, and I wanted all those intervals to come through clearly. I'm not really into distortion except for solos, feedback and stuff. There were a couple of times when I used a [Gibson] SG straight into a Marshall, which is the best kind of distortion. My favorite guitarist is Bernard Sumner of Joy Division, and that's what he uses." Frusciante mostly played a 1962 Fender Stratocaster with a rosewood neck, not the same guitar he used on the majority of the previous album. "That '58 [Strat] has a bit of a cleaner sound and it always seemed to sound better for what I wanted on *Californication*, but for this album, the '62 just sounded right straight away — the sustain's better — so I stuck with that pretty much all the way, apart from an SG on a couple of songs."

Using various Taylor acoustic guitars for the album, Frusciante's amplifier rig included a 200-watt Marshall Major and a 100-watt Marshall Super Bass, one of which he usually ran in a stereo setup with a Fender Showman Blackface guitar amp pushing the Marshall. Additionally, he used the Ibanez WH10 wah-wah pedal, kept in a trebly position. "I was using a lot of effects. We wanted to create a real sense of atmosphere. I used a few Line 6 Echo pedals, an Electro-Harmonix flanger and the Big Muff a lot . . . [As far as amps] I was using this big Fender spring reverb from the '60s. I used it with a modulation synthesizer — that's the sound you hear on the 'Throw Away Your Television' chorus. . . . It has 'great reverb' but also a really thick sound and a great tone. On 'Don't Forget Me,' I used an envelope filter and I was using the volume pedal a lot on that song too — and that Line 6 pedal in one of the analogue delay settings to where it's constantly feeding back. Just as it was about to feed back, I'd just turn the knob as I'm playing to prevent it from going into full-on feedback. It gives it that spooky kind of feeling." Flea recorded playing a Modulus bass with a Gallien-Krueger head on a Mesa/Boogie amp cabinet.

"When we made *By the Way*, I'd never recorded harmonies in a studio by my own will," said Frusciante to the *Austin Chronicle*. "Rick had forced me to do backing vocals for *Californication*, which at the time I wasn't into. It wasn't until Guy Picciotto of Fugazi was so complimentary about my harmonies that it made me think, 'Oh, wow — harmonies. Great!' Before that, I was like, 'Harmonies suck.'" Harmonies weren't the only new edition to the Chili Peppers' sound. "John did a lot of things we hadn't done before on previous records, like synthesizers and keyboard

parts," said Flea to MTV. "It brought a whole new color and feeling to the record that hasn't been there before."

Frusciante felt the keyboard sound fit the ethereal musical texture of the album. "I think a big reason for that is that a lot of elements on *By the Way* are mixed very soft. I did all kinds of little synthesizer things that are barely audible. A lot of the time my guitar is barely audible. The mix is definitely done in a really subtle way. When you have a lot of things that are just barely at the level of audibility, you tend to feel them more than hear them, and that creates a sort of ethereal quality." Said the guitarist of Rick Rubin, "I love the working relationship that we have. He really, like, [comes] in and makes everybody feel comfortable and he just, he lets things be when they're fine. . . . he understands that little imperfections are sometimes what makes something great and colorful." Frusciante took on additional responsibility during the post-production mixing stage, something he hadn't done before. "I was very present for the mix of *By the Way*. It was the first time I was in a production of this importance — a huge responsibility for a novice . . . poor Rick Rubin!"

With *By the Way* completed, Flea felt proud of the Chilis' accomplishment. "Both individually and as a band, we are growing and changing and finding new ways to express ourselves. This is definitely a different record for us because our lives are different, because we are different people every day and are always writing and changing and arriving in different places. I'm very proud of my playing on this record, but I'm also proud of being a part of something that is in touch with the energy around it." Reflecting on the album upon its release in July 2002, Anthony Kiedis said, "I can't even tell if it's good anymore. . . . I mean, there are days I feel like this is the greatest thing we've ever done, and there are days that I'm like, 'This is just going to die in the water.'" Not surprisingly, the album didn't die in the water; it stayed afloat on the Billboard Top 200 for months.

CHAPTER 22

Rick's a Believer

Weezer and Neil Diamond

RICK RUBIN WORKED WITH a wide range of artists throughout 2002 and 2003 — Limp Bizkit on *Results May Vary*, Jay-Z on the hit single "99 Problems," The Mars Volta, Joe Strummer, The (International) Noise Conspiracy, Lil Jon & the East Side Boyz, Sheryl Crow, and Slipknot. Among the full-length studio albums Rubin produced was Weezer's *Make Believe*. As the lengthy pre-production process began, Rubin said, "Rivers just gave me some demos, the first round for this album. I'm trying to get my head clear to really just dive in." And dive in he did. By the time Weezer and Rubin had wrapped pre-production, rhythm guitarist Brian Bell estimated they had "75 to 100 — not even exaggerating — cds of demos and B-sides — or what we consider might be B-sides, A-Lists that turn into B-Lists, B-Lists that turn into A-Lists."

In describing some of those tracks that made the final cut, lead singer Rivers Cuomo said "Haunt You Every Day" came about when Rubin asked him to write a Billy Joel or Elton John style song. "So, I didn't really accomplish that at all, but I did write a song on the piano.

So that's about as close as I could come. . . . It's the first song I wrote entirely on piano." What would become the album's biggest single, "Beverly Hills" originated from another one of Rubin's seemingly off-the-wall questions. Recalled drummer Patrick Wilson, "Rick said, 'Why don't you have a boom-boom-chop song?' And that's how it turned into that." Cuomo explained his inspiration for the lyrics to "Beverly Hills": "I was at the opening of the new Hollywood Bowl and I flipped through the program and I saw a picture of Wilson Phillips. And for some reason I just thought how nice it would be to marry, like, an 'established' celebrity and live in Beverly Hills and be part of that world. And it was a totally sincere desire. And then I wrote that song, 'Beverly Hills.' For some reason, by the time it came out — and the video came out — it got twisted around into something that seemed sarcastic. But originally it wasn't meant to be sarcastic at all."

Another of the album's tracks, "Pardon Me," almost didn't make the cut. Brian Bell had to fight for the song when the band was making final track selections at Rubin's house. "[I said,] 'Wait, we forgot about this song!' I remember running out to my car, and [grabbing it and] I made everyone listen to it, and I think three-fourths of the way into the song it comes back around to that one moment." It didn't hurt the song's chances that they were listening to it at the producer's place. "Everything sounds so good at Rick Rubin's house, because he has this über-soundsystem, and it just was, like, apparent that we had to do ['Pardon Me']. And I thought it was just an unbelievably sincere message that Rivers was conveying and that — I don't know if he knew the weight of what he was saying. It was really great."

Of the actual in-studio time with Rubin, Scott Shriner has an enduring image of the producer: "I just always think of Rick Rubin in the studio, just moving his head back and forth, rockin' in the control room." Released in May 2005, the album debuted at #2 on the Billboard Top 200 Album Chart; *Make Believe*'s Top 10 hit single "Beverly Hills" also won the band their first Grammy nomination for Best Rock Song.

* * *

Neil Diamond had the groovy rocker market cornered for over 40 years. With his signature sideburns and flamboyant stage shows, *Rolling Stone* has accurately dubbed Diamond "the Jewish Elvis." Seeking to refocus attention on his songwriting with 2006's simply titled *12 Songs*, the pop legend paired up with Rick Rubin in a move that reminded many of Johnny Cash's career revival in the '90s, with the Rubin-produced albums that focused solely on the songs and the man singing them. Rubin was eager to work with Diamond and unabashedly described his pursuit of the artist as "stalking." At first, Diamond found Rubin's enthusiasm "a little scary — I didn't know what to make of it." Diamond wasn't that familiar with Rubin's work: "I knew he cut a few artists, I knew he was very highly regarded, kind of a mysterious figure, kind of standoffish as far as what people saw." But Rubin knew Diamond's work well and held him in very high esteem as one of the greatest pop songwriters. "He's never been part of any style," said Rubin, "and he's crossed different boundaries of pop and rock and different kinds of music at different times."

Once they'd began working together, Rubin insisted Diamond track all of the album's songs playing acoustic guitar while he sang. The singer hadn't recorded like that since the 1960s, and he was reluctant to try it again. Diamond would later concede that Rick was right: "I was one of those radio stars killed by videos. It was hard to get back on track. With Rick, I found the right path. He picked up on the vibe of acoustic guitar and understatement, something I haven't done in years and wasn't able to replicate until this album." Rubin, who had "always just been a fan of his early records," wanted to bring back the Neil Diamond who "made those old records great" with a stripped-down sound. When Rubin and Diamond listened to those old records again, "he got to hear things in a new way," said the producer to the *New York Times*. "With an artist that tours as much as Neil does, the songs kind of take on a new life, much different from the records. I wanted to go back to the feel of a singer-songwriter, not a performer."

Part of Diamond's resistance to the idea came from a lack of confidence. "I stayed away from it for years, thinking that there were many,

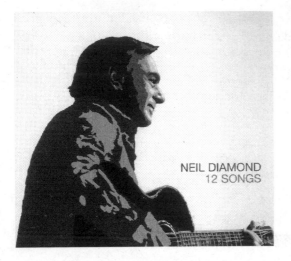

NEIL DIAMOND
12 SONGS

many better guitar players than I and that I should stick to what I do best, the writing and singing. Rick didn't want to budge, and we argued about it almost every day in the studio. I played on every track, which means I lost every battle." As he did with all the music he produced, Rubin put the emphasis on great material to create "more of a songwriter's album than a singer's album." Diamond's image had changed since the '60s to him being "viewed more as a cabaret artist," opined Rubin. "I missed that image of the singer-songwriter." Singing and playing acoustic guitar at the same time was "a different animal," the producer told *Rolling Stone.* "It's taking him back to being more of a singer-songwriter. He really blows me away."

As in his collaborations with Johnny Cash, Rubin stripped down a Neil Diamond song to its core for a more honest and revealing performance. Heading into the studio, Rubin tried not to "have a preconceived idea. . . . I think that's one of the secrets of doing it, is not having any expectation of what it's supposed to be. You just let it take on a life of its own. Our job is to pay attention and watch and know when it's good. We just wait for those moments and try to capture them." Despite Rubin's Zen approach to the outcome, Diamond described the producer as anything but uninvolved to the *Washington Post.* "He certainly wasn't easygoing in the studio. He's a passionate, obsessive person, like I am. . . . I have so much respect for the guy. He's talented, and he knows music and he brings a fresh perspective. . . . Despite his appearance, which can be really intimidating, Rick's a really good, sweet person." To *USA Today,* Diamond called Rubin a person with "inner peace. . . . He's a throwback to the '60s, a big lovable bear of a man. The only problem I had was his habit of hugging. At first, I was taken aback. After a while, I got to like it. He's like Father Earth taking you to his bosom."

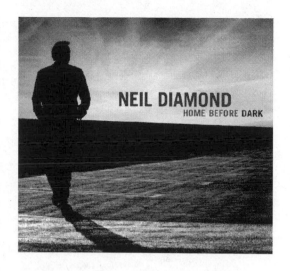

The pre-production for the album started with Neil Diamond hunkering down to write. "I locked myself in the recording studio with a whole box of number 2 pencils, a big stack of my trusty yellow legal pads and a funky old three-quarter size Martin guitar with an E minor chord that could break your heart. Rick was determined not to rush the process, but to wait until we got to the essence of the songs I was working on. I loved the sheer freedom of creating music for its own sake." With the producer's direction, Diamond "made a U-turn and went back 40 years to try to recapture those feelings. The major difference between this album and my first or second album is I think the lyrics now go to places I could never go to then." For Diamond's backing band, Rubin recruited fellow rock veterans Mike Campbell and Benmont Tench from the Heartbreakers and Billy Preston, among others.

Rubin felt Diamond had "hit a sweet spot in his writing, and there's an intimacy and vulnerability to how it was recorded and a natural quality to it that really affects me when I hear it. We went in with no expectations and it turned into what it is. I'm really proud of it . . . It really touches a spot in me." Upon the release of *12 Songs* in November 2005, critics celebrated it as Diamond's strongest, freshest, and most consistent in years, with *Rolling Stone* observing in its four-star review, "The hushed *12 Songs* isn't easy-listening: Diamond sings with a close-miked sincerity so disarming and lacking in his usual gruff bravado that it's almost refreshing when he lapses into over-statement. . . . He's as direct as he's ever been with his lyrics, which give them an extra poignancy." Of the critical accolades, Diamond quipped, "It's been a long wait," and announced excitedly that he was already working on the next album. That album turned out to be his first #1 on the Billboard Top 200 chart. *Home After Dark*, released in May 2008, was also produced by Rick Rubin.

CHAPTER 23

Out of Exile and Mezmerize/Hypnotize

IN 2004, AUDIOSLAVE BEGAN WORKING on their follow-up to 2002's successful debut, with Rick Rubin to produce. Because the band had already proven itself commercially and critically, for *Out of Exile*, the members of Audioslave felt a certain amount of freedom from those pressures. Chris Cornell spoke to MTV about the album: "On this record, I don't think we considered [album sales] in any way. . . . We didn't talk about direction, and yet, we went in a lot of different directions musically that I haven't done in my career before. So it really feels fresh." Guitarist Tom Morello recalled, "When we wrote *Out of Exile*, we had a great deal of confidence in each other in the creative process, and we felt confident bringing any idea in. We just make music to please ourselves."

The time between albums had allowed the members of Audioslave to form into a more cohesive unit. Said Morello, "When we wrote and recorded the first album, we'd played zero shows together as a live band. Our first show was on *David Letterman*." Rick Rubin echoed the guitarist in *Rolling Stone*: "On the first album, Chris didn't know the guys so well, and the guys didn't know Chris so well. The first album was like an experiment; this was more like 'This is what we do.' There was just less apprehension. Everybody was more comfortable with each other." Audioslave had experience performing as a group under their belt, and Rubin felt "like the potential is so much greater to do a really powerful album, better than the first one."

That familiarity, as Chris Cornell explained to MTV, made *Out of Exile* easier to record and also more diverse. "I think, in 10 months of touring, we did nothing but play Audioslave songs. Even though we have vast career catalogs, we didn't touch on that. We carved out, I believe, a spot for Audioslave on its own terms and by itself. That was pretty huge in terms of how we felt coming back into songwriting for this record. It was clear that, on every level, we worked great and it was also clear that the openness of the creative process the first time really helped. So we went right back to that." Morello, for his part, felt that the band's closeness brought "even more spontaneity to the new album's material. With the last record, each of us was inevitably bringing some of our musical histories into the room. This record, it feels like, is just Audioslave. A lot of the songs grew up out of this fresh soil of getting to know one another."

Bassist Tim Commerford agreed: "There's definitely a work ethic that the three of us, me, Tom and Brad have and Chris Cornell just jumped right into it and assumed the same ethic. Whenever we get together, we get work done. . . . I feel really comfortable that we'll make a really great second album that'll be even better than the first record because we're a better band now. We've played more and we've been on more tours. We're just better." Cornell described the sound of *Out of Exile* as "less riff rock than ever, but there's a lot of faster, more aggressive songs."

Going into the group's pre-production sessions, Rick Rubin said, "They have about 15 or 20 songs already. I'm really excited about that . . . because the last Audioslave album was more of a studio project." The guys in Audioslave were excited too, sending Rubin "two-way pages . . . on a pretty regular basis after rehearsal and they're like, 'We were good at work today, you're gonna be so excited,' so that's nice. What's exciting to me about this album is . . . they're so much more comfortable with each other now; they got along fine before, but it was so new. The potential is off the map."

Tom Morello described to *Ultimate Guitar* how he approached songwriting with a more adventurous spirit: "I consciously made the effort to rely more on spontaneity and intuition in my writing and my playing than in preparation. So, the night before rehearsals or the morning of, I pick up a guitar and maybe, maybe come up with an idea. Or just walk into rehearsal with nothing pre-planned and just sort of see what occurred . . . it was all purely day of, what can we come up with in rehearsal? I think it's really added to the excitement of the songwriting process and to the breadth of the music we were able to create. . . . What was very different about this record than any record I've ever made before, was my contribution to it. Normally, I'm very structured in my approach to songwriting. I have a tape recorder . . . where I catalog from the day we master the record until the day rehearsals begin for the next record — I'm cataloguing ideas. And I'm listening back and making meticulous lists and graphs and, 'Riff 72 is a four-star riff, Riff 101 isn't so good,' and then when it comes time to write an album, going back to those lists and referring and cherry-picking and doing a lot of self-censorship in that way to get the best ideas. . . . It felt very unsafe and it took a big leap of faith and then after the first couple of days, we had written songs that I thought were fantastic and gained a confidence in that process. By just following whatever thread musically I suggested or Timmy suggested or whoever suggested, we could make a fine Audioslave song out of it."

Cornell, like Morello, also preferred to write with the group. "I didn't really spend any time writing songs alone when I was in Audioslave. It was something I consciously wanted not to do for a while. I had so many years in Soundgarden writing alone, and obviously for [solo album] *Euphoria Morning*. So it really was something I wanted to get away from for a while." Audioslave eclipsed their own prolific songwriting sessions from two years ago. "Last time when we went in to make a record, we wrote a song a day," said Morello. "This time, we've done even more. Sometimes we've gotten the skeletons of two songs a day."

Said Cornell to MTV, "It was comfortable [to have Rubin back on board]. I actually personally learned more from him as a producer than I have from anyone else I've worked with. Oftentimes, I feel like there's sort of smoke and mirrors involved with a producer, and that really, if you have any kind of self-confidence and know your band, you don't need one." On why Rubin was the kind of producer that suited the band, Cornell said, "The way Audioslave works, where we write songs in a room live and can immediately play them live, Rick's whole focus is you should be a rock band that can write great songs and be able to play them live, and that is your record. That is his whole philosophy. So, for me, he's the perfect choice." And while Rubin was producing again, Cornell felt in some ways the producer had already done his job through his work on *Audioslave*. "I think we learned so much from him last time that this time, he wasn't as involved." From Commerford's perspective, Rick Rubin was "an ear guy . . . where Rick has just absorbed all the music he's ever listened to. And you as an artist, if you're working with him, get to run your ideas through his computer that has every song ever written in it and he gets it, to send it through there and go, 'Oh, those chords remind me of the chords that are in 'Let it Be,' and this might remind me of an AC/DC song. Why don't you try this?'" Tom Morello and Rubin didn't always see eye to eye, to understate their dynamic. "Rick and I behave much like an old married couple. . . . He knows what he's talkin' about [but] I have a lot of confidence and when I feel a thing is right, I'm gonna stick with it. . . . He can complain all he wants. . . . Rick Rubin is an excellent producer but he has never understood what I do as a lead guitar player."

The approach Morello took was "more traditional guitar playing in the solos whether it's melodic or fast technical playing or whatever as opposed to relying exclusively on sounds. From records like *Battle of Los Angeles* and even on the first Audioslave record, solos often didn't sound very much like a guitar at all. But on this I thought it's fine because I've done a lot of records exclusively like that. And sometimes I go back to one of the things in my arsenal, which is to 'rock a solo' solo. And I try to do that from time to time. . . . So the way that I approached the solos was different on this record than any other record I had done before."

In an interview with *Ultimate Guitar*, Morello explained the lengths to which he took spontaneity on *Out of Exile*: "Normally, in the songwriting and the rehearsing of the song, an idea for the solo will surface and from that day forward it will be the solo idea for the song with some variation. This time, much to the dismay of some of my band members who thought I had lost my everloving mind, whenever the solo sections of songs would come up, I'd kinda noodle along in an awful kind of C- Allman Brothers way. But the intention was, when I was going to really go for the solos, I wanted to feel like the first time I had ever heard that part. And so, I took some time before recording the solos and did something again that I hadn't done in a while — I went back to the woodshed and I just practiced. Hours of day with the technique stuff, hours a day jamming, trying to get my improvisational skills, sort of feeling I could bounce off chord progressions and grooves, and feeling pretty comfortable with that. I spent a couple days getting a number of guitar sounds together with and without the effects and then when it came time to record the solos, basically I just said, 'Put up any song you want, don't tell me which one it is, give me one bar before the solo, and let's just see what happens.' I would dial up a sound and it was pretty exciting. So there was no planning, like, wah-wah on this song. I'd think to myself, 'Whatever comes up, I'm gonna rock the wah with and let's just see how it happens.'"

Detailing his technical setup for the second album's guitar sounds, Tom Morello explained that "all the songs played in standard 440 tuning are either played on my Fender Strat Soul Power guitar or the old Arm the Harmless guitar, which I've played throughout RATM. The Fender Strat is a slightly modified guitar; they added a toggle switch for me to do the on/off clicking thing and the Ibanez whammy bar, the Floyd Rose knockoff which I have on my other guitars. It is three years old, a brand new guitar. . . . The songs in dropped D tuning are a Fender Telecaster, about an '82 Made in Mexico Telecaster that I, ages ago, traded my roommate a Marshall head for. Because I needed something I could go down to D with. And the

songs in dropped B tuning are played with a new Les Paul Standard." As with Audioslave's first LP, and in the tradition of most great rock albums, Rubin and the group agreed to make "a real conscious effort to record to 2-inch tape rather than to ProTools," said Morello. "We did overdubs with Pro-Tools, some vocals and some of the solos, because technology like ProTools allows creativity. You or I can make the *White Album* in our bedrooms now but at the same time, it changes the creative process. Whereas the creativity is happening in front of a computer screen rather than in a room with live rockin' drums. Like I say, we play to our strengths and our strength is rockin' live and so it's always been important to capture that warmth of the tones on the 2-inch tape."

Audioslave repeated the success of their debut album when *Out of Exile* reached the top of the Billboard Top 200 after its release in May 2005; the single "Doesn't Remind Me" was nominated for a Grammy.

* * *

Looking to push the artistic bar even higher, System of a Down and Rick Rubin plotted a double LP, *Mezmerize* and *Hypnotize*, for release in 2005. A politically focused concept LP, Rubin called the music "a whole new invention. . . . I saw them in rehearsal the other day, working on their new stuff . . . System's *awesome*." The albums were recorded at Rick Rubin's Mansion in Laurel Canyon (where Rubin had first recorded with the Chili Peppers on *Blood Sugar Sex Magik*) and Akademie Mathematique of Philosophical Sound Research in Los Angeles. Of the political subject matter, Rubin told MTV, "You can't help but write about that stuff when you have such strong emotions. I don't think it'll come out in an obvious way. System has a great way of taking the realities of their lives and things we see in the world and twisting them into these odd little puzzles. You don't know necessarily what they're talking about, 'cause they create this kind of surre-alistic picture." *Rolling Stone* called the double album a "one-two punch in six-month installments"; *Mezmerize* was released in May 2005 and *Hyp-notize* in November. Both debuted at #1 on the Billboard Top 200 Album Chart.

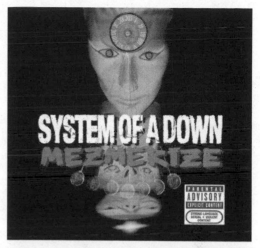

As perhaps the group's biggest fan, Rubin said that System of a Down "wanted to feel like they grew past their last album, which we're all very proud of. As musicians, the biggest improvements have been with John and Serj. There's not so much singing

on the last album — it's more characters and yelling and different great vocal things. But something happened over [the two years they spent on tour] where Serj has become a tremendous singer." The esteem was mutual; said drummer John Dolmayan, "Rick Rubin is an incredible artist himself." The group won the Best Hard Rock Performance Grammy for *Mezmerize*'s first single, "B.Y.O.B." Despite this success, the future of System of a Down was uncertain as 2007 began, with guitarist Shavo Odadjian explaining that while the band was "alive and well. We're just not working together right now. We kind of like split up at first, but you know, we're brothers, man, we'll take bullets for each other. So it's like, you kind of miss each other after a while and one guy makes the first move, then another starts making phone calls. . . . This is a juggernaut, man. System of a Down is my lifeline. It'll never go away. We could not make a record for 10 years — that's not gonna happen, but I'm just saying we could — and we'll come back strong."

CHAPTER 24

"The Best Album We've Done"

Stadium Arcadium

THOUGH HE NOW WORKED with mainstream artists like Justin Timberlake and U2 and Green Day, Rick Rubin stayed true to his independent roots, serving as executive producer on Slayer's sixth studio LP, *Christ Illusion*, after the band re-signed with American Recordings. Slayer won its first Grammy for Best Metal Performance for the single "Eyes of the Insane." On returning to work with Rubin, Kerry King said, "He knows what we want and we know what he will bring us."

The Red Hot Chili Peppers felt the same way, recruiting Rick Rubin for the double LP *Stadium Arcadium*. *Rolling Stone* described the record as "the most ambitious work of [the band's] 23-year career — an attempt to consolidate everything that is Chili Peppers, from their earlier, funnier funk-metal stuff to soul-baring 'Under the Bridge'–style balladry to Californicating vocal-harmony pop. And unlike . . . almost every other double album of the post-vinyl era, the band pulls it off."

Ironically, the original idea for what turned into an epic album was quite the opposite. "Our plan was to do a short, sweet, simple record. Something that was easily digestible," said Kiedis. "We just ended up writing enough songs for about three records. . . . So making a double record just seemed to fit. It's funny because making this one has been a lot less taxing than our past records have been. The workload was a lot more intense because we wrote so many songs and recorded them all. But we are getting along better, everyone was happy and confident, and when you hear the new songs, you can hear that everybody's hearts are in them all." Talking to MTV, Kiedis elaborated on how the band expanded its original concept. "I think we always [go into writing] with this mindset that this time, we're going to write the perfect 11 songs and just put out 11 songs like they used to do in the days of Buddy Holly and the Beatles. Those early records were so short and sweet, and had this kind of lasting profound impact on the world because they're very memorable and digestible and, I don't know, maybe it just takes less energy or effort to connect with smaller collections. But as has been the case with every single time we've tried to do that, we end up with 30 some-odd songs. The difference this time was we ended up liking all of those songs and finishing all of those songs and it actually became a very difficult process to even just whittle it down to 25."

Said Frusciante, "Usually we record 25 songs, Anthony records vocals on 20 and we end up releasing 15. This time, we finished 38 songs! At this point, I even consider that keeping 'only' 25 in a double album constitutes a regression, proportionally speaking. I battled for a double with 30 songs! When you write music that you judge satisfying, you want to transmit it to a maximum of people; it's human. Every song of this album deserves to be transmitted to the public. God didn't give us music for the only selfish pleasure of those who write it and play it." Pre-production for *Stadium Arcadium* took place in "this funky room in the Valley where we write music, and everyone felt more comfortable than ever bringing in their ideas," said Kiedis. "Everybody was in good moods. There was very little tension, very little anxiety, very little weirdness going on."

On writing lyrics and harmonies to the band's jams, Anthony Kiedis joked, "They don't make it easy for me. They could be an amazing jazz-fusion trio. But somehow I find songs in the bigness of what they're doing. It's not like I get to decide: 'I want this.' It's this unspoken moment of consideration, where as a unit we listen to these parts and meditate on what serves the song best."

John Frusciante described the intensity of creating *Stadium Arcadium* to Spanish *Kerrang*: "We started to record the album a year and a half ago and during that time we've been listening to the album for, like, 14 hours every day. Since we finished it, I haven't listened to it again. I think it's the best album we've done . . . the most psychedelic, the darkest, the deepest if you want, and the most eclectic. Sometimes when you pick the best songs to be part of the album, just by chance they all sound the same — funky, rock, fast, or slow. But in this album we've tried to pick the songs from a wider range. Personally I wanted to do songs that sounded harder, but at the same time, that they would transmit something deeper, more transcendental. The separation between funky songs and melodic songs started with *Blood Sugar* . . . *Stadium Arcadium* is the first time we mix these two elements in the same song."

Rick Rubin explained to *Rolling Stone* how the band crafts songs: one of the band members would "create one main element, a verse or a chorus, and from that find pieces to make other parts of the song. Most bands write a lot of riffs, then see how they fit together to make a song. The Chili Peppers are more organic: creating pieces to go with other existing pieces. . . . Once the foundation of a song is built, John takes the song over the top. It's not a lot of experimentation. John has the idea. And if he goes too far in any direction, the other members pull him back in."

Kiedis had nothing but growing admiration for Rubin as a producer. "He really has earned his place as the producer of this band," the singer told MTV. "He has improved his game consistently. He just gets better and better. He's willing to work harder and harder. His intuition flourishes. We have been so willing to grow and change as a band, and he's also come along for that ride. He has the same love for music today that I think teenagers get when they're 17 and they fall in love with the wonderful world of music." Frusciante also brought in an engineer he worked with on his solo albums. "I worked with my friend Ryan Hewitt who is a young engineer ready to experiment. . . . By the time I was doing my overdubs for this record with Ryan, we just had it 'down.' On this album we actually had 72 tracks, because we had to have a 24-track machine for the basic tracks, a 24-track machine for overdubs and treatments, and another 24 for backing vocals. So when we mixed there were three 24-track machines all synced up with each other."

The band's pace was more measured this time. "They decided to work shorter hours," Rubin explained to MTV. "In the past, [the] writing mode would be a very exhaustive process and they would be in there for a long period of time and it'd be tiring. In this version, they worked less days a week but carried it on as long as it took. And they took a lot of breaks. So there was much more of a freshness — there was never the drudgery of showing up on the 100th day and trying to [energize]. Just naturally, as an experiment, they decided to see what this felt like, and by cutting down their hours, they ended up being much, much, much more productive. . . . Recording-wise, it went very quickly. There was a very fluid momentum. Everyone always plays at the same time, but typically the instruments are really isolated from each other for control over the sounds later. John thought it would be an interesting concept for this album for all the instruments to be in the room at the same time, so all the instruments are bleeding into each other, and that was the first time we had done that." Engineer Ryan Hewitt said of the Chili Peppers, "They're pros, and they're incredibly talented. . . . They rehearse their stuff, they look at each other, they lock in, and they just go for it, and Rick really pushes for that. He wants a natural, organic feel, and so does the band. They don't play to a click track. Everything was done on tape. There's no ProTools involved. What you hear from the band is exactly what they played when they played it. There's no trickery involved in the music on this record. It all came out of the fingers and hands of these guys."

The Chili Peppers had nothing but praise for each other's work on *Stadium Arcadium*. Drummer Chad Smith described Kiedis's process for tracking vocals in the studio: "He's like a mad scientist in the studio . . . and we let him do his thing." Frusciante praised Smith to *Guitar World*: "He's great at [being] tight but not rigid. I was especially pushing for lots of sections to be at slightly different tempos than other sections. Like in 'Dani California,' I really wanted the chorus to be slower than the verse, and Chad can do that. In the studio, we're always talking about how many 'clicks per minute' something is. Chad's really in control of that. We'll tell him 'just slow down two clicks,' and he can do it. It's something we all do together; we all feel the tempo in a precise, scientific way."

The band recorded in the same Laurel Canyon mansion they had for *Blood Sugar Sex Magik*. Kiedis explained, "We had some new spirit to work on. We had new feelings, new emotions, new songs — it was a different time for the band. We were in a different psychological state the second time around than we were the first time around. We were looking to go to a warm and inviting place." Frusciante elaborated to *Total Guitar*, "It just seemed like the perfect idea because I live about one minute away and Anthony and Chad live about 10 minutes away. Flea's about an hour away in Malaga, but because of the way it's set up he could sleep at the studio. Flea made it his home for the weekends so it was just practical in that way. Also the studio we normally use, Cello Studios, closed down." But the mansion, like the band, had evolved in the intervening years. "It was a lot different now than it was back then," said Frusciante. "The feeling was a lot warmer, a lot cozier. A certain amount of work had been done on it: there were some nice carpets, and a parachute had been put up in the tracking room [as a ceiling hanging]. When we did *Blood Sugar*, it was just a big empty house when we brought in some equipment and started tracking. This time they had a couch in the tracking room. Little things like that. It didn't seem as devoid of life as it did the first time."

Frusciante described the technical setup to *Guitar Player*: "We recorded to three synchronized 2-inch, 24-track machines, running at 30 ips, and mixed to analog tape as well. . . . [The console was a] Neve 8068 with 31102 mic preamps, and Neve 1057 and 1073 mic preamps were also used for some tracks. The basic tracks, including most solos, were cut 'live' in the studio, with everyone playing together in the same room. For a lot of it we even had our amps in the same room with the drums, and we allowed for bleed, as I was really into trying to capture some of the atmosphere of '60s recordings, and also have that extra push you get when you know you've got to nail the take because you're all in the same room." For this album, Frusciante made more use of tape manipulation. "On the solo for 'Stadium Arcadium,' I flipped the tape over and processed the guitar through an old EMT 250 digital reverb that was then run through a high-pass filter from my modular rig. So it's backward reverb, filtered. I did three different passes of that, listening to the track backward and opening up the high-pass filter on the reverb. Then I flipped the tape over and took the best bits of the three passes — did a comp, basically — and then erased what I didn't need. I did the same thing at the very end of 'C'mon Girl,' where Anthony comes in singing and there's a guitar that answers him. The filtered reverb sound turns into the real guitar sound. If you tail it right, that's the sound it produces, as if sounds are coming out of thin air."

To capture the album's guitar sounds, Frusciante's microphone setup included "a Shure SM-57 positioned on axis a couple of inches from the cone. On some tracks the engineer, Ryan Hewitt, added a Royer R-121 ribbon mic, positioned about 15 feet away, in order to capture some of the room sound. We used a Telefunken Ela M 250 tube condenser mic on the acoustic guitars." The guitarist also "bought a bunch of different wah pedals because there were so many moments on the album that were going to have wah-wah that we didn't want them all to be the same. My favorite one is still the Ibanez [WH-10] one. . . . The Dimebag model was another one I used on certain spots on the album. . . . Sometimes I'm experimenting with the modular synthesizer, and sometimes I hear the sound clear in my head so I know exactly what I'm setting out to do. Some effects are impossible to control, like the new MURF pedal by Mooger Fooger. It's basically a series of 10 filters that go in a rhythm and you can turn up each frequency at any moment. I used that on the solo at the top of the verse on 'Dani California,' and I also used it on Flea's trumpet on 'Death of a Martian.'"

For his guitars and amps, Frusciante stuck with the tried and true. "My sunburst '62 Strat and white '61 Strat go into a Boss Chorus Ensemble, and the stereo output on that splits out to my 200-watt Marshall Major and Marshall Silver Jubilee. I also have a '69 Les Paul that I put through just the Silver Jubilee with one cabinet. But after the guitars went down to tape, I'd process them through my modular synth gear. A lot of people might think they're hearing effects or even a keyboard synthesizer, but that's not what I was using. There are parts of a synthesizer that make sound, and parts of a synthesizer that process sound. And I was using only the parts that process sound, like filters [low-frequency oscillators], and envelope generators. . . . [For effects] I did use the new POG [Polyphonic Octave Generator] from Electro-Harmonix, which is what's making the guitar sound just like an organ on 'She Looks to Me' and 'Snow.' I used the new Electro-Harmonix English Muff'n, too, which is a really cool tube-driven distortion box. And, of course, I always use a Big Muff and a Boss distortion pedal and my Ibanez WH-10 wah."

But despite all this gear, Frusciante didn't want the album to sound overly processed or "perfect," as he told *Total Guitar*. "Another part of my concept for this album was to make it more raw and to let certain mistakes fly. If you listen to 'Especially in Michigan,' I had my guitar on the wrong pickup. I like the way that riff sounds on the bass pickup, but when I was playing the song I looked down and it was on the wrong pickup. You can hear it when Anthony starts singing: there's a little commotion going on where I stop playing the riff for a second and you hear the sound change, then a little white noise for a second. I'm happy to leave it like that because it gives the recording personality. That's the kind of shit they would leave in during the 1960s but take out in the 1980s. Which time period was better? The Rolling Stones' recordings in the 1960s had the tambourines and drums going off on different times with each other; the guitars go off time with each other then come back together and it's beautiful. That's what gives it personality and a magical feeling. I am a perfectionist, but for me those kind of accidents are perfection." That approach spilled over to his guitar solos. "For the guitar solos on

Blood Sugar Sex Magik and *Californication*, I knew what I was going to do more or less in advance . . . or at least I knew how I was going to start and end them. I wasn't going out on a limb too often. On this album, almost every solo happened spontaneously. I had no idea where I was going to start or end, and that's also due to this rhythmic approach I've discovered."

Ryan Hewitt explained that Frusciante "has an instinct to leave imperfections in a record. . . . He's a huge fan of 1960s, 1970s music, where there's just stuff that's blatantly wrong on certain records. It's not perfect. John recognizes when to let go of things. There are other times when we'll sit there trying to fix one note forever until it is perfect. But there are some things that are, to me, really obvious — Chad dropped a stick in one song, and that was left in. You can tell because he's playing kind of weird. He's trying to find his other stick, but it keeps going, and he's playing with one arm. It's things you don't notice when listening to the song because it was so good and the groove is so tight. If you listen to the guitar by itself, it might sound a little funny in one spot. But because the band is so tight, that kind of thing is not going to stick out, and it will add to the cool factor."

Said Kiedis of the guitarist's approach on *Stadium Arcadium*: "There's this ongoing progression of everything else that has been slowly happening between *Californication* and *By the Way*, with harmonies and textures. John has really fallen in love with the art of treating sounds. [The album's] layered, but not in a heavy-handed way. John's work is definitely of the masterpiece quality, as a guitar player and sound treatment-ist. He has certainly gone to some weird über-level of hearing some Beethoven-sized symphony shit in his head. He really shines on this record." Flea felt Frusciante had managed to achieve something on this album that he hadn't on previous ones. "John often puts limits on himself as a guitarist," the bassist said to *Guitar World*. "He wants to make a stylistic statement, so he doesn't just let go and play. But on this album, he did both of those things. But there are also times when he just let fly with a Hendrixian, Pagian flurry of loudness." One model Frusciante had for *Stadium Arcadium* was Black Sabbath's *Master of Reality*, "where the guitars are in stereo, hard left, hard right, and it's just the simple power chord and sounds so thick as you'd ever want it to sound."

Hewitt described recording the guitar solo at the end of "Dani California" to MTV: "John wanted to double-track it, so it was a bigger, thicker sound. So really, there are two guitars playing at that point. And he did that solo in one take. The solo you hear on the record is the solo he played in the room, with the band — that was one take, done. And then he went in to double it. He listened to it a couple of times and played it exactly the same. Again, in maybe two takes. It was perfectly similar — or as perfect as you can get. . . . When you listen to 'Dani California,' the guitars are always changing, and there's all these effects going on, created with the modular synthesizer after he played them. So you have this endless palette to choose from to make those sounds, and John would never use the same sound twice. That was real exciting. At times, we would record the guitars at a different speed, so we'd change the speed of the tape so when he was listening to it, it was going really slow or really fast — at least compared to its normal speed. Then, when you play it back, it's like this totally different sound. At the end of 'Wet Sand,' it sounds like there's a harpsichord when really it's three guitars playing the harmony to each other at twice the tape speed."

Frusciante was left to his own devices when it came to his guitar parts, to experiment as much as he wanted. "We composed and recorded the base tracks all together, then I worked alone," he related to *Autopsy*. "Anthony worked with Rick Rubin to record his vocal parts, I did my overdubs on my own, with a sound engineer and an assistant. I got all the time I needed to experiment, and I did so 12 to 14 hours a day. I love all those songs and I wanted each of them to be perfectly completed. At the same time, my challenge was to create something I had never heard before. For that, my solo albums [had prepared] me to use the studio in a creative way. The fact I used the same sound engineer [Ryan Hewitt] who worked on my two last records helped me. He also mixed the Chili Peppers album. We gained by an experience we got working together, and we're faster today, cause we know how to get some sounds."

One of the only minor complaints Frusciante had about the process was that it was "a bit fast between the end of the mix and the release of the album. It's a bit my fault, I wanted to take a lot of time to perfect the production. I recorded a lot of backing vocals, guitars overdubs, electronic treatments. . . . I knew that the mix couldn't be finished in two days! We had to find a compromise — Anthony wanted to release the album last fall, I wanted to take my time." And while the band has nearly perfected their working relationship after so many years playing together, some conflicts still arise. Said Frusciante, "We had a little tension before the mixing started because Flea thought he was going to want it different than me. Anthony thought he was going to want it different. It ended up that once we mixed the first song, we realized that everybody was liking the same thing. But it is this huge pressure when you've gone as far as I've gone." But in the end, Frusciante's vision for the album was one that all the Chili Peppers shared. "[I wanted] to retain all the raw power of the band playing live in the studio but also to have additional guitars and sonic effects enhancing what was already there. But on the rough mixes it didn't really sound like that, so there was a lot of tension building, because some people though, 'Oh, John's going overdub crazy,' or 'He's turning it into a Beach Boys album.' The main problem was that we'd been listening to the band's basic tracks on a slave reel. It was transferred badly, so the mix sounded really dull, while the overdubs were much brighter. That was freaking people out. But when we synced up the overdubs on the slave reel to the original 24-track master reel, everything sounded awesome. It's not that the overdubs ended up being softer; it was that the band sounded so much burlier. So we all ended up loving the final mixes. There hasn't been a single instance of somebody not wanting to use something that I'd done. It all ended up serving the song well. So that was cool."

While Frusciante found the mixing process to be "a drag because it's not a very creative process," Anthony Kiedis thought the toughest part of making the album was "cutting down the tracks [which] was excruciating. . . . But we did it in a very scientific way, where everyone was involved in and petitioned for the ones they thought should make it onto the record. It was a long process and everyone had to suffer a bit. There was too much democracy!"

For engineer Andy Scheps, this album was the next step in the band's evolution. "*By the Way* seemed to be the first record in whatever direction they were going, and *Stadium Arcadium* is where they're starting to realize it. It's less grooves and more songs, and Anthony is just singing his ass off. . . . And now he's a great singer. They were doing more of the same, but they were a lot more confident at it because they'd been doing it for a while, and they were just better at it. It seems as though this could be — and it's ridiculous, because they have been making records for so long — but this could be the beginning of the next set of records they make."

Stadium Arcadium won an outstanding seven Grammy Awards, including Rock Album of the Year. The *LA Times* praised the album: "[*Stadium Arcadium*] overflows with the kind of music the Chili Peppers do best: a physical, often psychedelic mix of spastic bass-slapped funk and glistening alt-rock spiritualism. Only they've never sounded this good as musicians." *Billboard* described Rick Rubin's production as "airy" and praised it for "[squeezing] the essence out of a monster — without taming it." And the band was justifiably proud of their work, with Flea declaring, "I'm very in love with this record," and Anthony Kiedis calling it "the best thing that we've ever done."

CHAPTER 25

Dixie Chicks
Taking the Long Way

AFTER WORKING THEIR WAY UP through the country-fair circuit to the top of the country charts, Dixie Chicks' Martie Maguire, Emily Robison, and Natalie Maines found themselves Nashville exiles in 2003 when their statements against President George W. Bush and the Iraq War turned many in their audience and in the media viciously against them. By going against the grain of unquestioning faith in the Presidency, the Dixie Chicks were subjected to a country radio boycott. But the controversy brought them to a new home with producer Rick Rubin, who would work with an all-female group for the first time since The Bangles in 1987.

Natalie Maines explained to MTV that the group was drawn to Rubin because his focus was "on the music, he doesn't care when the label wants [an album] done, he doesn't care if there is a format that plays you or doesn't play you." The Dixie Chicks would take a step away from their signature sound on their 2002 album *Home*, and Rubin felt his role was to facilitate that leap, making sure they were confident enough not to "soft-pedal anything." The stylistic direction, said Rubin to *Rolling Stone*, was to make "a rock album that leaned country, like [Tom] Petty or Gram Parsons."

As many artists before her had felt, Natalie Maines found that having Rubin producing was a positive change from her previous in-studio experiences. "I think [this album] was really the first time that I ever made a record where I just loved the process," she told MTV, "because there was no pressure, no stress, there were no rules. We used to have rules for ourselves just about being the Dixie Chicks . . . she had to play something and she had to play something on the same song, and we all three had to sing on the choruses. And Rick just throws all of that out."

Rather than focusing on the political controversy of 2003, the Dixie Chicks chose to explore the personal growth that had resulted from it. Announcing the upcoming release of *Taking the Long Way*, Maines said, "Everything felt more personal this time. I go back to songs we've done in the past and there's just more maturity, depth, intelligence on these. They just feel more grown-up." In promotional interviews, Emily Robison said, "This album was about finding a balance in the different aspects of our lives but there's something thematic there, too — it's really about being bold." As was his style, Rubin approached the sessions organically. "So much of what we do is not premeditated," he told MTV. "We really show up and try to do our very best and get it flowing, and then when it's flowing, we try to let it flow until it runs out and then we see what we got. It's not dictated by us."

Rubin worked with the Dixie Chicks with an honest and direct manner, something they appreciated. Emily Robison recalled to *Time*: "It was a weird time for us, obviously. If he had come in like a car salesman and said, 'I can totally hear a sound for you all,' we would have been put off. But he said, 'I don't know what this record will be, but you guys have something to say, and it'll make itself clear as we work.' Then he made us work 10 times harder than we've ever worked before." Natalie Maines was a little unsettled at first by Rubin's strong interest in spirituality. To the *New York Times*, Maines quipped, "That's why they call him a guru. At first, I didn't know if I was down with all that guru stuff. I thought, 'We're making a record — I don't want to be

converted.' But Rick's spirituality has mostly to do with his own sense of self. When it comes to the music, he's so sure of his opinion that you become sure of his opinion, too. And isn't that what gurus do? They know how to say the right things at the right time and get the best out of you." Emily Robison found that Rubin, in appearance and manner, wasn't what she expected.

"He's the exact opposite of what you would think he would be. With the hard rock and rap background, this guy with the long hair and big beard, everyone was a little intimidated by him at first. But when you realize what he's like, he's just a big teddy bear," she said to the Associated Press. Of Rubin's skills as a producer, Robison said, "I think he knows when it's right and he's very decisive, which is refreshing. But he's also a very good listener. You just respect his ears and his taste so much. That's an earned trust. We knew the legend but we didn't know the actual reason [behind it]. . . . We came to learn that it's just that he has great ears." Natalie Maines told the *New York Times*, "He doesn't even take notes. He listens with his eyes closed, presses pause, and then says, 'You need another chorus,' or 'There isn't enough of a bridge.' He's really precise, and you go back to work."

Upon its release, *Taking the Long Way* debuted at #1 on Billboard's Top 200 Album Chart, moving an astonishing 525,829 units in its first week at retail. *Rolling Stone*'s four-star review said the album "embraces the depth and fury of classic rock while remaining true to the trio's Texas roots." *Entertainment Weekly*'s A-grade review of the album called it "a little bit country, a little bit rock 'n' roll — but also a little bit power balladry, alt-country, and roadhouse boogie. Along with the comments that got them into their recent mess, it's the least wimpy thing the group's ever done." Even the country music establishment had to acknowledge the band's success when the album took the top spot on the country music charts. The National Academy of Recording Arts and Sciences showed support for the album and group, who won Grammys for Album of the Year, Record of the Year and Song of the Year (for "Not Ready to Make Nice"), as well as Best Country Performance by a Duo or Group with Vocal and the Country Album of the Year. Following the win, Rubin commented, "It feels so good to know our work touched listeners enough to vote it the best of the year. During the process, we are making our own favorite music. This award is confirmation that what is true and real in the emotion of music is contagious."

CHAPTER 26

Linkin Park
Minutes to Midnight

LINKIN PARK HAD ALREADY ACHIEVED great success with their mix of nu metal and rapcore on *Hybrid Theory* and *Meteora*. In 2006, the group began working on its next studio album, *Minutes to Midnight*, for Warner Bros., and they were looking to explore new sounds instead of rehashing the same thing again. "We were looking back at the things that we had done in the past," said Linkin Park's Mike Shinoda, "and I think we just figured that we had exhausted that sound. It was easy for us to replicate, it was easy for other bands to replicate, and we just needed to move on." Shinoda reasoned that Rick Rubin would be the best producer for the band since he has worked with artists in so many genres of music. "Our whole style is based on the seamless mixing of styles. So who better to produce the next Linkin Park album?" he said to *Rolling Stone* when the band first announced it would be working with him. The members of Linkin Park had made a list of possible producers to work with and Rubin was the name at the top. Said lead singer Chester Bennington, "If you don't think about working with Rick Rubin then you're probably an idiot, you know what I mean? We decided to approach him, and after meeting with him we didn't even bother with meeting with anybody else. He seemed really into shaking things up as far as what we were going to do musically and lyrically. We were looking for a new direction and we knew he was going to get us there."

DJ Joseph Hahn said on the group's website, "Fortunately for us, Rick lives in L.A. and we got to meet up at his house and talk about music, life, and approaches to writing, and just kind of have real casual conversation and get to know each other as people. And we really took a liking to him as he did to us, and the more we talked to him it just kind of made sense that we'd try working with him." Chester Bennington said of Rubin, "He wanted to see how open the band was to maybe approaching making music in a different way. . . . He told us: 'Make music you're inspired by, regardless of the way you think you're supposed to sound.'"

In a note to Linkin Park fans on their official website, Shinoda wrote, "We were looking for someone with experience in diverse musical styles, whose music taste is as diverse as ours. Seeing that Rick has produced albums for groups like Red Hot Chili Peppers, Slayer, Beastie Boys, Neil Diamond, Jay Z, and Johnny Cash, I think it's safe to say that he's pretty versatile. The other guys have put me in charge of production on our end, so you'll see that the production credit on the next record will read, 'Rick Rubin and Mike Shinoda.' I have to thank the guys in a huge way for trusting me with this honor and challenge — we're going to make a great record. As for the sound of it, I think you will recognize our style and personality in the sound, but we definitely want to step outside the box and make something new and different. We have been challenging ourselves to do something that will keep all the things we/you like about Linkin Park, and then add new sounds and styles that you've never heard from us." To be co-producing an album with Rick Rubin was a landmark experience for Shinoda. "I was raised on his music and to now be working with him, to be mentored by him, is such a huge thing," he told *Rolling Stone*.

Said Rick Rubin to MTV as the band was working on the album, "They really are reinventing themselves. It doesn't sound like rap-rock.

There's very strong songwriting. I've heard guys in the band say that it transcends everything they've done before, like it puts them in a whole different light in their minds, and they really like that. It's very melodic. It's a progressive record." From the outset of the project, Linkin Park was clear that they didn't want to complete the "trilogy" with another album in the same ilk as their previous two. Rubin told Linkin Park, "Whatever you think your fans want to hear, whatever music you think you need to make, whatever limitations you think you have, just forget about it. Throw everything out of the window because none of it matters. What's important is making music you're inspired by." This advice was just what the band wanted to hear; the combination of the producer's adventurous nature and Linkin Park's desire to push its musical boundaries would prove magical. As Bennington said, "We went to great distances and lengths to change the sound of the band, discovering how to write songs that didn't corrupt what we'd already created."

The change for Linkin Park began by de-emphasizing the rap side of their sound, which left Mike Shinoda out of his traditional role. Recalled Bennington to *Rolling Stone*, "Mikes was like, 'I wrote myself out of the record.' There's not a lot of Mike on this record — there's a couple of songs he's rapping on, he has a couple of songs he's singing on, he's singing a lot of harmonies and playing a lot of guitar. And, you know, he produced this record as well, so it was interesting. I questioned that early on, like, 'Hey there, what are you doing? Maybe we should try some rapping or more of you.' And he was like 'No, no, no. This is all you, dude.'"

The group was completely open to Rubin's suggestions. "We took everything Rick said to heart," said Bennington. "We have a lot of respect for him and he's got great taste in music and a really good ear so if he was like, 'Let's try this beat,' we really tried everything." One of the major suggestions Rubin made was to fundamentally alter the way Linkin Park constructed songs. Lead guitarist Brad Delson explained to *Entertainment Weekly*, "We've made a number of records, and we went into this process thinking we knew what we were doing. In the past we wrote all our music, we structured it, it was pretty much set, and then we put vocals on for the very last part of the recording process. And Chester and Mike had the stressful challenge of coming up with melodies and words that were as good as the music. In this case, Rick didn't want us polishing anything. We would look at the song in its roughest form and see if it was great. And if it wasn't, we'd move on and write another song." Said Bennington of the process, "It's fun. We all get a chance to release and contribute creatively. . . . We'll come up with ideas individually then come together and work on it as a band. We decide together what direction the songs will go. . . . [In the early stages of writing] we're working out our individual parts first. Each of the guys write their own part for their own instrument. But we have a band meeting every week, and we partner up on a lot of what we're doing. We get together at the studio every week and listen to each other's stuff. Then we all get to decide what to keep, what to change and help each other with what we've been working on."

Bassist David "Phoenix" Farrell said of songwriting: "I think you'll always be striving to write that 'perfect song.' I think anytime I sit down and work on something that's kinda the starting goal? . . . *Hybrid Theory* is an album that, for us, will always hold a special place in our hearts, as far as being, you know, that first album, and the beginnings of everything we were doing . . . and *Meteora* was an extension on that, and us starting to really branch out and try different ways of approaching songwriting, different sounds, incorporating different keys for us and things like that. And that really opened the door for us to write the album we're working on now, as far as being comfortable saying, 'You know what, let's sit down and make music, and let's pick the favorite stuff that we're writing out of everything that comes out of it,' regardless of whether it sounds like 'Linkin Park,' and that's just what happens with it. And that's really what we're doing with this album. It still has our sound, I believe, but at the same time the feel of it is different, there's a lot of things going on differently, and there are lyrical themes and moods and feels on this album that are very new and exciting for us."

On the guys' different roles in crafting a Linkin Park song, Bennington said, "Usually, Mike and I write lyrics, and the rest of the guys write their parts to them. Brad is really great at structuring the songs. It's obviously a lot of work." Splitting up the lyrics between Bennington and Shinoda worked well, said Bennington. "We both have our own personal things we write about, so some of the songs start out separately then we put them together and work on them together. But we both have songs that we've written on our own. Usually we tweak each other's stuff and go from there." Shinoda found that the songs he was writing were more melodic than rap-heavy, perhaps due to his co-producer's influence. Rick Rubin encouraged Linkin Park to listen to other kinds of music while working on the album, like Pink Floyd, Elton John, King Crimson, and Emerson, Lake & Palmer among others. Said Shinoda to *Billboard*, "The thing about Rick that I love is he's unpredictable. He'll listen to a song and throw out an idea that seems completely out of nowhere, but it makes a lot of sense and it makes the song better." After a year of writing produced 150 completed demos, by the band's count, Rubin proudly felt, heading into principal recording, "These are really beautiful songs. They've outdone themselves."

Shinoda said of their producer, "At the core of his being, Rick understands so much. He doesn't have to work for it. So in the studio, there's no thought, there's just feeling." Comparing Don Gilmore, the producer who worked on *Hybrid Theory* and *Meteora*, to Rick Rubin, Mike Shinoda wrote, "Don was a lot of fun to work with . . . because he's really silly in the studio, and he makes great, exciting rock records. He has a very distinctive style. Rick is a legend. He's one of the most respected producers of all time. He can listen to a song one time, and immediately give you five things that you can do to it that will make it better. He knows his way around just about every type of music, and can really get your ideas and momentum going."

Minutes to Midnight was recorded at Rubin's Laurel Canyon mansion. The less formal environment suited Linkin Park. Said Delson to *Entertainment Weekly*, "It's a really famous — or infamous — place. It had a timeless feel. You're almost not sure which decade it's in. I think that's reflected on the record, whether it was the Motown-inspired drums, or different pianos we experimented with, or vintage amps, or totally new electronic sounds." While the group had traditionally kept to their principal instruments, Delson explained, "All six of us played really anything and everything instrument wise on this record. There were no boundaries in terms of what someone could contribute or how they could contribute to the creation of these songs. It was really a product of collaboration by all six of us." To create the sound of *Minutes to Midnight,* the band experimented with "many guitar sounds and styles," said Bennington. "[We] tried many drum kits, played banjo and xylophones, a lot of crazy stuff." Added Shinoda to *indieLondon,* "We wrote in new ways, and used instruments and equipment that we hadn't experimented with, from vintage guitars and amps to mellotron to Rick's original 808 drum machine he used on the Beastie Boys' first record." While exploring these new sounds, Rubin "brought in a lot of perspective and a kind of a really great way of being able to guide us through a really challenging process and to do so while simultaneously creating a really positive and open atmosphere," said Delson to *Ultimate Guitar.* "Rick is really a big picture guy."

On the album, Delson used Paul Reed Smith guitars as well as vintage gear. "Stuff like a 1950s Stratocaster, a vintage Les Paul, a Fender Jaguar, a Fender Telecaster and I completely abandoned the amps I was using. There really is no Dual Rectifier or any new Marshall on this record. I mainly used a vintage Soldano, a vintage Hi-Watt, a Sears amp and an AC-30 for my clean tones. I also had this really rare piece of gear which we called the 'Bo Diddley' amp. . . . Our engineer had only seen this amp in a magazine before. He had never seen one in person and we were able to find one and rent it for the recording sessions. And it had this incredible clean tone." Delson also experimented with other amps: "I found and got a lot of cool combinations between amps. I used a Soldano and Hi-Watt in combination and sometimes, I'd mix in, like, an old JCM800 amp where it created a really unique heavy tone. I wanted to do things differently with each song, so we weren't married to one particular setup. It was like whatever sounded the best."

A standout track for Bennington was "The Little Things Give You Away." Calling it "the pinnacle of what we can achieve as a band," he went on to describe it to MTV: "It's an epic song, but it's also kind of delicate in a lot of ways. There's a great guitar riff that comes in acoustically, and the words really say a lot. And I think that they'll touch people in a way Linkin Park haven't touched people before. And there's a breakdown that's my favorite moment on the record. It's beautiful and timeless-sounding, with this great synth sound . . . and Brad [Delson] breaks into this beautiful solo and it just builds and builds and builds until it breaks down into this a cappella section. It's a huge explosion of sound, over six minutes long, and it's truly, completely amazing. And I can't wait for people to hear it." A track like "In Between" epitomized many of the changes in Linkin Park's sound, featuring a cello, a sample beat, and Mike Shinoda singing lead vocals. To MTV, Bennington described "Bleed It Out" as "a song that rides the line of what you might expect from us. It's got rapping on it and a real big chorus, but it's also got these great Motown drums and a real party vibe to it. So it's something different too. It's fun."

Of *Minutes to Midnight* as a whole, Bennington said, "Rick has brought more of a stripped down, classic rock and hip hop kind of feel. We're using vintage guitars and drums carved out of wood and skin for more of a tribal sound. It's definitely not nu metal." Delson praised Rubin for providing the band with "really smart guidance" over the 17-month-long process that it took to create the album. Speaking to *Ultimate Guitar*, Delson reasoned that Linkin Park had "had a lot of success making songs with a definitive sound and style and so to really start over and to do something totally new and unproven was a huge risk for the band. And with great risk can also come great reward so our hope is that when people listen to this album that they can connect with, as much as [possible], all six of us — really all seven of us when you include Rick — connect with each of the songs that we chose."

Linkin Park had definitely shaken off their old sound with *Minutes to Midnight*, and Shinoda hoped that the band would soon lose the label the media and industry had given them. "People have always tried to lump us in with the whole rap/rock stereotype, but we don't intentionally want to be part of that scene. We've always had our own personality and I think it really shows on this record." Bennington echoed his bandmate when he spoke to Reuters, "There's still a hip hop element to us, and there'll always be. We've really moved away from anything that sounds like nu metal. I know that we kind of helped create, I guess, the sound of that genre, but I hate that genre. I'm not going to speak for everyone, but I can personally tell you

that I am not a big fan of almost everybody in that category. There are a few bands that I don't really believe belong in there, and we're one of those bands."

Said Linkin Park's bassist, "We've really challenged ourselves to do things differently than the way we've done them in the past. I think it's produced an album that is a little more broad in its emotional range, and it's a little more organic in how it came together." Delson was proud of the album and hoped that the band's enthusiasm for the album would translate to its fans. "We really just wanted to make the most honest record and the most exciting record for us," Delson told *Entertainment Weekly*. "We have the philosophy that if all six of us love a song, that there's a probability that someone else in the world will also like it. Every song [on] the record is a song that we all *love*."

The process of whittling down the 150 songs the band wrote to the final track list of 12 was laborious (and one of the reasons it took so long for the band to get the album finished). As with some of his other acts, Rubin suggested a democratic process for song selection. "There's a grading system for everything and there's also voting," said Bennington to *Rolling Stone*. "We graded everything, voted, graded them again, and voted again and that process just happened throughout. It was very tedious. Sometimes democracy felt like it wasn't a very good idea, but the end result was that we all walked away with a record that was lyrically stronger, very musical, really well written. [We all] thought we could live with this one. This one's good." And the sales figures for *Minutes to Midnight* agreed with the band's assessment. Released in May 2007, the album debuted at #1 in 15 countries, including on the U.S. Billboard Top 200 Album Chart, moving 625,000 copies in its first week of sales. Driven by the single "What I've Done," the album went platinum worldwide that same week.

CHAPTER 27

Metallica
Death Magnetic

AFTER 2003'S *ST. ANGER* WAS widely received as a failure, Metallica cleaned house, dismissing long-time producer Bob Rock, and enlisted Rick Rubin. The band's decision to part company with their producer was partly because of his over-involvement. Lead singer James Hetfield said to *Kerrang*, "On *St. Anger*, Bob Rock did everything. He was producer, engineer, bass player, babysitter, father figure — and Rick Rubin is pretty much the opposite, he's not there to babysit. When he first came in, his opening statement was 'I want you guys to impress me: I want you to feel like you're starting out again.' He really wants us to get in the mindset of *Master of Puppets*. It's impossible to recreate what we were 20 years ago, it's silly, but we had to get that hunger back." Drummer Lars Ulrich felt the band had exhausted their creative relationship with Bob Rock after so many years working together. "In 1990, when we started using Bob, it was because Bob made all the best rock records that were going on at that time — Mötley Crüe, David Lee Roth, The Cult — and he was involved in the engineering of all the Bon Jovi records. Everything that was going on in the late '80s was all about Bob Rock. And now, everything that's great about rock, from Slipknot to System of a Down to the Chili Peppers to Mars Volta, and even the Johnny Cash and Neil Diamond records, it's all Rick Rubin. The same thing that brought us to Bob 15 years ago is now kind of bringing us to Rick. We want to work with the guy who's got the total finger on the pulse. And Bob was the first one to bless it, to say, 'Look, I don't know what else I can offer you 15 years later.'" Rubin would bring "a whole new energy and dynamic" to Metallica.

Instead of trying out some new sound for the legendary band, Rubin pushed Metallica back to their roots. "I asked them not to reinvent themselves so much as to make a defining album, like the purest of what Metallica is. That's the aim," said Rubin to MTV. The producer had seen the 2004 documentary *Some Kind of Monster* and was justifiably a bit nervous to begin working with the band. "Then we started working, and it's the opposite direction of that. They're really productive, really communicative — it seems like they really like being in the room together. It's a great process. They say they're more excited than they have been in a long time about making music." Said Hetfield to *NRK*, "Rick is extremely good at getting the best out of any artist he's worked with. . . . He's got a good vibe, and a good ear, and we think we do too. So sometimes there's a little bit of this — we like our things the way we like them, he likes his things the way he likes them — but with two great powers putting something together, I think we'll come up with something pretty amazing."

Working with Rubin on the new album was a big change from working with Rock on *St. Anger*. Hetfield explained, "One thing that someone said on the last record — going through all of the cleansing, the therapy, the talking, the breaking down, the falls . . . you know, from one extreme to the other — from hating each other to not talking to hugging and crying over every note. . . . It's crazy — one [extreme] to the other. They're both unrealistic. Somewhere in the middle is where we need to live, and balance is difficult at times, especially for myself, who likes the extremes, or thinks I like them. All the work that we went through on *St. Anger*, it was said that it was not for *St. Anger*, it was for the next record, and that makes total sense. . . . This record is more us working together — in harmony, in friction, in happiness, in sadness . . . all of that put together. And we're able to get through it — we've walked though fire; we know how hot it can get, and we don't need to go through there again." The project felt full of possibility. Said Hetfield to *Revolver*, "It's like, 'Imagine if 'Tallica did a record with Rick Rubin? Whoa, what would that be like?' There's a lot of untapped stuff, and we don't know where we can go until we try."

As spring 2006 progressed, Metallica wrote material for the album and got to know Rick Rubin. "Rick's reputation is true," remarked Hetfield. "He's not showing up every day at the studio. He's there when needed and we are there flying on our own. It's very different from the last record. *St. Anger* was hours and hours of talking, talking about what was going on, what's going to happen, what will happen — all of that and going in and having coaches here and there. This one we're pretty much on our own and it does — it feels really free and really nice. There's no pressure. It feels good. Sometimes it's a little unfocused so we kind of have to crack the whip every once in a while to get everybody in there." The band wrote song after song, and when they felt they needed the producer's input, Rubin would come into the studio. "We've had half a dozen meetings with Rick," said Ulrich in *Revolver*, "and he just comes up and listens. We're just kind of feeling each other out, kind of getting to know each other. Once we start the recording phase of it, which should hopefully be this fall, that's when his big input will come."

Metallica toured in the summer of 2006 but didn't let that put a stop to their writing and rehearsing. Ulrich explained, "We did something we'd never done before: we carried a ProTools system with us. Twenty minutes before stage time, we would go into a room and play, to get the machinery moving. They were jams, riffs, fun, and games. And they were recorded. That's where 95 percent of this record came from. The working titles are the geographical locations where they came up." Touring and writing at the same time had its advantages, said Hetfield from the road. "It gets your chops up again, gets your voice back in shape, it helps you remember why you are doing it, you see all the fans out there, it inspires you, and you go back in the studio with a fresh new appreciation of why you have this gift. So the live show, the whole thing, inspires the studio." And playing songs from *Master of Puppets* during shows helped the band "revitalize some of that stuff in us," said Ulrich. "It's been kind of fun having that in the back of our mind."

Though they had written and recorded *St. Anger* at the same time, Metallica returned to the more traditional model of writing first and recording after. "It's James and me going through riff tapes and picking out the best riffs, and then molding songs around that," said Ulrich. "This is like what we used to do back in the day: sit down, write a bunch of songs, then uproot and go somewhere else and record them." Though Hetfield and Ulrich were at the structural helm, the rest of the group was involved too. The creative process for Metallica "changed a bit over time," Hetfield told *Blistering Metal News*, "from Lars and I sitting in a room putting things together to including everyone, and now it's kind of a combination of both. I'll bring some things into the hat that already have lyrics or something, or Lars will come in with certain ideas, and we'll all have individual ideas, but we'll also create things together." Ulrich found the amount of material the band came up with "a little overwhelming," he told *Revolver*. "So we're trying to be as self-critical as possible. It's great with Rick, because he doesn't really have any baggage with us. He just comes in and says, 'That's great. That's not so great.' . . . We're having fun again, which we didn't for many, many years in the '90s, and in some way, it feels to me like it's kind of come full circle in that all the external crap and all the extracurricular stuff has kind of subsided and now it's just a bunch of guys hanging out in a rehearsal space/studio, having a lot of fun together and sweating and laughing and making music, and kind of . . . to me, doing what this band has always been about, and . . . bringing it back to its kind of point of origin."

Metallica would only start recording once their material was as ready as it could be. Said Ulrich, "Rick Rubin doesn't want us to start recording until every song that we're gonna do is as close to 100 percent as we can get it." Hetfield explained, "Rick wants us to take care of all the creative elements first. He wants us to capture these songs in a recording environment instead of creating them there." Rubin continued to help the band choose the best of their in-progress material. Speaking to the *New York Times*, Rubin said, "Lars will play two things for me, and I'll say, 'This one is great and that one is terrible.' Lars will say: 'How do you know? They both sound good to me.' Well, I just know. The right sound reaches its hand out and finds its way. So much of what I do is just being present and listening for that right sound." Once the guys had chosen 20 songs, Rubin worked with them to whittle the list down to 14. (The album ended up with 10 tracks, some over eight minutes long.) "He won't say 'This fucking sucks,'" said Hetfield to *Kerrang*, "but he'll make suggestions and I'm definitely open to that. With *St. Anger*, it became so open-minded that it became unfocused. This time around, there's a lot of 'Sorry, it's not good enough.' We're aiming for excellence."

Ulrich was excited to start recording the final songs. Speaking to New York's Q104.3 before the band began recording, he said, "It's been about a year of writing and getting ideas together and the whole thing — going through a couple of years' worth of riffs and all this stuff. We started out about six months ago with about 25 songs and now we've narrowed those down to 14, and we're gonna start recording 14 songs. So we're all pretty stoked. . . . Rick's big thing is to kind of have all these songs completely embedded in our bodies [and] just go in [the studio] and execute them. . . . You leave the creative element of the process out of the recording, so you go in and basically just record a bunch of songs that you know inside out and upside down and you don't have to spend too much of your energy in the recording studio, creating and thinking and analyzing and doing all that stuff. His whole analogy is the recording process becomes more like a gig — just going in and playing and leaving all the thinking at the door."

Once Metallica entered the studio with Rubin they found the producer no less demanding of excellence — and willing to ditch the band's signature '90s sound. Revealed Ulrich, "He's questioning what key we should play in. We've played in E flat since the beginning of the '90s. Nobody questioned it. All of a sudden, Rick is going, 'Maybe the stuff has more energy and Hetfield's voice sounds better in E.' He's forced us to rethink big-picture stuff, something we haven't done in years." Though Rubin came to the studio every day, his role was not to nitpick, but to think about the album as a whole. "He's all about the big picture," said Lars to *Metal Hammer*. "He doesn't analyze things like drum tempos. . . . He's more about the feel: is everyone playing together? Rick's a vibe guy." From bassist Rob Trujillo's perspective, Rubin "makes suggestions, and you try them: some of them are great, and some of them aren't gonna work — but that's okay. Some of his words of wisdom were very inspirational in bringing the band back to the old school, and getting James and Lars to step back in time. It's pretty exciting, although it's not like there haven't been any head-butting contests: there's been a little bit of that, but sometimes that little bit of tension is good for the tracks."

Guitarist Kirk Hammett described the album as having "a lot of really, really fast songs, a whole lot of really heavy stuff. We changed our approach to writing the songs. . . . We tuned the guitars back up to what they originally were for the first five albums. Because we've done that, James' voice sounds more like it did in the '80s than it did in the '90s." The changes made the band feel like they'd gone back in time. Hammett said, "It's our eleventh studio album, but it feels like our sixth. It's just a really spectacular range of songs. This time we're not afraid to refer to our past music in order to create future music. People will see that we've kind of embraced our old vocabulary again and are using that vocabulary to express new things." Trujillo described the album as shaping up to be "dynamic, heavy, groovin' and you'll prob-ably be excited to know that there will be guitar solos on it! In addition, Lars remembered to tune his snare drum properly this time! For me, this album incorporates part of the dynamic and character of *Master of Puppets*, as well as the melodic style that people liked in the *Black Album*, as far as the melodies are concerned." With *Master of Puppets* as their main inspiration, James Hetfield said they also kept the spirit of deceased bassist Cliff Burton alive during recording sessions. "We talk about what Cliff would think and what he would have added. And now, especially with our new bassist Rob playing so powerful and with his fingers just like Cliff, I have a feeling that he likes what we're doing."

Hammett described the sound of the album to *NME* in July 2007, before the band went on the road again. "The music is really heavy — surprise, surprise — very, very progressive; different from anything we've ever done." Hetfield said of *Death Magnetic*, "The direction is embracing our past in the now. We know what we know. It's hard to erase that. But to strip it down again, and get back to why we're doing this? Why did we write songs that way? The template was *Master of Puppets* and the strength of that record. How can we do that now?"

Reflecting back on the two years it took to make *Death Magnetic*, Ulrich said, "When we met with Rick [Rubin] a couple of years ago, he said he really wanted to make a record that captures the energy we produce when we play together. He felt like we'd never captured that before. When I hear this record, it sounds like that kind of energy, that kind of in-your-face pummeling kind of thing. It sounds like it's got a lot of attitude and dynamics and energy; and it sounds like a bunch of people who are alive on planet Earth and playing music together and having a pretty good time doing it." With the album complete, Ulrich looked back on how Metallica's past had inspired its present. "Reconnecting with the past was something that definitely happened organically. Rick spends a lot of time just hanging out and talking about music, and during the first few months, he made us comfortable about revisiting and being inspired by some of the records that we put out in the '80s: *Ride the Lightning, Master of Puppets, . . . And Justice for All*. When we finished *Justice*, we felt there was nothing more to do on that progressive, thrashy side of Metallica, so we spent the better part of the '90s running as far away from those records as we could. Rick made us feel okay about revisiting those records. . . . Rick would suggest, 'Listen to the same records that you listened to in the '80s, or try and write the same way.' It was never, 'Copy what you were doing musically.' It was, 'Put yourself in that headspace.' And it felt really good to do that, finally. We avoided going there for so long, but when we finally went back, it was like: 'Yeah, we can hang out here — we can be inspired by those records and feel good about it.'"

On working with Rick Rubin, Lars Ulrich said, "I've known Rick for a long time. I've known him longer than I've known Bob Rock. He's always been a friend, and I've always wondered what it would be like to work with him. It was great. We needed to make a change, and we made a change. We kind of let Rick steer the ship; me and James especially tried to hang back and let Rick make all the big-picture decisions. Rick is very different from Bob. He has a very different way of doing things. Rick is not a musician; he's not a 'technical' guy. He's the kind of guy who hangs out on the couch and listens to songs with his eyes closed and says, 'Why don't we try this or that?' It's a very different kind of thing. He doesn't sit there and go, 'Double the last chords up' or 'Go to F-sharp instead of G. He's more 'big picture.' He says things like, 'You guys aren't playing together. Play together. Listen to each other when you're playing.' That's the kind of comments you get back, more so than, 'Play some different notes on the guitar solo.' He's not that specific. He's got a different kind of way of doing things than anyone we've ever worked with. . . . [He's] intuitive. It feels like there's an element of — and I mean this in a positive way — an element of chaos."

Lars Ulrich felt Rubin helped him play the drums more organically. "He pushed me to listen to the other guys. We have this tendency towards, 'You start with the drums, and then you add this, and this . . .' like you're building a house, with the drums the foundation and everything else an afterthought. But he didn't want that — he wanted us all to play together and interact with each other." For Hammett, it was Rubin's suggestion they recapture the energy on early Metallica records. "The attitude we had back then was a lot different to the attitude we have now. We were young, eager to prove ourselves — eager to prove that we were one of the heaviest bands around — and we wrote accordingly. So Rick said, 'Just put yourselves in that spot.' And it totally worked. It worked across the board: in the writing, the lyrics, the guitar solos, the attitude. . . . I really felt that we were going somewhere fresh and new."

Of the completed *Death Magnetic*, Ulrich said, "I love the way the album sounds. Rick pushed it as far as he needs to go. Did he push it too far, farther than some people wanted? Absolutely. In a world of compression, maybe it's too hot for some people. But there is some perverse beauty in knowing that a Metallica record is considered too loud." James Hetfield addressed the complaints some fans had on the overall sound: "Rick Rubin's opinion [was] that the production on *Death Magnetic* makes the album sound livelier. I'm inclined to agree with him. I think it sounds pretty cool. I think it sounds good and raw and in the moment. It's less than per-

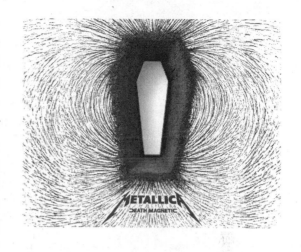

fect, but I like that aspect of it. In the past, we've gone to great pains to eliminate any kind of digital distortion or redlining. I think for these songs — and the concept of this record — it sounds good. . . . The kind of sound that Rick Rubin goes for — which is pushing the limits. We went back and forth with the sound of the record. I was one of the first ones to notice the compression was affecting the overall sound, but when we took it away, something was missing . . . some of the liveliness went away with it. So after comparing both directions, we said, 'This sounds better.'" Hetfield concluded, "*Death Magnetic* is Rick Rubin and us trying to capture the essence, the hunger, the simplicity, the skeleton of Metallica. And that's what I think we captured." Enthused Trujillo to MTV, "One of the coolest things was Rick actually suggested that we all stand up and rock out, like we would live. And we did, and it put a lot of life into the basic tracking of it all. It was almost to the point where, when I was retracking stuff, I was standing up, headbanging. I'd never done that in a recording situation before. He's a great song doctor, and he has great ears."

Released on September 12, 2008, *Death Magnetic* sold nearly half a million copies in just three days, debuting at #1 on Billboard's Top 200 Album Chart. The album was a triumphant comeback for Metallica. *Rolling Stone* declared in its four-star review that *Death Magnetic* was "a sudden act of aggression from a sleeping giant. . . . This album is Metallica becoming Metallica again. . . . At their best, they combine the melodic smarts of Metallica's mature work with the fully armed-and-operational battle power of their early days." *Billboard* said of the album's producer, "Rubin understands the core of Metallica's greatness and gently steers them back to basics." Certified platinum within a month of release, Metallica went on to receive four Grammy nominations and won Best Metal Performance, while Rubin won Producer of the Year for the second time.

CHAPTER 28

Rick Rubin,
Record Executive

In 2007, Rick Rubin's career came full circle, as he returned to the A&R focus of his earliest days with Def Jam. Lured away from American Recordings' parent label Warner Bros. by Columbia Records with the position of label head, *Billboard* reported that Rubin "would 'form a dynamic and creative executive partnership' with Columbia chairman Steve Barnett, under a new model devised by Sony Music topper Rob Stringer." The significance of this news was overshadowed only by Rubin's multiple Grammy nominations for his production work, including the much-coveted Producer of the Year award. Of his accomplishments, *Time* observed that "Rubin's dominance of this year's Grammy Album category is unprecedented" and described his range as "essentially limitless." That range was Rubin's greatest capital as a record executive: his platinum instinct crossed genres. His job at Columbia Records as co-chairman was fundamentally to listen and to tackle the larger issues facing the ailing industry plagued by declining CD sales and rampant illegal downloading. The deal's terms were as vague and non-specific as the record industry's future, with the *New*

York Times reporting that Rubin wanted freedom and not to have to "punch a clock" or work in a traditional corporate way.

While Rubin seemed nonchalant about a position which would terrify most fellow executives, the producer took his job as record executive as seriously as he did that of producer. He had started his career as both label head and in-studio producer, and while the Columbia job was more mainstream and corporate than anything he'd done before, Rubin had always kept a full vision of a project, and of his label, in mind as part of his work — artwork, marketing, videos, brand building, and so on. Not everyone was confident that Rubin would take to the role, given his historically unconventional approach to the business. But some industry veterans showed their support. Legendary record mogul David Geffen (whose label had once distributed Rubin's) reasoned that the decision to bring Rubin in made sense. The panicked industry may be focused on how to *sell* music, but Rick Rubin had always been focused on *making* great music first and that should be the aim of a record company. Said Geffen to the *New York Times*, "[Columbia parent company] Sony was very smart to hire Rick."

Antony Bland, director of A&R for American Recordings, described Rubin's focus on content and the crucial direction that it lends a record company: "Rick is really intriguing to work with because he is very, very calm, and driven by what is really great. He's very hard to please, and I think that has taught us all to really, really believe in something before we try to sign it. Having someone like that who is so musical and has such a history of working with great artists . . . makes you want to bring something in that's fantastic, and not just mediocre. Rick is going to have the final say as to what comes on [American]. If he's not passionate about something, it's probably not the greatest place for the band to be. I think his influence and his ability to direct the projects through the big Columbia system is paramount. I don't think there is anything that has been signed that he personally dislikes. . . . He's pretty harsh when it comes to things we bring him. I've walked in with things that I really thought had merit, and to his credit, he'll give it a listen and say, 'No, it's not there.' I can't say he's been wrong about anything I've brought in."

Rick Rubin at home in 2007. (© AP Photo/Damian Dovarganes)

Warner Bros. CEO Tom Whalley had recognized Rubin's tremendous impact back in 2005, when Rubin moved distribution of American Recordings to Warner Bros. Whalley noted, "Rick has been a driving creative force in popular music for two decades, discovering new artists, nurturing established ones, and bringing about their success time and again." Despite a very stormy time for the record industry, Rubin's move to Warner Bros. had reflected the importance he placed on patience and open-mindedness toward artist development. Rubin praised Whalley's continued emphasis on "grass roots development of artists and the importance of growing real careers in a time when most executives are looking for short-term success, which ultimately yields short-sighted goals. Tom understands that if artists are developed and nurtured the right way from the beginning, they'll stick around for a long time."

Arriving in his new role, Rubin thought Columbia Records was "stuck in the dark ages" with the rest of the majors. Addressing why he had opted to take on the monumental responsibility of turning that figurative Titanic around, Rubin initially quipped, "I thought it would be an interesting challenge." That the company recruited Rubin was a sign of the times, that the industry's future required revolutionary change and for Columbia that started with an unorthodox hire. Rubin described his purpose there as "protect[ing] the label from itself": returning the focus to the music and making the label relevant as the new business model for the industry as a whole evolves. The old model — of controlled retail and media channels for the majors to push their product through to the end user — was crumbling and Columbia wanted Rubin to find new ways for a "dinosaur" to survive and thrive. Of course there were no easy answers, but flexibility and conceptual change seemed Rubin's themes for the company's future.

Music fans had driven album sales since the dawn of the business, and Rubin felt the industry had fallen out of favor with the fans, and buyers, of its content. The proliferation of illegal downloading, said Rubin, may have something to do with the music not being worth the price being charged for it. Producer-driven recording, where artists are interchangeable and track after track ends up sounding the same, lends a disposable air to music, something that's supposed to outlast the generation who created it. Self-described as a music fan, Rick Rubin's own distaste for his industry had the potential to change it from the inside. Rubin thought the noise of the industry machine had drowned out the ability and objectivity to hear greatness, costing labels not only substantial financial losses but the vital flexibility and freedom to recognize "when something is revolutionary." Arguing that the current state of crisis is a telltale sign that the music industry's evolution is well underway, he encouraged bravery in the major labels' choices.

After the cheers that Rubin was in a new power position and cries that he had sold-out died down, it was difficult to ascertain what, in hard terms, was Rubin's grand vision for the industry. The music media grabbed on to the idea of a subscription model when Rubin mentioned it in a *New York Times* profile piece and made a fuss when he moved Columbia's offices to a cushier location in Beverly Hills. By the time the Grammys rolled around in 2009, with Rubin nominated again for Producer of the Year, there were rumors that his influence at Columbia was declining after nearly two years of producing hit records for other majors and not bringing in big-name or high-selling acts to his own. With three years left in his contract with the company and revolutionary change impossible to enact in a brief tenure, only time will tell what effect on the industry at large Rubin's role at Columbia Records will ultimately have.

But fans of the producer's work can rest easy: he continues to thrive in the studio. Winning that Producer of the Year Grammy again, Rick Rubin had a few notable releases for 2009, with the Gossip's *Music for Men* and The Avett Brothers' *I & Love & You*, both for Columbia. The producer continued to work with a wide range of artists who lined up for time with the legend — Josh Grobin, rapper The Clipse, ZZ Top, Crosby Stills and Nash. . . . Rubin also had a hand in the deal that saw Jay-Z leave Def Jam for Columbia sister-label Epic, in advance of the rapper's highly anticipated *Blueprint 3*.

While Rick Rubin has clearly begun the next chapter in his legendary story, it is his loyalty to his existing legacy that made him arguably the most influential producer for over two decades and is responsible for his continued success. Rubin attributes that success to very simple core principles: try to understand culture as well as music, surround yourself with people interested in music for the right reasons, and be true to the things you love. For Rubin, his great love and fandom for music has lead to honesty and purity in his work. And like any good documentary filmmaker, Rubin's fame comes from his invisibility. Rubin's close friend comedian Chris Rock sums it up succinctly: "Most producers have their own sound, and they lease it out to different people, but we know it's still their record. The records you make with Rick are your records. He makes it his job to squeeze the best out of you — and not leave any fingerprints." Still, without doubt, his impact has been felt by a generation of music fans who would readily credit Rubin with producing the soundtrack of their lifetime.

Selected Discography

Year	Song/Album	Artist	Label
1983	*Hose*	Hose	Def Jam Recordings
1984	"It's Yours"	T La Rock	Def Jam Recordings
1985	"Def Jam"/"Cold Chillin' in the Spot"	Jazzy Jay	Def Jam Recordings
1985	"It's the Beat"	Hollis Crew	Def Jam Recordings
1985	*Krush Groove — Music from the Original Motion Picture Soundtrack*	Various	Warner Bros.
1985	*Radio*	LL Cool J	Def Jam Recordings
1985	*Rock Hard*	Beastie Boys	Def Jam Recordings
1985	"This Is It"/"Beat the Clock"	Jimmy Spicer	Def Jam Recordings
1986	"Can You Feel It?"/"Knowledge Me"	Original Concept	Def Jam Recordings
1986	*Licensed to Ill*	Beastie Boys	Def Jam Recordings
1986	*Raising Hell*	Run-DMC	London Records
1986	*Reign in Blood*	Slayer	Def Jam Recordings
1986	"The Word"/"Sardines"	The Junkyard Band	Def Jam Recordings
1987	*Electric*	The Cult	Sire Records Company
1987	*It's Tricky (And More)*	Run-DMC	London Records
1987	*Less Than Zero*	Various	Def Jam Recordings
1987	*Yo! Bum Rush the Show*	Public Enemy	Def Jam Recordings
1988	*Christmas in Hollis*	Run-DMC	Profile Records
1988	*Danzig*	Danzig	Def American Recordings

Year	Song/Album	Artist	Label
1988	*Masters of Reality*	Masters of Reality	Def American Recordings
1988	*South of Heaven*	Slayer	Def Jam Recordings
1988	*Tougher than Leather*	Run-DMC	Metronome
1989	*Dice*	Andrew "Dice" Clay	Def American Recordings
1989	*Live Fast, Die Fast*	Wolfsbane	Def American Recordings
1990	*Danzig II: Lucifuge*	Danzig	Def American Recordings
1990	*Decade of Aggression Live*	Slayer	Def American Recordings
1990	*Seasons in the Abyss*	Slayer	Def American Recordings
1990	*The Day the Laughter Died*	Andrew "Dice" Clay	Def American Recordings
1990	*Trouble*	Trouble	Def American Recordings
1991	*American Grafishy*	Flipper	Def American Recordings
1991	*Blood Sugar Sex Magik*	Red Hot Chili Peppers	Warner Bros. Records
1991	*Nobody Said It Was Easy*	The Four Horsemen	Def American Recordings
1992	*Baby Got Back*	Sir Mix-a-Lot	Phonogram
1992	*Danzig III: How the Gods Kill*	Danzig	Def American Recordings
1992	*Dice's Greatest (Bleeped) Bits*	Andrew "Dice" Clay	Def American Recordings
1992	*King King*	The Red Devils	Def American Recordings
1992	*Manic Frustration*	Trouble	Def American Recordings
1992	*The Witch*	The Cult	Sire Records Company
1993	"Big Gun," *Last Action Hero*	AC/DC	Columbia

Year	Song/Album	Artist	Label
1993	"Disorder," *Judgment Night (Music from the Motion Picture)*	Slayer	Epic
1993	"Mary Jane's Last Dance," *Greatest Hits*	Tom Petty	MCA
1993	"Search and Destroy," *The Beavis And Butthead Experience*	Red Hot Chili Peppers	Geffen Records
1993	*21st Century Jesus*	Messiah	WHTE LBLS
1993	*The Day the Laughter Died Part II*	Andrew "Dice" Clay	American Recordings
1993	*Thrall-Demonsweatlive*	Danzig	Def American Recordings
1993	*Wandering Spirit*	Mick Jagger	Atlantic
1994	*40 Too Long*	Andrew "Dice" Clay	American Recordings
1994	*American Recordings*	Johnny Cash	American Recordings
1994	*Danzig 4P*	Danzig	American Recordings
1994	*Deconstruction*	Deconstruction	American Recordings
1994	*Dice*	Andrew "Dice" Clay	American Recordings
1994	*Dice Rules*	Andrew "Dice" Clay	American Recordings
1994	*Divine Intervention*	Slayer	American Recordings
1994	*Live Rare Remix Box*	Red Hot Chili Peppers	Warner Bros. Records
1994	*The Plasma Shaft*	Red Hot Chili Peppers	Warner Bros. Records
1994	*Wildflowers*	Tom Petty	Warner Bros. Records
1995	"I Found Out," *Working Class Hero — A Tribute to John Lennon*	Red Hot Chili Peppers	Hollywood Records

Year	Song/Album	Artist	Label
1995	"I've Been Down," *The Basketball Diaries (Original Motion Picture Soundtrack)*	Flea	Island Records (U.S.)
1995	"Piggy (Nothing Can Stop Me Now)," *Further Down the Spiral*	Nine Inch Nails	Nothing Records
1995	*Ballbreaker*	AC/DC	EastWest Records America
1995	*Empty*	God Lives Underwater	American Recordings
1995	*God Lives Underwater*	God Lives Underwater	American Recordings
1995	*One Hot Minute*	Red Hot Chili Peppers	Warner Bros. Records
1996	"I Make My Own Rules," *Howard Stern: Private Parts (Soundtrack)*	LL Cool J, Flea, Dave Navarro, and Chad Smith	Warner Bros. Records
1996	"Pictures of Matchstick Men," *Howard Stern: Private Parts (Soundtrack)*	Ozzy Osbourne and Type O Negative	Warner Bros. Records
1996	"The Ben Stern Megamix," *Howard Stern: Private Parts (Soundtrack)*	Charlie Clouser	Warner Bros. Records
1996	*Songs and Music from the Motion Picture She's the One*	Tom Petty and the Heartbreakers	Warner Bros. Records
1996	*Sutras*	Donovan	American Recordings
1996	*Unchained*	Johnny Cash	American Recordings
1996	*Undisputed Attitude*	Slayer	American Recordings

Year	Song/Album	Artist	Label
1997	"We Will Rock You (The Rick Rubin 'Ruined' Remix," *No-One But You (Only The Good Die Young)*	Queen	Parlophone
1998	*Chef Aid: The South Park Album*	Various	American Recordings, Columbia
1998	*Diabolus in Musica*	Slayer	American Recordings
1998	*System of a Down*	System of a Down	Columbia
1998	*VH1 Storytellers*	Johnny Cash and Willie Nelson	American Recordings
1999	"Angel on My Shoulder," *Goin' Down*	Melanie C	Virgin
1999	"How Strong," *MOM 3: Music for Our Mother Ocean*	Red Hot Chili Peppers	Hollywood Records
1999	"Suddenly Monday," "Ga Ga," "Be the One," *Northern Star*	Melanie C	Virgin Records America, Inc.
1999	*Californication*	Red Hot Chili Peppers	Warner Bros. Records
1999	*Echo*	Tom Petty and the Heartbreakers	Warner Bros. Records
1999	*Peasants, Pigs & Astronauts*	Kula Shaker	Columbia
1999	*The Globe Sessions (Europe)*	Sheryl Crow	A&M Records
2000	"I Wonder What It Would Be Like," *Never Be the Same Again*	Melanie C	Virgin
2000	"School of Hard Knocks," *Little Nicky — Music from the Motion Picture*	P.O.D.	Maverick

Year	Song/Album	Artist	Label
2000	"Shame," *Loud Rocks*	System of a Down and Wu-Tang Clan	Loud Records
2000	"Snowblind," *Nativity in Black II: A Tribute to Black Sabbath*	System of a Down	Divine Recordings
2000	*American III: Solitary Man*	Johnny Cash	American Recordings
2000	*Living in the Present Future*	Eagle-Eye Cherry	Polydor
2000	*Paloalto*	Paloalto	American Recordings
2000	*Renegades*	Rage Against the Machine	Epic
2001	"No Shelter (Live at Grand Olympic Auditorium, Los Angeles, CA)" *Rock Sound Volume 49*	Rage Against the Machine	Rock Sound
2001	*Amethyst Rock Star*	Saul Williams	American Recordings
2001	*The Final Studio Recordings*	Nusrat Fateh Ali Khan	American Recordings
2001	*The Id*	Macy Gray	Epic
2001	*The War of Art*	American Head Charge	American Recordings
2001	*Toxicity*	System of a Down	Columbia, American Recordings
2002	*American IV: The Man Comes Around*	Johnny Cash	American Recordings
2002	*Audioslave*	Audioslave	Epic
2002	*By the Way*	Red Hot Chili Peppers	Warner Bros. Records
2002	*Steal This Album!*	System of a Down	Columbia, American Recordings
2002	*The Zephyr Song*	Red Hot Chili Peppers	Warner Bros. Records

Year	Song/Album	Artist	Label
2002	*We Want Fun*	Andrew W.K.	American Recordings
2003	"99 Problems," *The Black Album*	Jay-Z	Roc-A-Fella Records
2003	"Long Shadow," *White Riot Vol. One: A Tribute to the Clash*	Joe Strummer and the Mescaleros	Uncut Magazine
2003	"Redemption Song," *Streetcore*	Joe Strummer and the Mescaleros	Hellcat Records
2003	*De-Loused in the Comatorium*	The Mars Volta	Universal Records
2003	*Fortune Faded*	Red Hot Chili Peppers	Warner Bros. Records
2003	*Heroes and Villains*	Paloalto	American Recordings
2003	*Live at the Grand Olympic Auditorium*	Rage Against the Machine	Epic
2003	*Results May Vary*	Limp Bizkit	Interscope Records
2003	*Unearthed*	Johnny Cash	American Recordings, Lost Highway
2004	"A Satisfied Mind," *Kill Bill Vol. 2 — Original Soundtrack*	Johnny Cash	Maverick
2004	"Stop Fuckin Wit Me," *Crunk Juice*	Lil' Jon & the East Side Boyz	TVT Records
2004	*Armed Love*	The (International) Noise Conspiracy	American Recordings
2004	*A Small Demand*	The (International) Noise Conspiracy	Burning Heart Records
2004	*Vermilion/Scream*	Slipknot	Roadrunner Records
2004	*Vol. 3: (The Subliminal Verses)*	Slipknot	Roadrunner Records
2005	"Lean on Me," "Why," *Greatest Hitz*	Limp Bizkit	Geffen Records
2005	*12 Songs*	Neil Diamond	Columbia, American Recordings

Year	Song/Album	Artist	Label
2005	*A Missing Chromosome*	The Mars Volta	Universal Records
2005	*Fijación Oral Vol. 1*	Shakira	Epic
2005	*Hypnotize*	System of a Down	American Recordings
2005	*Make Believe*	Weezer	Geffen Records
2005	*Mezmerize*	System of a Down	Columbia, American Recordings
2005	*Oral Fixation Vol. 2*	Shakira	Epic
2005	*Out of Exile*	Audioslave	Epic
2006	"(Another Song) All Over Again," *FutureSex/Lovesounds*	Justin Timberlake	Zomba Records
2006	"Announcement Service Public," *Underground 6*	Linkin Park	Machine Shop Recordings
2006	"Qwerty," *Underground 6*	Linkin Park	Machine Shop Recordings
2006	"The Saints Are Coming," *U218 Singles*	U2 and Green Day	Mercury, Universal Island Records
2006	*American V: A Hundred Highways*	Johnny Cash	American Recordings
2006	*Stadium Arcadium*	Red Hot Chili Peppers	Warner Bros. Records
2006	*Taking the Long Way*	Dixie Chicks	Sony Music Entertainment Inc.
2007	"Window in the Skies," *U218 Singles*	U2	Mercury
2007	*Better than I've Ever Been*	KRS-One, Kanye West, Nas, and Rakim	Nike, Inc.
2007	*Free Life*	Dan Wilson	American Recordings
2007	*Luna Halo*	Luna Halo	American Recordings
2007	*Minutes to Midnight*	Linkin Park	Warner Bros. Records

Year	Song/Album	Artist	Label
2008	*Death Magnetic*	Metallica	Warner Bros. Records
2008	*Home Before Dark*	Neil Diamond	Columbia
2008	*Live in Liverpool*	The Gossip	Columbia
2008	*Mercy . . . (Dancing for the Death of an Imaginary Enemy)*	Ours	American Recordings
2008	*Seeing Things*	Jakob Dylan	Columbia, Starbucks Entertainment
2008	*The Cross of My Calling*	The (International) Noise Conspiracy	Burning Heart Records
2008	*Weezer*	Weezer	DGC, Interscope Records
2009	*Music for Men*	Gossip	Columbia
2009	*I & Love & You*	The Avett Brothers	Columbia

Selected Sources

AllMusic.com.

Billboard.com.

Binelli, Mark. "The Guru." *Rolling Stone*. September 22, 2005.

Discogs.com.

Drakoulias, George. Interview with the author.

Droney, Maureen. "Rick Rubin: Life Among the Wildflowers." *Mix Magazine*. October 2000.

duLac, J. Freedom. "The 'Song Doctor' Is In." *Washington Post*. January 15, 2006.

Fremer, Michael. "The Musicangle Interview: Producer Rick Rubin." *Musicangle*. May 1, 2004.

Glickman, Simon and Ronnie D. Lankford, Jr. "Rick Rubin Biography." MusicianGuide.com. Last accessed March 13, 2009.

Gueraseva, Stacy. *Def Jam, Inc.* New York: Ballantine Books, 2005.

Gundersen, Edna. "Rick Rubin, Music's Rock." *USA Today*. July 7, 2006.

Heller, Greg. "Rick Rubin: Behind the Beard." *Rolling Stone*. December 17, 2001.

Hilburn, Robert. "A Balance of Rattle and Om." *LA Times*. February 11, 2007.

Hirschberg, Lynn. "The Music Man." *New York Times*. September 2, 2007.

Knight, Sirona and Michael Starwyn. "The Music Wizard." Blue Sky Link (www.dcsi.net/~bluesky). Last accessed May 4, 2009.

Moss, Corey. "Rick Rubin Calls His Year 'Not Unusually Special'; Grammy Nods Tel Another Story." MTV.com. February 6, 2007.

———. "Rick Rubin's 'To Do' List: Audioslave, Peppers, System, Cash." MTV.com. March 30, 2004.

————. "Rubin Turns to Linkin Park, Weezer After Winning Buckets of Grammys." MTV.com. February 13, 2007.

MTV.com.

Ogg, Alex. *The Men Behind Def Jam: The Radical Rise of Russell Simmons and Rick Rubin.* London, U.K.: Omnibus Press, 2002.

Rabin, Nathan. "Rick Rubin." *AV Club.* January 12, 2005.

"Rick Rubin, the Man Behind the Hottest Albums." Associated Press, MSNBC.com. February 5, 2007.

RollingStone.com.

Sager, Mike. "What I've Learned: Rick Rubin." *Esquire.* February 20, 2007.

Tyrangiel, Josh. "Rick Rubin: Hit Man." *Time.* February 8, 2007.

Welch, Will. "The Intuitionist." *Fader.* August 2004.

Williams, Joy. "Interview with Rick Rubin." *Shark* (Germany) via ArtistWD.com/Joyzine. Last accessed April 27, 2009.

Wikipedia.org.

Zulaica, Don. "LiveDaily Interview: Producer Rick Rubin." *LiveDaily.* March 17, 2004.

1. *Production by Reduction: Rubin's Approach in the Studio*

Leland, John. "Neil Diamond, Unplugged and Unsequined." *New York Times.* May 22, 2005.

Moss, Corey. "What's Up with that Bearded Guy in the '99 Problems' Video?" MTV.com. April 5, 2003.

"Metallica Heading Back to Studio." Jam.Canoe.ca. February 23, 2007.

"Rick Rubin, the Man Behind the Hottest Albums." Associated Press, MSNBC.com. February 5, 2007.

2. *Growing Up in Long Island*

Rubin, Rick. "The Immortals — The Greatest Artists of All Time: 72) AC/DC." *Rolling Stone.* April 22, 2005.

————. "The Immortals — The Greatest Artists of All Time: 7) James Brown." *Rolling Stone.* April 15, 2004.

3. DJ Double R and the Birth of Def Jam

Golus, Carris. *Biography: Russell Simmons*. Minneapolis: Twenty-First
Century Books, 2007.

JayQuan. "T La Rock Interview." Tha Foundation,
thafoundation.com. September 23, 2001.

Odell, Michael. "The Greatest Songs Ever! Fight for Your Right."
Blender. February 15, 2004.

Scoppa, Bud. "George Drakoulias Interview." Taxi.com. Last accessed
January 13, 2009.

4. Run-DMC: Raising Hell and Making History

Barkan, Ryan. "An Interview with DMC of Run-DMC."
BrooklynVegan.com. December 12, 2006.

Coleman, Mark. "*Raising Hell*." *Rolling Stone*. August 28, 1986.

"Hip Hop's Greatest TV Moments: Run-DMC's 'Walk This Way.'"
VH1.com. Last accessed February 2, 2009.

Kemp, Mark. "RS Hall of Fame: Run-DMC." *Rolling Stone*.
September 5, 2002.

"Rick Rubin: Got Hell If You Want It." VH1.com. June 17, 2002.

5. Beastie Boys: Licensed to Ill

Batey, Angus. *Rhyming and Stealing*. Shropshire, U.K.: Independent
Music Press, 1998.

Heatley, Michael. *Beastie Boys: In Their Own Words*. Van Nuys, CA:
Alfred Publishing Company, 1999.

Light, Alan. "Kings of Rap." *Rolling Stone*. November 15, 1990.

————. *The Skills to Pay the Bills*. New York: Three Rivers Press,
2006.

Levine, Daniel B. "Profile: Rappers' Delight." *Guitar World*, June 1994.

Owen, Frank. "Beastie Boys II Men." *Newsday*. April 12, 1992.

Sexton, Paul. "Don't Be a Faggot." *Record Mirror* (U.K.).
February 1986.

6. Public Enemy Brings the Noise

D'Ambrosio, Antonino. "Chuck D Interview." *The Progressive.* August 2005.

Fricke, David. "*It Takes a Nation of Millions to Hold Us Back.*" *Rolling Stone.* December 15, 1988.

Pareles, Jon. "Defiance and Rage Hone a Debut Rap Album." *New York Times.* May 10, 1987.

7. Rick Rubin Goes to Hollywood

Wright, Jeb. "Joe Perry: Still Letting the Music Do the Talkin'." ClassicRockRevisited.com. April 2005.

8. The Cult: Electric

"Cult in the Act," *Kerrang* via RockIsBack.8m.com. December 1987.

Forsythe, Thomas. "Personality of the Cult." Auroral.com. 2002. Last accessed February 2, 2009.

Johnson, Howard. "And the Wall Came Tumbling Down." *Kerrang.* November 1989.

————. "Super Sonic." *Kerrang.* March 1989.

Schwartz, Robin J. "*Electric.*" *Rolling Stone.* July 2, 1987.

Worley, Gail. "He Sells Sanctuary." Ink19.com. October 2000.

9. Slayer and Danzig: From Rock to Metal

Alexander, Lorena and Greg Fasolino. "Danzig: The Legacy Continues." *Faces Magazine.* March 1989.

Atkinson, Peter. "Songs about God and Satan — Part 1: An Interview with Slayer's Kerry King." KNAC.com. April 24, 2006.

Bennett, J. "An Exclusive Oral History of Slayer." *Decibel.* August 2006.

Blush, Steven. "DANZIG," *Seconds.* January 1989.

Burk, Greg. "The Spin Interview: Glenn Danzig." *Spin.* August 2007.

Carman, Keith. "Danzig: Often Imitated, Never Duplicated," CHARTattack.com. June 28, 2005.

Chirazi, Steffan. "Now Hear This." *Kerrang* via MisfitsCentral.com. Last accessed January 13, 2009.

Considine, J.D. "Careful with That Axe, John Christ." *Musician*.
     August 1994.
Davis, Brian. "Exclusive! Interview with Slayer Guitarist Jeff
     Hanneman." KNAC.com. July 26, 2004.
Epstein, Dan. "Rebel Meets Rebel: Brandan Schieppati Interviews
     Glenn Danzig." *Revolver*. February 19, 2009.
Gamble, Billy. "Interview with Kerry King (Part 2)." antiMusic.com.
     March 2007.
Gilbert, Jeff. "The Passion of Christ." *Guitar World*. August 1994.
"Glenn Danzig — Finally Some Words About 'The Misfits,' Movies,
     and Dolls." *Rock Brigade*. October 2004.
"Interview with Kerry King." *The Age* (Australia) via Slayerized.com.
     August 2001.
"Interview with Kerry King." AntiMTV via Slayerized.com. June 2000.
"Interview with Tom Araya About the new album." KNAC.com via
     Slayerized.com. May 2001.
Kitts, Jeff. "The Dark Knight Returns." *Flux* via MisfitsCentral.com.
     September 1994.
Kulkarni, Neil. "Interview with Kerry King." *Metal Hammer*. June
     2001.
Ma, Maria. "Danzig: Def New Music." *Concrete Foundations*.
     December 10, 1988.
McNeil, Legs. "Glenn Danzig." *Spin*. January 1991.
MisfitsCentral.com.
Natanael, Christine. "Danzig with Danzig." *Metal Mania*. 1988.
Neely, Kim. "Danzig II: Lucifuge." *Rolling Stone*. October 4, 1990.
Nieradzik, Andrea. "Moaning Misfit." *Metal Hammer*. Spring 1989.
The Official Danzig Website. danzig-verotik.com. Last accessed
     May 15, 2009.
Press release for *Danzig*, 1988.
Sherman, Lee. "Danzig into the Light," *Faces*. December 1990.
"Slayer Interview." antiMusic.com. Last accessed April 28, 2009.
Slayerized.com.
Smit, Jackie. "A New Cycle Begins." ChroniclesofChaos.com.
     September 30, 2004.

Ternes, Chris. "Glenn Danzig 'Satan's Child.'" The7thHouse.com.
      November 10, 1999.
Young, Jon. "Danzig Knows the Power of the Dark Side." *Musician*.
      August 1994.

10. Building Def American

Andrews, Rob. "Danzig: Metal Muscle." *Hit Parader*. August 1992.
Browne, David. "*Seasons in the Abyss.*" *Entertainment Weekly*.
      November 9, 1990.
Kitts, Jeff. "The Dark Knight Returns." *Flux*. September 1994.
Levitan, Corey. "Danzig's 'Mother' Ship Comes In." *Circus*. May 1994.
O'Connor, Chris. "Is Glenn Danzig Rock's Rebel Angel or . . . The
      Devil, You Say?" *Eye*. May 13, 1993.
Palmer, Robert. "*Danzig III: How the Gods Kill.*" *Rolling Stone*. Posted
      on RollingStone.com January 29, 1997.
"Sympathy for the Devil." *Entertainment Weekly*. October 14, 1994.
Wild, David. "The Devil Inside." *Rolling Stone*. March 24, 1994.

11. Red Hot Chili Peppers: Blood Sugar Sex Magik

"Anthony Kiedis: Blood Synergy Sex Meltdown." *Ultimate Albums*,
      VH1.com. Last accessed April 4, 2009.
Apter, Jeff. *Fornication: The Red Hot Chili Peppers Story*. London:
      Omnibus Press, 2006.
Blackett, Matt. "Return of the Prodigal Son." *Guitar Player*.
      September 1999.
Di Perna, Alan. "Getting Better All the Time." *Guitar World*. August
      2002.
"Flea: Bass Specters Sex Madness." VH1.com. May 30, 2002.
"Funky Monks." *Guitar School*. July 1992.
Gore, Joe. "The Red Hot Chili Peppers: Gods of Sex and Funk."
      Guitar Player.
Grossman, Patrick. "For Me, There's No Difference Between the Joy
      of Life and the Joy of Death." *Galore* (Germany). March 2004.
"Is Rick There?" NME.com. January 4, 2001.
Kiedis, Anthony. *Scar Tissue*. New York: Hyperion, 2005.

"Making of *Blood Sugar Sex Magik*." Warner Bros. press package interview.

McPherson, Brian. *Get It in Writing*. Milwaukee: Hal Leonard Corporation, 1999.

Miserandino, Dominick A. "Interview Kiedis, Anthony — Lead Singer for the Red Hot Chili Peppers." TheCelebrityCafe.com. January 2005.

Roach, Martin. *Red Hot Chili Peppers: Inside the Veins of the Velvet Groove*. Chrome Dreams, 2004.

"Socks Away!" *Q Magazine*, June 2002.

Thompson, Dave. *Red Hot Chili Peppers: By the Way*. London: Virgin Books, 2004.

"Tonal Telepathy." *Guitar* (Germany). 2002. Translation via Invisible-Movement.net.

13. *The Man in Black:* American Recordings

"10 Questions with the Man in Black." *Livewire's One on One*, ConcertLivewire.com. April 1, 2003.

Berkowitz, Kenny. "No Regrets." *Acoustic Guitar*. June 2001.

Cash, Johnny. *Cash: The Autobiography*. New York: HarperOne, 2003.

Hall, Russell. "Rick Rubin on Johnny Cash." Gibson.com. December 19, 2007.

Miller, Adam D. "Meet Me in Heaven: The Final Years of Johnny Cash." BeingThereMag.com. Last accessed May 13, 2009.

15. Ballbreaker *and* One Hot Minute

Hiatt, Brian. "Can't Stop the Rock: A Conversation with AC/DC." SonicNet via sg.wilkes.edu/spengler/. Last accessed May 13, 2009.

"Interview with the Chili Peppers." *iMusic Modern Rockshow* via RocknWorld.com. 1999. Last accessed May 14, 2009.

"Interview with Cliff Williams." *Hard Rock*. December 1996.

Malandrone, Scott. "Flea Interview." *Bass Player*. October 1995.

"Phil Rudd Interview." *Rhythm* via sg.wilkes.edu/spengler/. Last accessed May 13, 2009.

16. Three Legends: Tom Petty, Donovan, and Johnny Cash

Avadhuta, A.V. and Gary Levinson. "An Interview with Donovan."
    New Renaissance. April 1998.

Greene, Briane. "Donovan Interview." *Grip Monthly*. March 6, 2007.

"Interview: Donovan." Uncut.co.uk. Last accessed May 18, 2009.

Knight, Sirona and Michael Starwyn. "The Long Path Traveler." Blue
    Sky Link. Last accessed May 18, 2009.

Phipps, Keith. "Donovan." *AV Club*. November 30, 2005.

Weisel, Al. "Johnny Cash." *Us*. February 1997.

17. Slayer and System of a Down

Harris, Keith. "*System of a Down*." *Rolling Stone*. September 4, 2001.

Marshall, Brandon. "Interview with Slayer." SonicExcess.com. Last
    accessed May 13, 2009.

Nalbandian, Bob. "System of a Down." Shockwaves. HardRadio.com.
    Last accessed May 14, 2009.

Oliveira, Daniel. "Interview with Kerry King." *Hard Force* (France).
    June 1998. Translation from Slayerized.com.

O'Neil, Luke. "Interview with Kerry King." *Metro* (New York). June
    2006.

Zulaica, Don. "LiveDaily Interview: System of a Down's Serj
    Tankian." *LiveDaily*. April 13, 2001.

18. Dream of Californication

"A Conversation with Anthony Kiedis." MTV.com. 1999. Last accessed
    May 14, 2009.

Albert, John. "Sons of the City." *LA Weekly*. December 12, 2002.

Cromelin, Richard. "His Guitar Just Wouldn't Let Go." *LA Times*.
    January 8, 2005.

Ehrlich, Dimitri. "Anthony Kiedis Interview." *Interview*.
    December 2000.

Gabriella. "Interview with the Red Hot Chili Peppers." *NY Rock*.
    July 1999.

"Interview with John Frusciante." *Guitar Magazine* (Australia). 1999.

"Interview with John Frusciante." Virgin Radio (U.K.). February 18, 2004. Transcript via Invisible-Movement.net. Last accessed May 14, 2009.

"Interview with Red Hot Chili Peppers." Cousin Creep (Australia) radio interview. 2000. Transcript from Invisible-Movement.net. Last accessed May 14, 2009.

Kaufman, Gil. "Red Hot Chili Peppers: Back in the Saddle." *Addicted to Noise*. June 1999.

Payne, John. "Changing Channels." *LA Weekly*. July 29, 2004.

Plauk, Dennis. "John Frusciante: He Will Surpass Pop." *Musikexpress* (Germany). April 3, 2004.

Simmons, Sylvie. "California Love." *Yahoo! Music*. June 29, 1999.

Turner, Dale. "Red Hot Once Again!" *Guitar One*. September 1999.

19. *"We'll Meet Again"*: American III: Solitary Man *and* American IV: The Man Comes Around

Edwards, Bob. "Johnny Cash: The Man in Black's Musical Journey Continues." *Morning Edition*, NPR. November 5, 2002.

Grossman, Lev. "Johnny Cash: A Final Interview." *Time*. September 22, 2003.

Mansfield, Brian. "Johnny Cash: He Won't Back Down." *Allstar*. January 24, 2001.

———. "Man in Black Expands Palette." *USA Today*. November 7, 2002.

Zafiais, Alex. "Blood, Sugar, Sex, Magic." *Papermag*. March 24, 2004.

20. *The Rise of the Supergroup: Audioslave*

"Audioslave." RollingStone.com. Last accessed April 27, 2009.

"Audioslave Guitarist Tom Morello: 'I'm a Great Believer in a Good Riff.'" *Ultimate Guitar*, March 6, 2009.

Baldwin, Joe. "Interview with Chris Cornell." *Undisputed Music and Entertainment Journal* via Blabbermouth.net. June 20, 2007.

Corbett, Ben. "Axis of Metal." Atlanta. CreativeLoafing.com. March 5, 2003.

Edwards, Gavin. "Rock's Mega-Merger." RollingStone.com. November 5, 2002.

Fricke, David. "The Last Days of Rage?" *Rolling Stone*. January 10, 2001.

Gabriella. "Interview with Tom Commerford of Audioslave." *NY Rock*. January 2003.

"Interview with Audioslave." *Rockline*. July 28, 2003.

"Interview with System of a Down." Wolfshead.co.uk. Last accessed April 24, 2009.

Kara, Scott. "No Longer an Audioslave to Rage." *New Zealand Herald*. May 28, 2005.

Moon, Tom. "*Renegades*." *Rolling Stone*. November 21, 2000.

Morello, Tom. "Joe Strummer." Axis of Justice. AxisofJustice.org. December 23, 2008.

Parillo, Michael. "Audioslave's Brad Wilk Reborn." *Modern Drummer*. April 2003.

Sidwell, Jason. "Tom Morello." *Total Guitar*. August 2003.

vanHorn, Teri. "System of a Down Measure Growth with *Toxicity*." MTV.com. June 27, 2001.

Wiederhorn, Jon. "Morello Says Audioslave Have Songs for Second LP Already." MTV.com. October 22, 2002.

21. *Red Hot Chili Peppers:* By the Way

Dalley, Helen. "Interview with John Frusciante." *Total Guitar*. August 2002.

Davis, Darren. "Red Hot Chili Peppers' Next Album Ready by June." Launch.com. February 15, 2002.

Di Perna, Alan. "Basic Instinct." *Guitar World Acoustic*. April/May 2005.

———. "Death & Axes." *Guitar World Acoustic*. April/May 2004.

———. "Getting Better All the Time." *Guitar World*. August 2002.

Gabriella. "By the Way — The Chilis Are Back." *NY Rock*. August 2002.

Grant, Kieran. "Water Muse Surfaces." *Toronto Sun*. February 17, 2001.

Hernandez, Raoul. "Me and My Friends." *Austin Chronicle.*
    November 26, 2004.
"Lost and Found." *Mucchio Selvagio* (Italy). March 2004. Translation
    via Invisible-Movement.net.
McCormick, Carlo. "Red Hot Chili Peppers." *Interview*. August 2002.
Moon, Tom. "*By the Way*." *Rolling Stone*. July 2, 2002.
Moss, Corey. "Chili Peppers Want to Spank You, in a Good Way."
    MTV.com. April 15, 2002.
Sullivan, Kate. "Red Hot Chili Peppers — Icons." *Spin*. August 2002.
Wiederhorn, Jon. "Red Hot Chili Peppers' New Single About Joy, Car
    Crashes, Playing Dice." MTV.com. May 24, 2002.
———. "Red Hot Chili Peppers Relax, Let the Magic Flow on New
    LP." MTV.com. June 19, 2002.
———. "Red Hot Chili Peppers: The Secret Sauce." MTV.com. Last
    accessed April 27, 2009.
Williams, Mary. "Kiedis Gives It All Away for Chili Peppers' New
    Album." *Daily Bruin* (U. California). March 11, 2002.

22. Rick's a Believer: Weezer and Neil Diamond

Araya, Eric. "How Jay-Z's Producer Brought Neil Diamond Back to
    the Future." MTV.com. December 5, 2005.
Baltin, Steve. "Diamond Teams with Rubin." RollingStone.com.
    March 29, 2005.
Kipnis, Jill. "Diamond in the Rough: Pop Star Pares Down." Reuters.
    October 29, 2005.
Sheffield, Rob. "*Make Believe*." *Rolling Stone*. May 19, 2005.
Sullivan, Kate. "I, Songwriter." *LA Weekly*. June 9, 2005.
Walters, Barry. "*12 Songs*." *Rolling Stone*. November 3, 2005.
Zahlaway, Jon. "Neil Diamond Brings his '12 Songs' to the Stage."
    LiveDaily. November 3, 2005.

23. Out of Exile *and* Mezmerize/Hypnotize

Fricke, David. "*Hypnotize*." *Rolling Stone*. November 17, 2005.
———. "*Mezmerize*." *Rolling Stone*. June 2, 2005.

Fury, Jeanne. "System of a Down on Ho's, Bad Asses, and Columbia Records." *NY Rock.* September 2001.

Harris, Chris. "Audioslave: Beyond the Sum of their Parts." MTV.com. April 4, 2005.

Hiatt, Brian. "Audioslave Shake It Up." RollingStone.com. March 17, 2005.

Knopper, Steve. "Audioslave Find a Groove." RollingStone.com. June 14, 2005.

McKay, Chris. "Audioslave: Two Great Tastes that Taste Great Together." *Flagpole.* March 5, 2003.

Moss, Corey. "Audioslave, at Work on *Exile* Follow-Up, Promise 'A Lot More Music.'" MTV.com. September 8, 2005.

———. "Audioslave's Morello Says New LP Feels Less Like Soundgarden + Rage." MTV.com. July 29, 2004.

Roberts, Michael. "Chris Cornell, Together and Alone." *Denver Westword.* July 11, 2007.

Stevenson, Jane. "Audioslave Returns with New Disc." *Toronto Sun.* May 22, 2005.

Wiederhorn, Jon. "Audioslave 'Surprised' by Adventurous New Songs, Morello Says." MTV.com. March 11, 2004.

24. *"The Best Album We've Done":* Stadium Arcadium

Ascott, Phil. "Red Hot Chili Peppers." *Total Guitar* (U.K.). Summer 2006.

"Autopsy of a Mad Scientist." *Guitare Extreme.* June 2006. Translation via Invisible-Movement.net.

Baltin, Steve. "Chili Peppers Get Busy." *Rolling Stone.* June 10, 2005.

Barras, François. "Bad Seed of a Genius." *Tribune de Geneve* (Switzerland). April 25, 2006. Translation via Invisible-Movement.net.

Bryant, Tom. "Being Addicted to Heroin? I Really Value that Period of Time!" *Kerrang* (U.K.). May 27, 2006.

Cleveland, Barry. "Red Hot Chili Peppers' John Frusciante." *Guitar Player.* September 2006.

Di Perna, Alan. "Guided by Voices." *Guitar World.* July 2006.

Endelman, Michael. "*Stadium Arcadium*." *Entertainment Weekly*.
    May 5, 2006.

Fricke, David. "Tattooed Love Boys." *Rolling Stone*. June 2006.

Harris, Chris. "Peppers Says Return to *Sex* Scene Yielded Different
    Magik." MTV.com. April 11, 2006.

———. "Red Hot Chili Peppers' *Stadium Arcadium* Has Some
    'Retardedly Painful Funk.'" MTV.com. January 13, 2006.

———. "Road to the Grammys." MTV.com. February 8, 2007.

Hiatt, Brian. "Red Hot Chili Peppers: *Stadium Arcadium*." *Rolling
    Stone*. May 3, 2006.

Martinez, Nako. "John Frusciante." *Kerrang* (Spain). May 2006.
    Translation via Invisible-Movement.net.

Philipp, Sven. "*Stadium Arcadium*." *Billboard*. May 13, 2006.

"Red Hot Chili Peppers Get Set to Bounce Back Stronger than Ever
    with 'Stadium Arcadium.'" *Kerrang*. February 2006.

Waters, Emilt. "Red Hot Chili Peppers." *X-Press Online* (Ireland) via
    Invisible-Movement.net. May 2006.

25. *Dixie Chicks:* Taking the Long Way

Browne, David. "*Taking the Long Way*." *Entertainment Weekly*. May 19,
    2006.

"Dixie Chicks." Creative Artists Agency, CAATouring.com. Last
    accessed May 1, 2009.

"Dixie Chicks Pulled From Air After Bashing Bush." Reuters,
    CNN.com. March 14, 2003.

"Dixie Chicks Will Release Fifth Album, 'Taking the Long Way,' in
    Late May." CountryStandardTime.com. March 20, 2006.

Nelson, Sean. "*Taking the Long Way*." Music.MSN.com. Last accessed
    May 13, 2009.

"Rick Rubin Rules Grammys." AntiMusic.com. February 13, 2007.

Sullivan, James. "Nashville Pines for Dixie Chicks." *Rolling Stone*.
    January 20, 2006.

Walters, Barry. "Dixie Chicks: *Taking the Long Way*." *Rolling Stone*.
    May 2, 2006.

26. *Linkin Park:* Minutes to Midnight

Baltin, Steve. "Linkin Park Team with Rick Rubin." *Rolling Stone.*
    February 9, 2006.

Cohen, Jonathan. "Linkin Park Mixing Album, Single Due Next
    Month." *Billboard.* February 2, 2007.

"Exclusive Interview: David 'Phoenix' Farrell Speaks with
    LPAssociation.com." LPAssociation.com. December 16, 2006.

"Exclusive: Mike Shinoda Discusses Linkin Park's New Record." Rock
    & Roll Daily, RollingStone.com. March 6, 2007.

Foley, Jack. "Linkin Park Talk New Album, *Minutes to Midnight.*"
    indieLondon.co.uk. Last accessed April 27, 2009.

"Folhateen Interview with Chester." LPTimes.com. April 2, 2007.

Fricke, David. "Linkin Park: *Minutes to Midnight.*" *Rolling Stone.*
    May 30, 2007.

Graff, Gary. "Linkin Park Inspired by Prog Rock on New Album."
    Billboard. November 15, 2006.

Hahn, Joseph. Postings on LinkinPark.com. February 9, 2006.

"Linkin Park Update from Chester." cBennington.com. April 18,
    2006.

"Manic Makeover." *Today Online* via LPTimes.com. April 6, 2007.

Matera, Joe. "Linkin Park Guitarist: '*Minutes to Midnight* Is a Huge
    Departure for Us.'" UltimateGuitar.com. May 12, 2007.

"*Minutes to Midnight* Review." HiCelebs.com. Last accessed April 24,
    2009.

Montgomery, James. "Linkin Park Finish Apocalyptic Album, Revive
    Projekt Revolution Tour." MTV.com. March 6, 2007.

———. "Linkin Park's *Minutes to Midnight* Preview: Nu-Metallers
    Grow Up," MTV.com. May 4, 2007.

———. "Mike Shinoda Says Linkin Park Halfway Done with New
    Album," MTV.com. May 2, 2006.

Moss, Corey. "Linkin Park Say Nu-Metal Sound Is 'Completely Gone'
    on Next LP." MTV.com. September 27, 2006.

———. "Linkin Park Say They're Going to 'Break Outside the Box'
    with Rick Rubin." MTV.com. February 10, 2006.

O'Donnell, Kevin. "Q&A: Chester Bennington, Linkin Park." *Rolling Stone*. April 19, 2007.

Shinoda, Mike. Postings on LinkinPark.com. March 6, 2006.

———. Chat transcript, LPUnderground.com. August 22, 2006.

"Spotlight on the Park." Faces.com. May 1, 2007.

"That's a Wrap: Linkin Park Are Saying Goodbye to Their Rap-Metal Roots on Their New Album." Reuters. April 9, 2007.

Vozick-Levinson, Simon. "The Q&A: Rappin' with Linkin Park." *Entertainment Weekly*. March 7, 2007.

"We're Not Just a Bunch of Kids Anymore." *The New Paper* via LPTimes.com. April 6, 2007.

27. *Metallica:* Death Magnetic

Andert, Christopher. "Kirk Hammett: 'No, I'm Not Gonna Cut My Hair.'" Krone.at. Last accessed April 28, 2009.

Appleford, Steve. "Metallica Play Intimate Los Angeles Benefit Show, Plus James Hetfield Reveals Latest Album News." Rock & Roll Daily, RollingStone.com. Ma 15, 2008.

Blackett, Matt. "Welcome Home: Metallica Revists the Past, Cranks the MIDS, and Humbles All." *Guitar Player*. February 2009.

Epstein, Dan. "Rebel Meets Rebel: M. Shadows Interviews James Hetfield and Lars Ulrich." *Revolver.* February 19, 2009.

Erlewine, Stephen Thomas. "*Death Magnetic.*" AllMusicGuide.com. Last accessed April 28, 2009.

Goodman, William. "Breaking News: Metallica Tells All About New Album." Spin.com. May 15, 2008.

"Hammett Says a Bit More About New Metallica Album." NME TV via MetalUnderground.com. July 14, 2007.

Harris, Chris. "Lars Ulrich Talks New Metallica Album: 'It's More Like Some of Our Earlier Records.'" MTV.com. May 15, 2008.

———. "Metallica Compare Hands-Off Producer Rick Rubin to Longtime Hand-Holder Bob Rock." MTV.com. August 8, 2008.

Hiatt, Brian. "Metallica: *Death Magnetic.*" *Rolling Stone*. September 18 2008.

"Interview: Metallica." Bombshellzine.com. September 19, 2008.

"Interview with James Hetfield." *Dagens Nyheter* (Sweden) via Blabbermouth.net. October 5, 2006.

"Interview with James Hetfield." SVT (Sweden) via MetallicaWorld.co.uk. July 12, 2007.

"Interview with Lars Ulrich." *Metal Hammer* via MetallicaWorld.co.uk. Last accessed April 27, 2009.

"Interview with Lars Ulrich." *Revolver*. March 2007.

"Interview with Robert Trujillo." *Rock Hard* (Greece) via Blabbermouth.net. May 22, 2007.

Iwasaki, Scott. "Producer Rubin Pushed Metallica to a Higher Level on Latest CD." *Deseret News*. October 31, 2008.

"James Hetfield: '*St. Anger* Was a Statement that Failed.'" *Kerrang* via MetalUnderground.com. July 20, 2007.

"Lars Ulrich: 'Death' Is 'Very Human.'" The Star/B2R via BacktoRockville.typepad.com. October 22, 2008.

"Lars Ulrich Interview." *Rhythm* via MusicRadar.com. October 2008.

"Lars Ulrich: New Metallica Album Probably Early 2008." KNAC.com. July 3, 2007.

McIver, Joel. "James, Kirk & Rob Interview (New Album . . .)." Blabbermouth.net. May 9, 2008.

"Metallica Drummer on Producer Rick Rubin: 'He's Forced Us to Rethink Big-picture Stuff.'" *Rolling Stone* via Blabbermouth.net. February 13, 2007.

"Metallica in K-Rock's Hostile Takeover on Monday." *Kerrang!* and NRK (Norway) via Blabbermouth.net. July 20, 2007.

"Metallica's James Hetfield: New Album Is 'Coming Along Exactly as it Should.'" Blistering Metal News, Blistering.com. June 13, 2006.

"Metallica Studio Update." Metallica.com. February 16, 2006.

"Metallica Talk About New Album." NME.com. December 8, 2006.

"Metallica Too Loud? Too Bad, Says Drummer Lars Ulrich." MetallicaFan.net. February 2, 2009.

"Metallica to Record 14 New Songs Starting Next Week; 2008 Release Expected." Blabbermouth.net. March 5, 2007.

"New Songs for Album." Artisan News Service via Blabbermouth.net. May 22, 2005.

"Rick Rubin: 'I Asked Metallica Not to Reinvent Themselves So Much as to Make a Defining Album.'" MTV.com via Blabbermouth.net. February 14, 2007.

Acknowledgments

Project thanks: I would first and foremost like to thank Jack David and ECW Press for giving this book a home and for the amazing job you did with *Heart: In the Studio* — looking forward to *Tori Amos: In the Studio* in 2010! Crissy Boylan, my editor, for *all* of your hard work on this project, thank you; Simon, David, and everyone else at ECW Press. I would also equally like to thank Tony and Yvonne Rose at Amber Books for giving me my start 20 books ago and for continuing to support my career as an author with the release of *Prince: In the Studio*; as well as anyone and everyone else who has played a small or large role in the aforementioned. Thanks as well to super-publicist Heidi Ellen Robinson Fitzgerald, George Drakoulias for the interview, as well as Mr. Rick Rubin for inspiring much of my musical direction over the course of my childhood/teenage years as a musician with the *amazing* catalog of records you produced and for producing the Beastie Boys' *Licensed to Ill*, the best rap album ever made — period. As a young adult starting my label at 23, modeled after Def American, and throughout the last 10 years as a writer leading up to this book, which I began writing freehand on a hotel notepad sitting stranded in a Canadian airport in the spring of 2006! This book represents some of what I feel is the best writing I've ever done, and, as such, I hope you enjoy this tribute to your mastercraft!

Personally, I would first like to thank my parents, James and Christina Brown, for tirelessly pushing me to keep an equal focus on this craft as I have on my other professional endeavors (i.e., Versailles Records). You have always supported me.

To my brother, (Ret.) Sgt. Joshua T. Brown. As of the publication of this book, you'll be celebrating your first summer retired from what has been a *long* decade of service to the U.S. military. After two tours in Iraq, one in Korea, and one in Cuba, we're very proud of you but look forward to having you back and more present in our lives. Congrats on Triple Crown! Also, thanks to my Grammie, Auntie Heather, Cousin Maddy, and the extended Thieme and Brown families.

To my Shannon, thank you for everything, I love you more each day. To my long-loyal group of friends who keep in my corner in spite of the increasing amounts of time that your growing families take on as our 30s unfold, I'm happy it's together with all of you: Alex, Lindsay, and Jackson Schuchard (congrats on your first child!); Andrew and Sarah McDermott; Alexandra Federov, MFC; Chris Ellauri; Richard, Lisa, and Regan Kendrick; Sean and Amy Fillinich; Adam "The GD Skipper" Perri; and Penelope Ellis, Matt and Eileen Pietz (congrats on the little one!), Paul and Helen, Bob O'Brien, Tim Woolsey, Reed Gibbons; and anyone else who deserves mention here.

Finally, to my Versailles Records label fam: first and foremost Richard Kendrick (it's been a great 10 years!); Burt, Larry, and everyone over at Big Daddy Music; Ed Seamen et al at MVD Music Distribution; our longtime engineer Joe Viers; Harry Slash; and everyone else who is still hanging in what has become an increasingly challenging business. We do it for rock, or money, or a mix of both, among other reasons, but the point is we continue to get it done!

Nashville-based music biographer **Jake Brown** has published 20 books, including *Heart: In the Studio, Prince: In the Studio, Dr. Dre: In the Studio, Suge Knight: The Rise, Fall and Rise of Death Row Records, 50 Cent: No Holds Barred, Biggie Smalls: Ready to Die, Tupac: In the Studio* (authorized by the estate), as well as titles on Kanye West, R. Kelly, Jay Z, the Black Eyed Peas, Red Hot Chili Peppers, Mötley Crüe, Alice in Chains (fall 2009), and the *Behind the Boards* Rock Producers anthology series. Brown was also a featured author in Rick James' recently published autobiography, *Memoirs of Rick James: Confessions of a Super Freak*, and in February 2008 appeared as the official biographer of record on Fuse TV's *Live Through This: Nikki Sixx* special. Brown has received additional coverage in national publications such as *USA Today*, MTV.com, *Vibe*, and *Publishers Weekly*. Brown is the owner of the hard-rock label Versailles Records, which is distributed nationally by Big Daddy Music/MVD Distribution and is celebrating its 10th anniversary this year.